gorgeous girl

Mary K. Pershall has written novels for children and young adults, including a trilogy co-authored with her daughter Anna: *Two Weeks in Grade Six*, *A Term in Year Seven* and *Escape from Year Eight*. As well as the Ruby Clair trilogy, *Hello Barney*, *Stormy* and the award-winning *You Take the High Road*, Mary has titles published in the Aussie Bites and Aussie Chomps series, two of them co-written with her older daughter Katie.

For many years she worked as an editor and writer for the student magazines published by the Education Department of Victoria, and later as a relieving assistant principal in ten different schools. More recently, through the Royal Children's Hospital Melbourne, she tutored students with chronic illnesses or brain injuries. Mary is an active member of the international online community The Addict's Mom. She lives in Melbourne.

Mary visits Anna twice a week at the Dame Phyllis Frost Centre, Melbourne's maximum-security prison for women, where she has come to know many families of women in crisis.

gorgeous girl

MARY K. PERSHALL

VIKING
an imprint of
PENGUIN BOOKS

VIKING

UK | USA | Canada | Ireland | Australia
India | New Zealand | South Africa | China

Penguin Books is part of the Penguin Random House group of companies
whose addresses can be found at global.penguinrandomhouse.com.

First published by Penguin Random House Australia Pty Ltd 2018

Text copyright © Mary K. Pershall 2018

The moral right of the author has been asserted.

Cover design by Louisa Maggio © Penguin Random House Australia Pty Ltd
Cover photographs: Paper tears by Shutterstock / Tim Benham; texture by
Shutterstock / Supa Chan; girl on swing by Shutterstock / Antonio Guillem;
cactuses in flowerpots by Shutterstock / KashtykiNata; paper fold by
Shutterstock / benzcanon; two childhood photos supplied by the author
The quote on page vii is © Julie Myerson, 2009, *The Lost Child*,
Bloomsbury Publishing Plc.

Typeset in Sabon by Midland Typesetters, Australia
Printed and bound in Australia by Griffin Press, an accredited ISO AS/NZS 14001
Environmental Management Systems printer.

  A catalogue record for this
book is available from the
National Library of Australia

ISBN: 978 0 14378 992 5

penguin.com.au

*To all the parents who give so much
to help their troubled children*

. . . you can make your babies and you can love them with every single cell of your being, but you can't make them safe, you can't in the end choose how their lives turn out.

The Lost Child by Julie Myerson

Chapter 1

The Call came on a sunny afternoon in spring. Every parent dreads The Call, a sombre voice informing you that something unspeakable has happened to the precious being you've used your every trick to protect since they were just a clump of multiplying cells. But when your child has told you countless times that she wants to die, and on several occasions has very nearly made that happen, I think you dread it more.

I was already on my mobile, chatting to a friend, out in our unruly backyard. Thirty years before, when John and I jauntily referred to ourselves as 'young homebuyers on the march', we were thrilled to find this big block with its many trees and a house full of light, in a little suburb called Oak Park in the northern suburbs of Melbourne.

The friend I was listening to was deeply upset about a row she'd had with another friend of ours, and she needed to vent. So I stood out there beside my veggie garden, occasionally voicing a courtesy 'hmmm', while gazing with frustration at the yellowing snow pea vine and the gangly tomato plants. Despite having grown up on an Iowa farm, I hadn't inherited the knack of coaxing salad from the soil. Herbs were a more satisfying story. The chocolate mint was shining with health, sending out exuberant tendrils from its corner of the bed.

That's when the two little beeps came, plonked in the middle of one of my friend's sentences. I reminded myself not to panic. Over the last few months I'd been practising the discipline of not reacting instantly to Anna's dramas. I told myself the beeps might have nothing to do with her. I mean, I did have other friends who called me. It could well be the one on the other end of the row I was hearing about.

So I waited till the conversation came to a natural end, then I checked my missed calls. Voicemail. I pressed the green light, the one in the shape of an old-fashioned telephone receiver. Easy. No warning that a tiny light would slice my life in two, dividing it neatly between Before and After. It was a man's deep voice, a police officer. This was about Anna. The officer stated his name; I don't recall what it was, even though I'm usually good with details like that. I've kept a diary since I was fourteen, so I have a pretty comprehensive record of my post-childhood life. There is no entry for that day. On the night of the 22nd of November 2015, I couldn't bear to write what I'd learned had happened. Across the space allocated for those twenty-four hours, two words are scrawled: Black Sunday.

I think the police officer said in his message that he was calling from a station in the CBD. Again, I can't be sure. I pressed in the number he gave me and a receptionist answered. I do recall what went through my head when I was waiting to be transferred. Surely she hasn't killed herself, I thought. Lately she had exhibited an uncharacteristic liking for life. She was eighteen weeks pregnant, so proud of offering her father and me our first grandchild. 'Wouldn't Dad love a grandson?' she had asked. Her dad had a trio of older sisters and a duet of daughters. Of course he would love a grandson.

And then there were the kittens. Even as a toddler barely able to talk, Anna had adored kittens. A few months before Black Sunday, when Anna was having her latest go at a detox program, she needed a place to live. She met a guy at the program who told her about an older man called Johnnie who lived in a big house in the northern suburbs. Johnnie slept in the lounge room and rented out his bedrooms, no deposit or references required. Anna moved in, amid the clutter and the collection of men who, like her, needed shelter. Anna was delighted to discover several cats in residence. She adopted the tamest one, a sweet tortoiseshell she called Chi Chi. I was grateful to Chi Chi for producing five babies, five furrily enchanting reasons for my daughter to keep living a little longer.

'Miss Pershall?' The police officer who'd left the voice message had come on the line. 'We have your daughter in custody.'

'What? *Why?*'

The previous summer, her brain marinated in ice, Anna's behaviour had escalated to the point where her long-suffering dad put his foot down and said that she could no longer live at home. And I had been vastly relieved. When she was growing up, if someone had told me I'd be relieved to have our daughter barred from our home, I wouldn't have believed them. But then, how could I have imagined the exhaustion, heartbreak and fear that would drive us to that decision?

Anna had calmed down a lot since we made that difficult choice. She swore she wasn't doing ice. She so wanted to have a healthy baby that she was hardly even drinking, only smoking a little weed to help with her persistent morning sickness.

'What's she done?' I asked the police officer. I couldn't imagine her even shoplifting, as she spent most of her time these days pinned to the bed with nausea, her kittens in her arms.

'Umm,' the officer hesitated. 'Are you close with your daughter?'

'Yes.' I'd seen her two days before, when I had driven to Johnnie's house at 8.30 a.m. to take her to her antenatal appointment at the Northern Hospital. She'd looked terrible and had been throwing up so much she couldn't even keep down water. I'd insisted that the hospital admit her for a few hours and put her on a drip.

'You realise she was living with some older men?' the officer inquired.

'Yes . . .'

'You know the elderly gentleman there?'

Well, come to think of it, you would call Johnnie a gentleman. He was a big Macedonian who spoke broken English at top volume, and he always made me feel more than welcome in his home. 'Anna mama!' he would boom when I arrived. 'You good mama. You the best mama!'

He wasn't actually ancient; I thought he might be in his late sixties – making him only a few years older than me. But he was so crippled by arthritis that he couldn't really walk. He could only shuffle a few steps with the aid of two sticks and plenty of painkillers. He spent his days on a chair in his kitchen, and he was always surrounded by friends. Some of them lived in the house, while others were regular visitors. They interrupted each other with gusto in a variety of languages as they drank glass after glass of white wine from a cask perched on the edge of the kitchen table.

If I stepped into the kitchen, Johnnie would order one of the younger men to vacate their chair. 'Anna mama . . . you sit! You want drink? Have drink!' He would tell me what a fine job I had done raising Anna. At least a hundred times he had said to me, 'She good girl. She like my daughter. I call her Daughtie!'

'Unfortunately,' the police officer informed me, 'there's been an assault involving your daughter. The elderly man has passed away.'

I'd heard of people feeling like they were outside themselves, watching a terrible event unfold as if to another person, and now I know that phenomenon is real. I could hear someone screaming, moaning 'Noooooo!' over and over again. I'd wandered from the garden into the house by then, and I was sitting on the edge of our bed. John appeared at the door. My husband, with whom I had made a perfect, blue-eyed baby twenty-seven years before.

'What's wrong?' There must have been alarm in his eyes, but that's not what I remember. What I remember is what I sobbed to him. 'She's killed Johnnie!'

When I stopped screaming, I still had the phone clamped to my ear. The police officer was there and sounded surprised at the level of my distress. 'Did you know the gentleman well?'

'Yes! Of course I knew him!' Perhaps my tone overstated my relationship with Johnnie. But I certainly knew he did not want to die. He had dreams and plans. He often told me, with hope in his eyes, that he had a booking at the Northern Hospital to get both his knees reconstructed. And the guys in his house teased him about a Russian girlfriend, telling me he was trying to get her to Australia.

Two days earlier, while Anna was lying in the hospital having fluids dripped into her veins, I had taken Johnnie to the post office. It was quite a business, helping him from his front door to my car, then lowering his bulk into the passenger seat of my little Honda Jazz. It was even harder getting him into the post office, but I parked illegally right out the front, and we managed. After I'd parked the car in a proper spot and then gone into the post office to help him, I found him leaning heavily against one of the waist-high desks provided for customers, signing and parcelling up documents. Being an inveterate stickybeak, I certainly would have read any bits of the documents that I could. But they were printed in a script indecipherable to me.

'Would you like to speak to your daughter?' the police officer asked.

My daughter. My squishy, giggly baby who I breastfed for fifteen months. My little toddling angel with the white-blonde hair.

'No!' So many times I had called her number and longed for her to pick up because I desperately needed to hear her voice. 'I don't want to speak to her! I can't speak to her!'

'All right.' His voice was kind. 'Ring me back on this number when you're ready.'

What happened then? Did John and I hold each other? Probably. The day exists in snatches in my head. Later, I was out in the garden again, and saw John through our big kitchen window. He didn't know I was looking. He was standing by the sink, with his head in his hands. The classic gesture of despair and horror. His hair was silver but he was still the lean, tall, strong guy who took me in his arms for a waltz at a colonial dancing class thirty-five years before and never let me go.

I called my older daughter, Katie, desperately hoping she would pick up. I remember having a deep, primal need for her to be with me. Thank goodness she answered her phone. She and her partner, Tom, were living on a property that his mother owned, on a billabong near Wangaratta. She said she would come down on the next train. Just as she has done since before she could talk, she would do what she could to help me whenever I needed it.

If only I could have willed the train to arrive immediately! I so wanted Katie by my side. But I had to wait four hours. Somehow the minutes passed, and as they did my shock began to morph into my default feeling towards Anna: concern. She would not have meant for Johnnie to die. She must have been so sorry. Just like she had been a few weeks ago when she rang me, sounding devastated. I was standing in Coles, in the aisle they keep at Arctic temperature, between the milk and the frozen fish.

'I hit Johnnie!' I could hear the shock in her voice.

'What?'

'I hit him with his walking stick, twice.'

'Why?'

'Because he wouldn't stop yelling!'

'Is he hurt?'

'No, he's okay . . . But Mummy, I hit him!'

I gave her a piece of advice then. Just one. This was our arrangement, honed over the months since she had moved out. I wouldn't nag, wouldn't tell her to be positive, because she hated me doing that. But I couldn't just watch and say nothing. So I was allowed one piece of advice per phone call or visit.

'Just walk out when you get that angry,' I said. 'Get out of there. Walk to the library or shops until you feel like you can control yourself.'

'Okay,' she whispered. But in my heart I knew she wouldn't walk to the library. It had been over a year since she'd had the courage to go anywhere on her own, unless she was fuelled by ice, and she didn't want to do that now.

This conversation beside the frozen fish had replayed itself over and over in my head, and each time I was shocked again. But it had never occurred to me that Anna would actually hurt Johnnie. He called her Daughtie and she called him Daddy. I had watched her lean over his chair and plant a kiss on his balding head. On Black Sunday, my mind was hurled into a dark mishmash of images where time was meaningless, so I don't know how long it took for me to prepare myself to hear Anna's voice. Maybe half an hour after I first talked to him, I rang the police officer back. He told me that Anna was not available. She was being questioned. The officer would arrange for her to ring me when she could. Now I was waiting for both my daughters.

My phone rang. A private number. It wasn't Anna. It was another young woman, with a voice full of light and energy. 'Hello, I'm Gina. I'm looking after Anna this afternoon.' She sounded like a waitress at a trendy restaurant. But she was a lawyer, putting in a few hours of pro bono work.

'Is Anna okay?' I asked.

'Well, she's emotional, but she's coping.'

'Is someone watching her, so she can't hurt herself?'

'Oh, yes. We'll be keeping an eye on her,' Gina assured me brightly. 'She's still being questioned right now. I'll stay in touch with you through the afternoon.'

'Did she hit Johnnie with his stick?'

'Sorry?'

This is how I imagined it. She got mad at him, like before, she lost control and this time she hit him more than twice. 'He must have died of a heart attack,' I suggested.

'No.' With that monosyllable, Gina's chirpy voice had changed dramatically. Suddenly it was full of sorrow. 'No, Mary, that's not how it happened.'

She didn't say any more, just that she'd talk to me later.

Finally, I went online to see what the papers had to say. *The Age* had an item about the incident. There were no names yet, just that on the previous night, the 21st of November, a 27-year-old woman had assaulted a 67-year-old man, and he had died of upper-body injuries.

Upper-body injuries . . . I knew what that was shorthand for. She had stabbed him.

Chapter 2

The young woman mentioned in that brief news article was the baby girl I carried in my heart decades before she was born.

Growing up on our Iowa farm, I was more or less an only child. My sisters are much older than me and had grown up and left home by the time I was six. I spent a lot of time outdoors: riding horses, exploring abandoned farmhouses with my cousins from up the road and, my favourite, building rudimentary tree houses over in the timber so I could climb high into the branches and read a book for hours. I was also devoted to my brood of dolls. I remember one evening when I was putting them to bed, swaddling a plastic baby and gently lowering her into the little wooden cot that my dad had made, I looked up to see my parents gazing at me from my open bedroom door. Mother said to Dad, 'Mary Kay's gonna have a big family some day.'

I fantasised about the real babies I would one day have. Watching my sisters and my many older cousins with their children, I formed theories about how I would raise my own. For example, I decided that three years would be the ideal space between children, so I could thoroughly enjoy each baby before the next one came along. I imagined the weight of my little daughters in my arms, as I fervently hoped they would be girls.

When I turned thirteen, my cousin, who lived down the road and who was also my best friend, began to tease me about the plastic babies lying in their cot beside my bed. I still loved my dolls. But I had fallen intensely in love with Paul McCartney as well. It was too confusing. I took the dolls down to the disused henhouse, and stored them in there, where I could visit them without anyone knowing. By the time I went to university, I am happy to report, I had found other passions, like writing for the university newspaper, working for our campus chapter of the Young Democrats and joining protests against the Vietnam War. This even led me to take a long, smoky bus ride to Washington DC, where the contingent from my university joined thousands of other students from all over the country. We marched down Pennsylvania Avenue, chanting, 'One! Two! Three! Four! We don't want your fucking war!'

I also longed to travel, and with that goal in mind, I majored in Teaching English as a Second Language. When I was in my final year, I saw a notice on the bulletin board in the careers office, announcing that the Education Department of Victoria was recruiting newly graduated teachers. Fireworks went off in my soul. Australia!

So I landed here on a winter's morning in 1974. My plan was to spend a couple of years here and then move on to a different country. But I fell in love with Melbourne, and my students, and the librarian at my school. During my twenties, I was having too much fun and was too focused on my career to think about having babies. I joined the Women's Movement Children's Literature Co-operative and helped to write, edit and publish Australia's first counter-sexist books for kids. This led to a magical position in the Publications Branch of the Education Department, where I was part of a team writing and editing the department's highly popular and well-regarded magazines for primary and early secondary schools. It was hard to believe I was getting paid a good salary to spend my days with the most creative, funny and spirited group I could imagine.

Then, when I was twenty-nine, a few major things happened. Not the least was the big three-O staring me in the face. Oops, I was definitely about to be an adult now, and I had better decide whether to stay in this country or heed my mother's pleas to return to Iowa. Meanwhile, the librarian and I had fallen out of love. He went to a new school and met a new woman, while I went to colonial dancing classes and met the man I would marry.

Like me, John was twenty-nine. He was the best dancer in the class, and waltzing with him took me to a magical place, which led to his bed. I admired the muscles of his thighs, firmed from riding his bike every weekday morning from his share house in inner-city Kensington, through the parklands, to his work at the Commonwealth Serum Laboratories in Parkville, where he made vaccines. Though he wouldn't have known a ragweed from a cocklebur, John reminded me of my farmer father. They were both able to see through the smokescreen of popular opinion and make up their own minds, based on the facts available to them. This is what made Dad a Democrat amid a sea of Republicans. As for John, he was the only person I ever met who read through every single section of *The Age*; he could not only discuss the news, but cars and movie reviews and business trends as well. On the downside, right from the beginning of our relationship, John could make me angrier than I ever knew I was capable of. When he sat beside me as I drove my car, pointing out to me in strong language the idiotic mistakes I was making, I experienced an intense desire to shove him out onto the road and leave him there, gaping. Then I would speed off, demonstrating the skills I had been employing since I earned my learner's permit at the age of fourteen. But no matter how mad he made me, I always had to forgive him. He was the one I saved up all the funny little things that happened in a day for, and packaged them into stories. Because he was the one who would listen to me with all his attention and chuckle at exactly the spots I intended. Plus, I have never doubted that he would stand between me and a raging razorback to protect me.

John made it clear almost from our first date that he very much wanted me to stay in Australia, and he thought we should make babies together. But I wasn't as sure as I had been when I was eight years old that I should have kids. I was keen on expanding my writing career beyond the school magazines, and I figured parenthood would be a major impediment to that. And there was another, deeper reason.

As a child and teenager I loved my mother a lot. She was so smart, and a fabulous cook, and she could be very funny, slicing through the fabric of our rural community with her incisive wit. I knew I was desperately important to her. But it was so difficult to keep her from getting angry. I tried hard to be exactly the sort of good little girl she wanted, and as I grew into adolescence, I learned to never express an opinion that was even slightly different to hers. Yet, inevitably, I would slip up. I might not be able to stop myself from making some aside that was not entirely polite. Or maybe I would look a little askance at something she said. Then I would be in trouble. 'You only ever think of yourself!' she would shout. I would soon be in tears and so would she. But still she would keep on through her sobs. 'You're so selfish and lazy! You're good for *nothing*!'

These judgements were locked firmly at the centre of my psyche. With my accomplishments, I tried to dislodge them. I wrote my mother a letter every week, first from college and later from Australia. The details of daily life varied, but I always included something which I hoped would make her proud.

> *Dear Mother . . . I earned all A's this semester . . . I've got my own column in the college newspaper . . . Look, I won a short story competition . . . I got a promotion at work . . . Here's our latest magazine with four articles written by me . . .*

Of course, what I was really saying was, *See? I'm not lazy. I'm not good for nothing!* I'm not sure I ever convinced my mother and at that stage I certainly had not convinced myself. It would require decades, and professional help, for me to challenge the characteristics my mother had assigned me, and to begin to see myself as a truly worthwhile person who didn't deserve to be described by demeaning adjectives. Back then, at the end of my twenties, hiding inside my carefully constructed fortress of accomplishments, I was deeply unsure that I had what it took to be a good person, let alone a decent mother.

When I was a kid attending our little country church, we were often told about prophets who would sooner die in excruciating ways than deny the word of God. I would imagine myself alone in a freezing cell, far away in some foreign land. Menacing men with black beards like in Bible pictures would be poking fiery sticks at me through the bars. 'Say you don't believe in Jesus or we'll cut your fingers off, slice by slice, *very slowly*!'

The only reason we were in this world, I was vehemently informed every Sunday, was to get ready for the next life, and that involved proving how much we loved God. I wanted to believe I could withstand anything rather than betray Him, but I strongly suspected that the moment the glistening knife bit my skin, I would blurt out whatever those bad men wanted to hear.

As a university student I silently pondered the quandary of the sinking lifeboat. Surely there was someone in the world for whom I would give up my place. My niece, maybe? Mother Teresa? A starving African toddler who would grow up to cure cancer? No, as deserving as those candidates were, and as selfish as I felt this to be, I still valued my own existence more than anybody else's.

So I guess it wasn't surprising that at thirty I was daunted by the maternal declaration I had heard and read so many times, *I would give my life for my child*. I just couldn't believe I was selfless enough to feel that way about anyone. But after John and I had been together for a couple of years, and I'd observed how much he loved playing with and teaching our friends' children, the old longing to hold my own daughter in my arms became stronger than my doubts. So, for the first time since my early twenties, I stopped taking the pill, and Katie was conceived in a combi parked near a Mornington Peninsula beach, during the Christmas holidays of 1984.

As soon as she popped out, my dilemma became a no-brainer. Of course I would jump into the water and drown if that was the only way my daughter could be safe in the lifeboat. Because, once I'd looked into her luminous navy-blue eyes, I knew life without her would be too bleak to contemplate.

Chapter 3

Another reason why I'd hesitated to have a baby was that so much of my self-worth was tied up with my career. My identity depended on getting up early, putting on good clothes and heading off to my wonderful job. How could I give that up for family leave? Therefore I found it utterly surprising, amazing even, how much I loved being with Katie while John was at work. She was such a delightful little companion. In the afternoons we would head off somewhere on the train, to the zoo or the National Gallery or off to visit John's sister and her two boys. Katie at a few months of age found everything fascinating. In a cafe, propped up in a highchair, a person would catch her fancy and she would stare at them with her impossibly big blue eyes, somehow managing not to blink for what seemed like minutes. She would even forget to swallow, so I'd have to reach over with a serviette and wipe the dribble off her chin.

I'd also worried about the pram in the hall, that famous symbol of a writer's thwarted literary ambitions. But it turned out that being home with Katie was the right time for me to start working on my dream of becoming an author. She had a three-hour nap every morning after breakfast, and that's when I wrote the draft of my first novel, *You Take the High Road*. John, who had never doubted that he wanted to be a parent and enjoyed Katie as much as I did, playfully informed his sisters that we planned to have six more kids. I agreed to one. As I'd already figured out when I was a kid, observing the babies in my extended family, a three-year gap would be a good idea. So when Katie was two years and three months old, I went off the pill and, just like the first time, became pregnant immediately. Ha! At least it was easy to get Anna.

Her birth was pretty spectacular as well. We all love that story. Katie claims she remembers it vividly, even though she was only three years and one day old when it happened. Her recollection could have a lot to do with the number of times she, John and I retold it, to Anna's delight, sitting around our kitchen table over dinner.

We always began the story by laughing at the memory of toddler Katie. I finished work when I was six weeks from giving birth, and Katie spent those weeks by my side, copying everything that I did. 'I don't walk like that!' I would protest, as she stuck out her little belly and waddled along like a cartoon pregnant woman. At one obstetrician's appointment, she clambered onto the examination table next to me, lay down and insisted that her baby needed to be checked as well. The doctor, himself a father of three little girls, felt her tummy and assured her, 'Your baby is growing nicely.'

A part of the tale we found especially amusing was that Anna was nearly born in the back of an Alfa Romeo. We were sure Anna would arrive on her due date, just as Katie had, so a few days before that we booked our only car, an aging orange Renault, into the trusty local garage for some overdue repairs. Wouldn't you know it? On that day, Katie and I were having our afternoon nap when I realised that the contractions I was feeling were not just Braxton Hicks. I called John at work and he called the garage, only to learn our car was in bits. By that time I was in full-blown labour, so I informed John he had better get me to the hospital somehow. He turned to his colleagues for help, and the one who came through drove him home in his Alfa Romeo.

On the way to the family birth centre at the Royal Women's, Katie and I rode in the back seat. My contractions were one minute apart by then, and I was coping with the increasingly intense pain by doing the pant-breathing we had been taught at prenatal classes. I looked across to see my tiny daughter with her chubby arms braced against the seat in front of her, panting away with her breaths perfectly matched to mine.

Thank goodness the hospital was only twenty minutes away from our house, because even in the state I was in I could sense that our driver, whom I'd never met before, was very keen for me not to make a huge mess in the back of his flash car.

We managed to make it into the room at the birth centre . . . just. Immediately after stepping inside, I collapsed onto all fours, and with a bit of help from a surprised midwife, our baby popped out – with the amniotic sac still intact. Although the midwife later told me she had never before seen an 'en caul' birth, she liberated our infant with no fuss and said to John, 'Do you want a cuddle?' John stripped off his shirt so it wouldn't get messy, and that's how we'd end the story: with John clutching his slimy, seconds-old daughter against his chest and Katie jumping up and down on the bed shouting, 'Baby! Baby! Baby!'

When did I first notice there was something different about my youngest girl, who was welcomed into the world with such delighted cheering? Certainly not during her infancy or toddlerhood. She reached all her milestones early, crawling at six months and speaking clearly in simple sentences by the time she was two. Apart from not sleeping through the night until she was a year old, she was an easy baby, and a cheery little toddler with a cheeky sense of humour. She couldn't have been more than two and a half when, one workday morning, I was trying to hurry her and Katie to get ready for day care. I had left a naked Anna absorbed with a toy in front of the heater, and now I called out to her from the kitchen where I was washing the dishes, 'Anna, get your underpants on.' A few seconds later she appeared at the kitchen door and announced with a chuckle, 'I've got my underpants on, Mummy.' I turned to see that she was indeed wearing her Care Bear pants . . . on her head!

As a preschooler she was an elegant little beauty, tall for her age but also fragile-looking, with her blonde hair and big blue eyes. Adults found her adorable, not only for her looks, but because she was never shy. She would go up to total strangers in the supermarket, or a park, or on a train, and prattle on about anything that was on her mind. So many people would look at me over her downy head and marvel, 'She's gorgeous.' And I would smile proudly in agreement.

I only remember one early instance when I felt concerned for Anna. It would have been the summer shortly after she turned four. The little girl next door, almost exactly the same age as Anna, had come over to play. They were out in our huge backyard and from inside, where I was trying to get some writing done, I could hear their voices. No, actually . . . I could only hear Anna's voice. Minutes went by and it was still her doing all the talking. I went to the back door so I could hear what she was saying. She was chattering about a bug she had caught, and how it was an orphan and very lonely and searching for its mummy and she was going to look all around the garden until she found a sister for her and that reminded her of a lonely shark she'd spotted at the swimming pool and how she'd reported this to the attendant and they rewarded her with the hugest icy pole ever and . . . on and on and on without a pause.

That's not play, I thought. That's not two kids interacting. No wonder the other girl hardly ever wanted to come over. But I didn't say anything to Anna. I didn't want to make her feel bad. My mother had attacked my personality and character so regularly when I was growing up that I entered adulthood harbouring, deep inside, only the tiniest kernel of belief in myself. I wanted Anna to know she didn't have to strive to be who I wanted her to be. I wanted her to never have to question, even for a millisecond, that her family would always love her exactly as she was.

When I was pregnant with her, I wondered how I could love another baby as much as I did Katie. It didn't seem possible that anyone else could be as important to me. But that's one of nature's miracles, isn't it?

Over the years, I've often thought of the spring morning in 1988, Australia's bicentennial year, when Anna was two days old. In those days you could go from the family birth centre to Frances Perry House, a private maternity unit at the same hospital, and stay for up to a week if you wanted to. I remember waking up there one morning and in that first fuzzy second I was aware that something was missing, of an absence of light beside my bed. Not yet fully conscious, I knew that something infinitely precious had been in that spot when I went to sleep, and now it was gone. It took another waking moment for me to realise it was a hospital-issue, wire bassinet that was missing. With my baby in it.

I looked around and there they were, all the bassinets from the ward lined up on the other side of the room, under a long window. The nurses had wheeled them over there, past exhausted mothers, into shafts of dawn sunlight. The newborns were asleep, neat little bundles wrapped up tight in pastel blankets. They reminded me of some candy babies my sister Joan brought back for me from a vacation when I was seven. There were eight sugar newborns in a padded pink box, each an inch long, swaddled in pale colours, each nestled in her own fluted cup. My sister teased me because I wouldn't taste even one, but couldn't she see they were too perfect to eat?

I didn't imagine how they might melt in the brutal humidity of a Midwestern summer, or get their tiny heads bitten off by my ornery cousin. I thought I could keep them forever, just as they were.

Chapter 4

A week after Anna turned six she had her first involvement with the police.

We had just returned from a four-month trip overseas. John and I had taken long service leave and pulled the kids out of school for a couple of terms. We'd splurged on round-the-world tickets and flown to Rome via Hong Kong, then made our way through Italy, Greece, Holland, England and Wales on our way to the US and our family in Iowa. It was the Friday evening of our first week back in the work–school routine, the final term for Katie in grade 3 and Anna in prep. The first four days of that week the girls had gone to after-school care, but for a Friday treat, our good friend Margie had picked them up from school and taken them to her place to play with her two boys, aged two and four.

When I pulled up in front of Margie's unit around five o'clock, Anna and Margie's older boy, Christian, were out in the communal front yard. Anna ran over and proudly announced, 'Look, I can fit into Llewellyn's tracksuit pants!' Llewellyn was the two-year-old. His pants were a tight fit on Anna and only came to her knees, but she did indeed have them on. She wasn't wearing a top. Around her neck was a lei made of plastic flowers, and her blonde head was adorned with a paper chef's hat.

'Aren't you cold?' I asked, noting that she also had no shoes on.

'I never get cold! I'm a unicorn!' With that she ran off to tell Christian what he was meant to be doing in her fantasy world.

I went into the unit to debrief with Margie about my long first week back at work. Katie had Llewellyn on her lap. She had known him since he was born, considered him her personal baby, and had missed him a lot while we were travelling. But as soon as she spotted me, her mind turned to more corporeal matters. 'I'm hungry,' she announced piteously. 'Can we order the pizza now?'

Katie was big on plans, and we had planned to order pizza. Margie and I agreed to go ahead and order, since we figured it might take a while to be delivered on a Friday night, and by the time it arrived our husbands would be there to enjoy it with us. While Margie phoned in the order, I went out to check on Christian and Anna.

They weren't in the front yard. My chest was already beginning to tighten as I looked around the side of the units. Surely they wouldn't have gone out into the street? Like all city kids, they had been warned countless times about the dangers of traffic. Now my heart was hammering. I stepped out into the quiet court and scanned up and down . . . cars arriving home from work . . . no kids in sight.

I went back into the unit to check if they'd somehow gone in without me noticing. Hoping, hoping . . . Margie's puzzled look didn't change to alarm straight away. 'I bet they're hiding,' she said. Less prone to panic than me, she led a search under beds and in wardrobes, but no giggling little devils emerged. We moved on to the wheelie bins lined up outside, Katie chattering along behind us with Llewellyn in her arms.

With all hiding places explored, Margie led us up to the end of the court, to the intersection with the busier street. God, please let us see them! I looked both ways, willing my eyes to make out the figures of a little girl and boy, barely six and four years old. That's when I heard the dread in Margie's voice. 'I think someone's picked them up in a car.'

As soon as she said it, I knew that's what had happened. In any moment of stress, my mind had a habit of racing straight to the worst possible scenario. Someone had stolen my baby.

'I'm going to call the police,' Margie said.

We didn't have mobiles in those days. She headed back to her place with Llewellyn, while I bundled Katie into our car. I couldn't sit still. I had to look for the kids. I don't know how I thought I was going to find them if a paedophile was speeding away with them, but to say I wasn't thinking straight was an understatement. In those moments I realised I had never felt pure fear before. During the previous few days I had been worried about my sore right ankle. Was I getting arthritis? What if it got so bad I couldn't walk or drive without pain? Now, as I drove our familiar streets whirling in a white vortex of panic, it seemed incredible that those questions had seemed even the tiniest bit important. Nothing was important, except finding our children. How could I live without my little girl?

Katie, a practical little person who already had years of practice calming me down, assessed the situation and pronounced, 'Well, Mum, if a bad man has got her, we just have to accept it.'

After cruising the streets for about twenty minutes, I headed back to Margie's, praying that the kids had magically appeared there. As I turned into the court, I saw a police car parked outside the units. A middle-aged cop was standing beside it, talking with Margie. When I approached, Margie told me our husbands had turned up. John had gone off on his bicycle to search along the creek, and Peter was looking beside the railway line.

The police officer turned to me. 'Are you the mother of . . .' he consulted his notes. 'Anna?'

'Yes.'

'Is she in the habit of running away?'

'No! She just turned six! She's never been out of my sight before except at child care, or with one of my friends . . .'

'Okay, I see,' he said kindly. 'Can you give me a description of what she was wearing?'

'Uh . . . size 2 black tracksuit pants. With a plastic lei and a chef's hat.'

He wrote that down without comment.

'And she wasn't wearing a top. Or shoes!'

He must have heard in my voice that I was about to cry, because he took on a reassuring tone. 'We've got two cars out looking for them. And . . .' He gestured towards the sky. There it was, whirling overhead, the police helicopter. As I gazed up at it, the searchlights suddenly went on, and I realised that as I'd been blindly searching, dusk had drawn in. I never guessed that anything could feel as horrible and bleak as that, to know there was nothing I could do to stop the darkness enfolding my darling.

The helicopter cast a circle of amazingly bright light. It was heading slowly away from us, going north. The officer got into his car and spoke to someone over the crackly radio. Through his open window he informed me, 'They've spotted them, running up Waterloo Road.'

'Really?' She was alive? My soul couldn't believe it.

The cop listened to the crackles again, answered something, listened some more, then turned back to me. 'They're at Tuckerbag.'

This was a grocery store in the next suburb to the north, more than a kilometre away, on the other side of the railway line.

'Another car is bringing them back, so I'll be off.' With that he was gone, on to his next job for the night.

John and Peter had returned by this time, so all four parents were waiting at the kerb when the police car pulled up with our kids in the back. They were both sucking on Chupa Chups.

The police officer, this one much younger than the first one, got out and opened his back door. Anna climbed out and I couldn't help registering my distress. 'Why did you *do* that?'

She didn't answer, just kept sucking on her Chupa Chup, while in her other hand she clutched another, unopened one.

'Don't be too hard on her,' the young officer said. 'They don't know what they're doing at that age.'

But John didn't want Anna to remember running away as a fun excursion. He confiscated her lollipops, led her into the house and smacked her bottom. Maybe two or three whacks. John and I both realise now this was not a good thing to do, but it was the only spanking she ever got. We couldn't know how deeply we would come to regret that action, which in those days was a common and accepted method of discipline. We thought we had taught her a lesson. I certainly learned a lesson that night. For years afterwards, the sound of the police helicopter overhead set off an involuntary, visceral reaction inside me. It made me feel like throwing up. But then I would rejoice, because it reminded me that as long as my daughters were safe, I had all I really needed.

Chapter 5

For many years after the running-away incident, Anna refused to talk about it. If anyone brought it up in front of her, she would get upset and leave the room.

I turned the night into a tale I loved to tell: I experienced the worst horror I could imagine and then, like a miracle, the agony was reversed. My child, my heart, was ripped away from me . . . and then restored, complete with a paper chef's hat.

I liked my version of the story so much, I never really considered hers. Now, I think I have pieced it together. Before she started kinder, Anna was a happy little cherub who delighted her extended family with her antics. Even kinder itself she didn't find too bad. It was only a few hours a day, and mostly she could choose what she wanted to do. She loved painting. She must have used up a whole roll of butcher's paper over that year, judging from the plethora of mulicoloured creations she brought home.

But school . . . that was not so free and easy. She had to stay there most of the day and do what the teacher decided she should, at the same time as all the other kids. Two weeks into the year, Anna's teacher asked, 'Have you had her hearing tested? Her speech seems very delayed.' I knew her hearing was perfect, and that she could talk the leg off a donkey. It was just that when she was deep inside one of her fantasies, she wasn't interested in listening to anyone. Also,

although her vocabulary was extensive and she was capable of verbal eloquence unmatched by people much older
than her, she often preferred to express joy or surprise by
squeaking like a mouse. And when she was frustrated or
angry, she yowled in cat language. Apparently Anna's feline
side had been much in evidence since she started prep. 'She
screeches so loudly,' the teacher complained. 'It upsets the
other children.'

With hindsight, John and I know we should have sought
a diagnosis for Anna much earlier than we did. Should we
have done it back then, when she was five years old? I think
we shouldn't have dismissed the prep teacher's suggestion so
easily. Even though we knew Anna didn't have hearing problems, things might have turned out better for her if we'd heeded
the teacher's concern and tried to find out why our daughter
needed to meow and hiss at the other kids.

But there were deep-seated reasons why we hesitated for so
long to seek professional help. For one thing, neither John nor
I had fitted in at primary school or made good friends there.
It hurt so deeply when my mother repeatedly pointed this out
to me, comparing me to my sisters, who were finishing their
school years just as mine started. Apparently they had adored
primary school and were always wanting to bring friends
home. Though I couldn't have put it into words then, I longed
to be loved for who I was, not some ideal version of myself that
I had no idea how to be. I know, after many years of chatting
with John about our childhoods, that he experienced similar
feelings. Both he and I wanted to give Anna what we didn't
receive: the gift of loving the whole little bundle that made her
our child, complete with her oddities.

So we didn't take Anna for a hearing test. 'Just make it

through this one term,' I encouraged her. 'Try to stop screech-ing, okay? When Easter comes, we're flying to Hong Kong!'

Anna endured school for a term, and then we took her on a four-month trip. Whoopee! her five-year-old mind must have rejoiced. No more school. During our two months travelling in Europe, among the fun and adventure, John and eight-year-old Katie and I had more than a few moments of boredom, frustration and generally getting sick of being with each other 24/7. But Anna was ecstatic the entire time. The world was full of people she could chatter to: the older, the better! It didn't matter to her if they couldn't understand English. In Hong Kong restaurants, on Italian trains, on ferries chugging between the Greek islands, Anna would scamper among the tables or train compartments and find adults to enchant with her stories. As we strolled along the impossibly narrow streets of Naxos, grandmothers sitting atop stools on their stone front steps would reach out to touch Anna's golden hair and her pale, flawless skin. *Koukla*, they would murmur. Little doll.

When we arrived in Iowa, she had our scores of relatives to dote on her. I never knew my mother to love someone as unre-servedly as she did Anna. We'd taken the kids to Iowa on two previous trips, when Anna was eight months and then two and a half. Katie was much more worldly than Anna. The first time we took Katie to Iowa, when she was three and a half, she had opinions on everything and expressed them with great convic-tion. I was amazed by her confidence and admired it heartily, but Mother found her 'too sassy'. While there was something about dreamy little Anna that touched her in a way I had never seen. The first time Mother spent time with her, when Anna was eight months, I was on family leave from the Education Department. After John flew back to Australia for work, the girls and I stayed on for a couple of months and lived with my parents. Mother and Dad were able to see Anna learn to walk and demolish her first birthday cake. They heard her first words. My mother pronounced her 'an angel of a baby'. The next time we visited, Mother found two-and-a-half-year-old Anna 'the cutest little girl I've ever seen'. This phrase stuck in my head because Mother always compared whatever beautiful thing she was looking at or delicious tidbit she was eating or TV show she was watching to a far better one she'd experienced in the past – but not in the case of Anna.

To my relief, Mother found Anna just as charming at the age of five. My parents had retired from the farm a dozen years earlier and moved to Maxwell, a small town about 15 miles away. My sister had bought our old farmhouse and 20 acres surrounding it. The girls and I spent part of each day there, and Anna adored it. She and Katie got to ride the horses bareback and run around with the friendly collie. But the biggest attraction for Anna was the litter of newborn kittens in the machine shed. Regardless of how hot it was, she spent hours at a time in there, making up elaborate stories about the kittens and cuddling them tight from when they were a week old, making my sister complain years later that Anna had turned them into the sookiest cats she had ever known.

Iowa must have seemed like heaven to Anna. But then we led her onto a plane and took her back to . . . well, not hell, obviously, but something she must have felt wasn't far from it. When I think back now to that night when Anna ran away, I believe she was telling us with all the eloquence of her already tortured little soul just how much she hated school. She desperately wanted to escape from grown-ups who gave her reading tests and forced her to stay in a room full of people who happened to be her age but were unfathomable to her. She tried so hard to tell us . . . and we should have listened, because I knew what it was like to hate school. But I'd never considered not going. I'd just figured I had to do it, and we thought Anna had to as well.

By the end of prep, Anna had stopped making animal noises in class. She was learning to read and would go on to cope well academically. It was recesses, lunches and group activities that were torture to her. None of the other kids in the class wanted to play with her or be her partner. And why was that?

It had something to do with the trait that adults found so endearing in Anna, best described as 'she's off with the fairies'. Years after most children had learned the difference between reality and fantasy, Anna was still confused. One day Anna wore her favourite hairclip to school. It was a distinctive little ceramic flower we'd bought her in Hong Kong. It wasn't much of a surprise when we found it missing from her hair at the end of the day, as she was always losing things. What made me really sad was what she told us over dinner the next night. 'Amber had a special hairclip for show and tell. It's exactly like mine from Hong Kong.' When John, Katie and I chorused that it undoubtedly was her hairclip, Anna reported, 'No, Amber said it's one just like it.'

Naturally, kids exploited her gullibility. Years later, when Anna was in her twenties, she told me how at recess a group of girls would sometimes invite her to join in a game, savour her look of relief, then giggle with delight as they ran away from her.

It seems obvious now that we should have screamed out for help for our lonely little girl. But mental illness was not in the public consciousness nearly as much as it is today, especially where children were concerned. Also, we didn't know then how things would turn out for her. As Kierkegaard put it, 'Life can only be understood backwards, but it must be lived forwards.' John, Katie and I liked the quirky way that Anna's mind worked, and rather than try to change her, we hoped she would find a soulmate, someone who would share her passions and appreciate her way of looking at life.

We knew this may not happen at school, so we made an effort to expose her to other groups, where she might find that special little friend. John and I had been going to the local Anglican church since we moved to Oak Park. There weren't many kids in the small congregation, but we hoped more might turn up. Meanwhile, both John and I wanted to offer our girls the opportunity to take music lessons, as we had both highly valued them when we were young. Katie learned piano and because Anna had a lovely voice, we signed her up for the Australian Girls Choir. She participated in their beautiful productions with grim determination rather than joy, and to our disappointment she never palled up with any girls there. She gave up the choir after a couple of years. Later she took up karate, which she enjoyed a lot more, and some of the kids there actually seemed to like her, but this didn't translate to friendship outside the club.

By about grade 2, Anna was still baffled by reality, but she had finally learned that she couldn't always trust other kids. Katie and her best friend, who was also named Katie, would usually let Anna hang around with them in the schoolyard. Anna loved them both with the whole of her easily confused little heart, and called them collectively 'the Kates'. Then, when Anna was at the end of grade 3, something happened that was inevitable, but terrible for Anna: the Kates graduated from primary school. After that, Anna spent far too many soul-destroying recesses and lunchtimes alone, forlornly wandering the yard or hiding in the school library. As each year of bearing the labels of 'loner' and 'loser' passed, she become quieter and sadder at school. I remember her grade 4 teacher asking John and me at a parent-teacher interview, 'Doesn't Anna ever smile?'

To the school's credit, around this time the principal organised an evening class for anxious children and their parents, run by a professional counsellor. Once a week for about a month and a half, Anna and I went along, listened to the counsellor and filled out exercises in a workbook. We were supposed to follow up by practising the exercises at home. So each evening, sitting beside her bed, I would encourage Anna to employ one of the suggestions, such as naming three good things that had happened that day at school. I remember the first time we tried that one. 'Nothing good happened,' she claimed. It was dark in the room, but I could hear her frown.

'Can't you think of one thing?' I challenged.

She lay there, pondering. Finally, she conceded, 'Well, I liked the Twisties I had for recess.'

Despite my initial hopes, Anna didn't seem to get much out of the anti-anxiety class, and prodding her to produce a positive thought about school became increasingly difficult. But I found the simple techniques surprisingly beneficial. It's where I learned one of my best mental health tools: to recall, as I drift off to sleep, five good things I've experienced that day.

By this stage I was back at full-time, salaried work. While I had been away on six years of family leave, the children's magazines that I had been working on were privatised, meaning the job I'd loved so much had vanished from the

Education Department. Instead I was offered a position as a relieving assistant principal, filling in for secondary school assistant principals on long-service leave. This turned out to be a fascinating job, which led me to work at ten different high schools over a period of six years. It certainly was a challenge, with some schools more difficult than others. But overall, I savoured the opportunity to experience a raft of new responsibilities, to meet so many students and their families, and to work to help them, even though my skills had evolved using a different professional route to most school administrators. Those years were, in many ways, a lovely time for our family. John had always wanted a stint as a stay-at-home dad, and this change in my career gave him his chance. He resigned from his job to take up the ushering of our two girls through primary school and around their various activities, as well as doing the cleaning, shopping and cooking. I worked long hours, but when I got home I was able to collapse into the rocking chair in the corner of our big kitchen, sip a glass of wine and debrief with my husband as he whipped up dinner. The four of us always ate our evening meal together, with Anna happily joining in the jokes and anecdotes. Both girls, and John too, loved the tales I brought home as an assistant principal. 'Tell us another naughty kid story!' became their nightly refrain.

Katie and Anna never fought like siblings usually do. They were so different, it seemed like they were born a decade apart rather than three years. Katie was eager to grow up, to understand the practicalities of life, always striving to reach the next rung on the ladder of independence. Whereas so much of Anna lingered in the shadowland of early childhood, where magic and fantasy play equal parts with reality. Perhaps we would have found these characteristics in our little girl horrifying, rather than enchanting, if we'd known she could never grow out of them. Anna idolised Katie, and even after Katie started high school and became very busy, she went out of her way to make time for Anna, to join in with her fantasies. As for me, I kept trying to fix Anna with words. I'm a passionate reader, and I've been recording my life in a journal since I was fourteen. By the time Anna was born, Katie and I had established a nightly routine of 'cubbyhouse time', and this continued for many years. After my girls were in bed, I would sit beside the wooden bunks John had made for them and tell them stories. We read plenty of books before we turned the lights out, but it was even more special to be in the darkness, just the three of us, taking off in our imaginations to other times and places. The girls loved tales I spun from my own childhood, and the three of us would also make up stories together, each contributing different characters or plot lines.

By the time she was twelve years old, Katie had become an independent girl who scoured op shops for clothes she wanted, and each day rode the train and tram for an hour to get to and from the inner-city high school she had chosen all by herself, even though not a single one of her primary school pals went there. She decided it was time to have a room of her own, so she moved out to the bungalow behind our house.

So it became just Anna and me sharing the dark. She still loved my stories and coming up with her own, and often we would weave our tales together to make a new and even better one. But sometimes Anna's mind couldn't settle to stories. She was so sad at school. I spent a fair amount of cubbyhouse time comforting her. *Don't worry about the girls at school. It's just that they don't understand you. I had trouble making friends as well, but eventually I realised that one of the girls at church thought deeply about the same ideas that I did, and we became best mates. You'll find a soulmate too, one day. In the meantime, you have so many people who love you.*

I tried to pass on to Anna the tools for good mental health I had acquired over the years. *You can decide what to think about. Make a list of what you are grateful for. Smile! You have a beautiful smile. People will respond to that, I guarantee.* I believed that if I could articulate my advice in just the right way, she'd be able to use it. It took a couple of decades to sink in to the alphabet soup of my mind that words, no matter how well planned and lovingly delivered, were not going to fix my troubled daughter.

When I look back at Anna's lonely childhood years, I find it hard to regret that we didn't seek a name for what troubled her earlier than we did, because this was a decision that we both believed was best for her. We didn't want to burden our daughter with labels. Knowing now how things have turned out, and having learned so much about mental illness, if we could go back to when our daughter was five or eight or ten, I think both John and I would make different decisions. What I do regret deeply is not trying another sort of school for her. I brought up this possibility more than once, but John was adamant that Anna was at a good school; he felt it wouldn't matter where she went, she would still struggle. I could see his point, and it was easier not to make a fuss. But now, when I'm lying awake at 2 a.m. with questions clanging around in my mind, this is a biggie: Why didn't I insist we spend less money on travel, and use it instead to send Anna to a private school, perhaps in the Montessori system, where her differences might have been celebrated rather than scorned?

If she had gone to a school like that, she might today be the forensic psychologist she dreamed of being, and certainly had the intellectual ability to achieve. And Johnnie might be alive, sauntering along jauntily with his new knees, with one of his many friends by his side.

Chapter 6

There was another reason why I sat beside Anna's bed as she was falling asleep when she was nine and ten and eleven years old. She was tormented by ghosts. When Katie moved out of Anna's room and into the bungalow behind the house, the spirits moved in. They floated outside the window beside Anna's bed and tapped on the glass. Even though she locked the windows, pulled down the blinds and closed the curtains, the ghosts crept in. They sat on her bed and chattered. They breathed in her ear.

'You're so lucky,' she whimpered to me. 'You don't have to sleep by yourself!'

I think most kids fear the monsters under the bed at some stage. But this tends to occur at a much younger age than Anna then was, and her level of distress went beyond what I now believe would be classed as normal. Should we have sought professional help for her? Looking back I think yes, we probably should have. But at the time it didn't occur to me that Anna might be experiencing auditory hallucinations. When I was young, I heard ghosts as well. So did my sister Linda and my mother. Our farmhouse was teeming with them, and as a kid they terrified me. When I was a teenager, Linda and I tried talking to them using a ouija board. Over several years we had hundreds of hours of 'talk' with departed souls; they were some of the most fascinating conversations of my life.

Did that communication with the other side come from our combined subconscious? That is certainly the most rational explanation. But I was raised to believe that a person's real life, the important and eternal part, began when they died. It was hammered into my brain every Sunday, and reinforced by my mother during the week, that every soul who had ever lived still existed. I figured that some had left their bodies peacefully, and hopefully they were safe in heaven. But many others had been ejected with no warning from their earthly moorings. Might they need to hang around for a while, till they got used to the idea of being dead?

As an adult I became highly sceptical about the existence of an afterlife. But the idea of it, which is a constant in all the religions I've heard about, continued to intrigue me. I explored this theme in my 'Ruby Clair' trilogy for tweens, making young Ruby more courageous than I ever was, bravely forcing herself to communicate with the departed without the prop of a ouija board.

In Anna's tween years I tried to reassure her that ghosts had been given a bad reputation in horror movies. If they did exist, they were most likely confused rather than vengeful, needing to face something or reaching out for help before they could rest in peace. But Anna was still afraid, so I would sit beside her until she went to sleep. This wasn't easy for me because I'm not very patient, and I don't like to sit in one place for long. But sit there I did, silently keeping the ghosts at bay, and gradually I would become more relaxed than I remember being before or since. This was long before I had a smartphone to play with. It was the closest I've ever come to meditating.

I now wonder if Anna also experienced visual hallucinations as a young child. When I was on family leave, before she went to school, she used to love being out in our big backyard with the cat and the slaters and other bugs, which she was a champion at spotting and catching. But once in a while she would run in, crying harder than she did at any other time. 'The eyes!' she'd sob. 'The eyes are looking at me again!'

'What eyes?' I'd ask, holding her on my lap, trying to soothe her. Her little body would be shaking: she was truly afraid. 'Whose eyes did you see?' I'd coax. 'Was it an animal, or a bird?'

'No!' she'd insist. It was just eyes, someone's eyes, but she didn't know whose. And when I'd go out to investigate I could never find anybody.

One day Sarah, a lovely woman I'd met at a writers' class, came over for lunch. We were chatting in the kitchen and Anna was playing outside. Suddenly she burst through the back door, ran over to me and clambered onto my lap. 'The eyes!' she gasped, clinging to me. I explained to Sarah about the eyes.

'I'm a medium,' Sarah said. 'I can communicate with spirits. I'll go see if there's anybody out there.'

A few minutes later she came back into the kitchen. Anna had calmed down by then. Sarah took her onto her lap and told her, 'It's a little Aboriginal boy. He told me he never means to scare you, he just wants to play. A long time ago, way before your house was built, he used to love playing here. But I told him how he makes you really afraid, and I asked him if he'd mind playing somewhere else.'

After that, Anna never mentioned the eyes again. Was it the suggestion Sarah planted in Anna's mind that made them go away? Quite possibly. Yet when I think of that autumn day with Sarah holding Anna on her lap in our kitchen full of light,

I always feel sad for the lonely little boy who only wanted to play.

Maybe I shouldn't have been so whimsical. Perhaps we should have taken Anna to a child psychologist back then. Were John and I actually harming our girl, by telling her to ignore the pain of school, by trying so hard to make her life at home safe, comfortable and fun?

It makes me ache to think we might have done that, when all we wanted was to smooth away Anna's angry scowl and see her gorgeous smile, the one we'd adored since we first saw it at five weeks of age. When she was eight and her heart was broken yet again because another girl in her class had flamboyantly distributed birthday party invitations without including Anna, I couldn't stand to see her in so much pain. I immediately wondered what I might do to make her feel better. 'How about a visit to the pet shop on Saturday?' I enthused. 'I bet your budgie would love a girlfriend.'

By providing an instant fix, was I setting her up for addiction? A bigger cage for her budgie did make her smile. As did the scores of fancy little fish who swam around the tank in our lounge room over the years. And the lizards, and the hermit crabs. We'd had a cat since Anna was three. He was our big, beautiful boy, Basil, the best cat I ever knew. And then there was a series of guinea pigs, cute little squeakers which, over the course of a couple of days, would produce their own weight in poop.

Anna was pretty good at feeding and cleaning up after her creatures, but of course they were ultimately my responsibility, with practical backup from John. This was disheartening sometimes, particularly with the hermit crabs, which needed a tank of sand kept at exactly the right temperature. If they were too cold they would burrow into the sand and hibernate, refusing to stick their eyes out on stalks the way Anna loved. Getting them too hot was even worse: the tiny one, which Anna named after my mother, crawled out of her shell one night and we couldn't figure out how to coax her back in. In those days we couldn't do a frantic Google search. All we had was a thin book from the pet shop and it did not address our particular emergency.

But the frustrations of trying to keep tropical crustaceans alive was nothing compared to the anxiety I felt attempting to keep the joy alight inside my daughter. Once, when she was in grade 5, Anna announced over dinner that she'd had a fantastic day at school. That got our attention! 'There's a new girl in our grade,' Anna sparkled. 'Miss Thompson got me to show her around. Her name's Sophie. She's really nice. Me and her are friends!'

Her enthusiasm made her look so beautiful, causing cold fingers of fear to close around my heart. Maybe Sophie *would* be the soulmate Anna was waiting for. But she was eleven years old by this stage, and the friend-keeping skills we'd hoped she would acquire just didn't seem to have developed. She seemed unable to decode the rules of childhood society.

For the next couple of days, Sophie was all we heard about at home. On the weekend, Anna wanted me to take her to buy a pair of those best-friend necklaces, the kind that is broken in two so each friend can wear half the heart. I made some excuse not to go.

I was afraid, so afraid, that when Sophie sussed out the power grid of the grade and gained a little confidence, she would drop my funny, needy daughter. And that's exactly what happened. Now I had to think of another quick fix: buy a new hermit crab, bake a batch of brownies . . . anything to ease her pain.

During the second half of grade 6, we dared to hope that Anna's troubles were beginning to resolve because she finally made an actual friend. It was a composite class and Anna's friend, Ellie, was in grade 5. She was a bouncy little thing with big brown eyes and a sense of humour that matched Anna's.

Of course, I feared her power over Anna, dreading the grief that might crush my girl if she was dumped. But when she came to our house, Ellie was so smiley and chatty, so full of light, I couldn't not like her.

It was a shame when Anna had to go off to high school alone, while her friend remained at primary school. John and I decided not to send Anna to Katie's high school, which I knew well – I'd worked there as a relieving assistant principal for three terms a few years earlier. It suited Katie perfectly. Multistorey and squashed into a tiny block in an inner suburb, it was staffed with terrific teachers, many of whom were also successful writers or artists. They treated their charges as young adults who did not require their education to be spoonfed.

Students who thrived there were mature for their age, independent and organised. Mature? Anna at the end of grade 6 didn't give a hoot about fashion or pop culture. Her idea of a great Saturday afternoon was hauling out her collection of Duplo and creating a safari park on the lounge-room floor, populating it with small stuffed animals while she did a running commentary in a David Attenborough accent. Independent? She could get lost walking back from the toilet to our table at the local shopping centre food court. As for organised . . . she was unbelievably hopeless with her possessions. Anything that left the house with her was in grave danger of never being seen again: sunglasses, purses, school books, even school shoes . . . I know, try to figure that one out. Anna was often in tears over what she had lost, and John at the end of his tether. 'Think!' he would demand. 'Where did you last have it? Why don't you put things where they *belong*?' She didn't know. She couldn't remember. With Anna, it seemed that physical objects had a life of their own, and could at will float off into the ether, never to be seen again.

There was one other important characteristic a student needed at Katie's school: being able to make informed decisions about whether, or how much, to partake in the smorgasbord of drugs that were conspicuously available in the area. We trusted Katie to make her own decisions on this score, as we had when we were young. But we didn't want Anna to be tempted. She was so gullible.

With the skills required for Katie's school pretty much entirely lacking in Anna, we decided that the local girl's secondary was a better choice for her. One of the few single-sex government secondary colleges in Melbourne, it was thriving – with over a thousand students – and had an excellent reputation. The principal, a well-known figure in our community, looked like she had stepped from the pages of a nineteenth-century novel. She and her loyal band of dedicated but traditional teachers attracted families from a wide area who preferred their daughters not to be educated with boys. Katie would have hated the protective atmosphere of the place, but we believed Anna needed the guidance.

At the beginning of 2001, the year Anna started high school, I was on a high. With John's blessing, I had resigned from the Education Department to pursue my dream of working full time on my writing. Actually, it wouldn't be quite full time. I wasn't adventurous or confident enough for that, and I still wanted to keep my hand in with education, so I signed on at the local high school to do emergency teaching. But I stipulated I could only do two days a week. And sometimes, if I was working towards a book deadline or travelling, I would be unavailable for much longer chunks of time. The chance to write seriously, combined with well-paid and flexible work, felt wonderful. I'd only been this excited a few times before in my adult life: like when I found out I was pregnant for the first time, or when Penguin informed me that they would love to publish my first novel.

John relinquished his position of stay-at-home dad and went back to paid employment, this time as a quarantine officer, one of those guys at the airport who, when you're coming into Australia, X-ray your luggage and inspect your shoes, to keep nasty biological surprises out of the country. The girls and I were proud of John for gaining this important job.

Katie got a job too, working after school and on weekends at the local McDonald's. So the three of us were happy when Anna began year 7. We encouraged her to be happy too, to view high school as a new start. Almost all of her classmates from primary school were going to the local co-ed secondary college; we only knew one girl from up the street who would also be going to the girls' college, so we felt this would give Anna the chance to create a whole new image. Katie and I were generous with advice on how to make friends.

Me: *I hated school too until I was in year 10. That's when I decided to stand up straight and look everyone in the eye and say hello. It was like a miracle. People liked me!*

Katie: *I didn't know anybody on my first day of high school, so I made sure I learned as many names as quickly as I could. You should smile a lot, but you also gotta know when to give a good greasy.*

Anna claimed that she tried out our methods, they just didn't work. Thank goodness she still saw Ellie on the weekends, although at school it was the same old story: sometimes she would make a friend, but the friendship wouldn't last for more than a week or so. Academically she was fine. And it was obvious, at our first parent-teacher conference for year 7, how much her teachers liked her. I remember the burly science guy telling us, 'Anna's a lovely little girl.'

Like at kinder and primary school, the other kids soon found her a weirdo, a dork, a loser. I'd see gaggles of girls walking home from school, giggling together, stopping at the local 7-Eleven for Slurpees and gossip. Anna plodded home alone in her green-and-white checked summer dress, her legs looking too skinny to lift the heavy school shoes she hated. As the weather cooled, she switched to the forest-green jumper and woollen skirt, but still she found no one to walk beside her.

I kept urging her to challenge her image, to employ the smile she so seldom displayed, which lit up her heart-shaped face. She told me one day she had gathered the courage to try. She'd sat down beside a likely girl in class and smiled at her and said a friendly hello, but that girl had gathered up her books and moved to a different seat.

Oh, God. What could I do to make her happy? I tried to spend even more time with her. I suggested that we turn some of the stories we made up during our cubbyhouse time into books, and Anna loved the idea. Katie and I had already done this when she was eleven, which resulted in a little novel called *Too Much to Ask For*, published in the Aussie Bites series. Katie had enjoyed writing with me in cafes on Saturday mornings while Anna was practising with the Australian Girls Choir, but she'd found the business of editing, revising and waiting for publication too tedious to repeat. She did like the money, though. I split the proceeds with her fifty-fifty, and even though the royalty cheques petered out pretty quickly, to this day the book earns money through the Public and Educational Lending Rights schemes, in which writers and illustrators are paid a few cents each time a book is checked out from a public or school library.

Anna was very keen to try writing a book with me, and she didn't mind the tedious parts. Together we created a trilogy of novels for tweens, which went on to be published by Penguin as *Two Weeks in Grade Six*, *A Term in Year Seven* and *Escape from Year Eight*. The books featured Kaitlin, a girl who finds it hard to fit in at school. During cubbyhouse time, as I sat beside her bed in the dark, Anna and I would work out the basics of the plot. While she was at school, I'd go to the local library and write broad outlines. Then on weekends and during the school holidays, she was my trusty little apprentice; she would sit beside me in the study, typing out the story as we worked on how to phrase every single sentence. Anna came up with some of our best lines, like the one when Kaitlin finally confronts the class bully by blurting out to her, 'I'd rather be fat than have lip gloss for brains!' Anna loved the book launches, where she amazed the guests with her assured and eloquent speeches. But at school, where our hero Kaitlin in the end prevails, Anna couldn't.

Through the challenges she faced in her childhood and early teenage years, Anna had one champion, an admirer who identified with her and was firmly on her side: her grand-mother. My mother. She and Anna wrote to each other every week. Long before Anna could write letters herself, when she was still a toddler, I would transcribe her stories and put them in an envelope along with one or two of her drawings, and send them off to my parents. As Anna's competence grew, she would write the letters herself, and make elaborate creations out of cardboard and glitter and fluorescent paint.

I encouraged Anna to do this. Each week I would remind her when it was time to write to Grandmother. I'd make suggestions of what she might draw or stories she could relate. Often I'd photocopy something to include: perhaps one of her school reports, which were always excellent, or a review of one of our books (not always excellent, but I only sent the good ones). In return, Mother would write to Anna, telling her over and over again how proud she was of her, how she was the best granddaughter ever. Was this just another way I enabled my daughter, making sure she got a serotonin rush in the letterbox every week? Maybe. But it was also a way to encourage the lovely relationship that Anna and my mother had. Mother never badmouthed other people in her letters to Anna, never exposed the bitterness and pain with which she had soaked my childhood.

This is partly because my mother really did want to be a good person. She might not have been able to keep her pain from spurting out in verbal attacks against those she loved, but writing uses a different part of the brain. When she was inhabiting that part, she was very careful. Also, Anna's childhood coincided with the happiest years of Mother's, and my dad's, life. They retired from the farm in their mid-sixties and moved 15 miles up the highway to Maxwell, a little town of about 900 people. Mother's favourite aunt had lived there and Mother had long envied her thriving community, based around the church. The deal that clinched Maxwell for my parents was that they found Mother's dream house there; it had two storeys with a full basement, and was as neatly painted and gabled as a home in a child's storybook. To Mother's delight, the church in town lived up to her expectations, offering not only groups to join but women who she considered her intellectual equals. I never understood, when I was growing up, how lonely Mother must have been on the farm. She didn't fit in with the other wives in the neighbourhood, or with Dad's seven sisters. In Maxwell, for the first time in her adult life, she had friends.

And so, with Mother's support, we helped Anna through to year 9. We kept hoping that as each year passed, life would become easier for her. As Anna and her classmates got older, we counted on her peers to gradually become less concerned with everybody acting the same. Differences would begin to be tolerated and then, we thought, Anna would shine. But there was no sign of this happening quite yet. As a result, I hatched a plan intended to make her smile: I'd take her on an extended trip! I would take her away from year 9 for most of the second and third terms. This was my present to her, something to take her mind off the classmates who caused her so much pain, to get her that much closer to an age when they would appreciate her quirky gifts.

This present to Anna would mean spending four months away from Katie and John. Katie was about to begin her final year at high school, and though many mothers would never consider leaving the country for that amount of time during their child's year 12 studies, I wasn't really worried. While

Katie and I have always been incredibly close emotionally, she showed me from an early age that she would experiment with life in her own way, thank you very much. My favourite example of this happened about a week after she began prep. When I arrived to pick her up at the end of the day, her teacher informed me that Katie had had to spend lunchtime with the principal. Apparently, after recess, Katie had not appeared in the classroom with the rest of the class. The principal had to search for her, and found her playing in a far corner of the yard.

'Why did you do that?' I demanded of Katie.

'Well,' she calmly replied, 'I saw all the others kids go in when the bell rang, but I wanted to see what happened if I didn't.'

Having not particularly enjoyed lunch with the principal, Katie went back to obeying the school bell. But this didn't squelch the clear-eyed need, which she had inherited from her father, to think for herself. Long before she began VCE, I'd learned not to suggest how or when she should do her homework because it would likely end up in tears on both our sides.

Many nights, Katie wasn't home for me to observe whether she was studying anyway. During years 11 and 12, Katie often stayed with Helinka, her best friend at high school. Helinka lived near the school so it meant less travelling for Katie. Helinka's mother, Jodie, had plenty of room for both girls in her spectacular renovated warehouse, and loved being Katie's 'second mum'. Helinka was a quiet girl whose passions were thick fantasy novels and horses, so at a glance she seemed very different from our loud and colourful Katie. But they were, and still are, united in their determination to live life in their own way.

As for being away from John, that was a challenge I savoured. Then, as now, our marriage formed the bedrock of my life, and I didn't want to imagine a time when he would not be available to deal with my computer issues or share a good story with me. But sometimes I hankered for a taste of being single again, for the chance to make plans and decisions without always considering his wishes, to make mistakes and mop them up using my own methods, minus his sometimes less-than-compassionate commentary. He didn't mind having some time off from me once in a while, either. In fact, while I was away, he was planning to take a month of long-service leave to do some intensive bushwalking. I'd tried that with him when we first got together, in the wilds of south-western Tasmania, and it was harder than being in labour. I didn't care to encounter either of those experiences again in this lifetime.

When I told my mother of my plan to give Anna a break, she couldn't have been more supportive. She sent us money to help with airfares and suggested, 'Do some travelling on your way here.' I also withdrew funds from a bond I'd invested in before I met John, which I'd kept all these years to use for something special.

This was indeed special. We planned a wonderful trip: stop off in Hawaii for a week, then fly to Seattle and stay with my best friend from uni, spend two summer months in Iowa, a place Anna loved, then move on to England where my oldest Australian friend, Anna's godmother, was living for a while in a village near Cambridge.

My heart danced when Anna's eyes lit up as we surfed the internet together, researching hotels in Hawaii. We chose a room with a glorious view over the beach, and booked it.

For a few precious weeks I looked forward to Anna being happy. Then one night, about a month before we were due to leave, the cry of the phone sliced through my dreams. It was my sister Joan ringing from Iowa, forgetting that it was the middle of the night for me. 'Can you come home right away?' she asked. 'We took Mother to the hospital about her headaches. She's got a brain tumour and they say she only has weeks to live.'

Chapter 7

With disappointment and worry clutching at my throat, I cancelled our booking at the beautiful hotel in Hawaii and emailed my dear old pal in Seattle to tell her that we wouldn't be visiting after all. Our travel agent rearranged our tickets so we could leave within the next few days and fly straight to Iowa.

I was mad. Why did things always go wrong for Anna? She'd really been looking forward to meeting my friend from college. And instead of enjoying the Midwestern summer with her beloved grandmother, she was flying over to watch her die.

But actually, the change of plan turned out to be good for Anna. We touched down in Des Moines in the chilly rain of early April. My nephew Phillip picked us up from the airport and we drove down the highway into the rural heart of the state. My parents lived in Baxter now. They'd hated to move away from their community in Maxwell, but when they reached their mid-eighties and Dad's robust health suddenly plummeted, they needed to be close to my sister Linda, who lived on the farm. I'd loved our country community when I was growing up, and some of our neighbours still shine in my mind as the most eccentric, and best, people I ever knew. But a handful of miles down the blacktop was Baxter, where I'd gone to school. I'd never felt totally accepted in that town. Neither had my parents. Every little town has its own personality, and Baxter's was so conservative that we didn't really fit in.

Several years earlier, Linda and her husband Jack, whom she adored, had bought from my parents the farmhouse where we grew up, along with a sizeable chunk of the land surrounding it. Linda and Jack's dream was to turn it into a picturesque ranch for breeding horses. They made a start by investing in half a dozen Arabian mares. After these lovely creatures were impregnated, but before the foals were born, Jack died of esophageal cancer. Linda stayed on the farm, devastated but stoic. She didn't have the heart to try running a breeding business on her own, but she did keep her favourite mares and some of their baby girls.

My parents had stayed healthy and active into their eighties, but then an abnormality my dad was born with, but had been unaware of, betrayed him. It was a tangle of blood vessels at the base of his brain, and one night it ruptured. He recovered from that mentally, but not physically. As he put it, 'I can't see worth a darn.' His balance was also totally out of whack, making it very difficult for him to walk, let alone negotiate stairs. So Mother had to say goodbye to her beautiful, impeccably decorated home, and to her beloved church. Her health was deteriorating, too. She was determined not to give up their independence entirely, but knew she and Dad needed help, and Linda was willing to provide this. In Baxter, my parents found a one-storey house with no stairs that was ideal for them at that stage of their lives. Mother hated it.

Linda's proximity meant that she spent lots of time looking after Mother and Dad, even though she was still teaching, working full time as head of the history department of a high school near Des Moines.

As the cornfields whizzed by outside the car windows, Phil tried to prepare us for how much Mother had degenerated in the two weeks since the diagnosis. 'She's bad,' he said, 'really bad.'

My stomach was tight with apprehension as Phil parked in my parents' garage and led us in through the side door of the house into the kitchen. Thank goodness Dad was still his sardonic self. I was relieved to see that even though he was leaning on a cane, he was at least standing. When I hugged him and asked how he was, he huffed, 'Old and fat!' He said I had got too skinny and Anna too tall since we last visited. Mother, huddled in a chair in the corner, with the plastic prongs of an oxygen hose in her nostrils, smiled and reached out to Anna, saying, 'Come here, honey.' As Anna leaned over and hugged her, Mother observed, 'You're still mighty pretty.'

Those were more or less the last positive words I heard my mother say. In the past, she would always sprinkle our conversations with compliments as well as criticism, but dying made her really grumpy.

Arriving earlier than planned was a boon for Anna, as school was still in session. Anna actually liked school in Iowa. She'd had a taste of it during our previous visit, when she was eleven. Now, at fourteen, I was able to enrol her as a freshman in the same high school that I had attended. Anna spent six weeks there, till school broke up for the summer.

Why was she able to head off to my old school every morning with her face lit up by a smile? Because the Iowa kids put any weirdness she projected down to her being a funny blonde Aussie with an adorable accent? Because she loved the elective subject where she learned about hog breeding and got to go on excursions to working farms? Because she joined the track team and used her long legs to help with the relay races? I suspect that having boys in the class was also part of the allure. That's one area of life Anna never had any trouble with: attracting male attention.

At the time, my mind wasn't focused on why Anna was happier than usual. She was staying out at the farm with Linda, because she liked both the farm and Linda a lot. And I knew she was getting a kick out of riding the big yellow school bus, just like the ones on American TV. So I was glad for Anna . . . and also I was totally distracted, instantly sucked into my mother's powerful orbit.

In the weeks before Anna and I arrived, Mother had become too sick to be left with Dad for hours at a time, so my other sister, Joan, had been staying with them. As soon as I'd stepped in the door, Joan took the chance to return to her own home and husband further north in Cedar Falls. She promised to be back soon.

My sisters and I had different ways of dealing with being raised by our mother.

Joan said that she hadn't experienced any bad times while growing up. But in my head, there vividly existed several painful scenes from the time before she went away to college, involving her and Mother. When I asked Joan about these episodes, she said she had no recollection of them. Over the years, whenever she came to visit the farm, she always talked sweetly to our mother. But sometimes, when Mother aimed one too many snide remarks at her, I would see the pain flame in Joan's eyes. Usually she would make it to her car before she started to cry, but she might not return for quite a while.

Unlike Joan, Linda and I have TGR (Total Grievance Recall) where Mother is concerned. When I was a teenager, Linda was in her twenties, working first as a secretary in

Des Moines and later studying at university to be a teacher. It was my greatest joy to go and stay at her house, sometimes for days at a time. During the evening and deep into the night, as well as chatting to spirits via the ouija board, we would discuss the escalating horror of the Vietnam War and our fervent hope that Bobby Kennedy would become president. Our other main topic was our mother. We engaged in a strange sort of competition, comparing insults that Mother had hurled at us over the years. Sharing the hurt did not extinguish it, but it was an enormous comfort to me to know my adored big sister was on my side.

Before Joan returned to her home, she and Linda had thoughtfully hired a wonderful local nurse who stopped in to see Mother twice a day, so that I wouldn't be left entirely in charge. The nurse had arranged for a hospital bed to be put into Mother's bedroom, with a commode beside it and a supply of morphine pills.

With Joan gone and Linda and Anna at their respective schools, there was just me and Mother and Dad in the little house for long stretches of time. I had to admit Mother was right. Compared to her storybook abode in Maxwell, this house was a big comedown. It was a practical rectangle sitting on a concrete slab, with the long side of the rectangle running parallel to the street. The front half of the house was a long room, with the kitchen down one end and the living area down the other. The back half was divided into two large bedrooms, both with ensuites. One also had a purpose-built closet for the washer and dryer.

The house was neat and clean, and the furniture was functional, but it was obvious that since she moved in, Mother had been too sick or disheartened to put any care into decorating the rooms. I especially missed the many lusty pot plants she had always nurtured so expertly. The home's sterility put me in a bad mood, and that made me angry at myself. I had recently read a novel about a daughter caring for her dying mother. The daughter had been grateful and the mother graceful. I was mad at both of us for not being them.

One morning I was feeling especially tired and cross. I'd slept, or more like attempted to sleep, in the single bed next to Mother's. She had woken me up every hour or so needing to use the commode. Not only was I tired, I was also still smarting from the night before. Linda had called by with Anna after school as usual, to see if there was anything she could help with. Afterwards, she and Anna went out to the farm to have supper, the Iowan term for the evening meal. For her supper, Mother announced, 'I'll just have me a bowl of strawberry ice cream.' I'd had a salad, and for Dad I'd fished a beef-and-mash dinner out of the freezer. For a TV dinner, it looked surprisingly appetising, complete with a brownie in its own tiny compartment for dessert. Mother had eyed it disparagingly. 'Why didn't you get Shurfine?' she demanded.

Shurfine was the house brand carried by the local grocery store. Dad's dinner was the more expensive and well-known Swanson.

'I didn't buy it,' I protested. 'It was already there. Linda or Joan must have got it.'

There was pain in Mother's eyes that morphine couldn't touch. Only a few weeks ago she could drive to the grocery store and do the shopping herself.

'Swanson tastes better,' Dad remarked.

'No, it don't!' Mother fumed. She turned to me, 'You shouldn't be spending so much money. You should be cooking.'

I knew she didn't begrudge me money. All my life she had been more than generous with me in that department. Also, all my life, bitching at her family – or raging at us – had been her way of easing her internal agony. That understanding didn't stop me from feeling bad about her chastising me.

So on this particular day, even though I was cranky from lack of sleep, I was determined to cook. Actually, I'd started to look forward to it.

It was midmorning and finally Mother had fallen into a deep sleep. Dad and I were sitting at the kitchen table sipping coffee and munching cookies. Not the store-brand ones but Oreos with double filling. I flipped through a few pages of the *Better Homes and Gardens New Cook Book*, which was far from new. Its red-and-white checked cover looked as familiar as the oilcloth that used to cover our kitchen table on the farm. In the fish and seafood section, I spotted a recipe Mother used to make, for potluck dinners in the church basement. It was nutritious and easy to chew.

'How about salmon loaf for supper?' I suggested to Dad.

He was half deaf and I braced myself for his 'Huh?', but he hadn't even noticed I'd said anything. He was staring longingly at the closed bedroom door.

'Are you sure your mother's all right?' he asked plaintively.

'She's fine,' I said. Of course she wasn't fine, but she was definitely still alive. 'I can hear her snoring.'

'I better wake her up.'

'Why?'

'She ought to be out here visitin' with us.' There was so much pain in his voice. After sixty-seven years of marriage, he was still in love with his bride. Linda and I could never figure out why he felt like that, since Mother often spoke to him in the same mean way she did to us. Somehow, he was able to look past that and see in his wife only the goodness, which no one could dispute was also there.

I said, 'She needs to rest, Dad.' But he was already up, opening the bedroom door. Ten years before, Dad had still been a strong man. There was no way I could have physically stopped him getting to her bedside. Now I could, easily, but I didn't. I stood in the doorway and watched as he shook her arm. 'Lela, wake up. You don't want to be sleepin' all day.'

She woke up. And boy, was she grumpy. 'Don't help me!' She snapped as Dad tried to assist her onto the commode beside the bed. 'You helped enough already by wakin' me up!'

I helped get her onto the pot. 'Bring me a morphine and two Tylenol,' she instructed me firmly.

I got the pills, and a glass of water, but by the time I took them to the bedroom, she'd changed her mind. 'I better eat me something before I take those. You could fix me some oatmeal.'

She managed to shuffle into the kitchen with her walker, with Dad in her wake, by the time I'd prepared the instant oatmeal. She ate about half of it, then put the spoon down with a pained look on her face. 'I had enough.'

'You gonna take those?' I pointed to the three pills she'd requested, which I'd put beside the bowl.

'Why didn't you give them to me *before*?' she whined, poking at them. 'Then I might be feelin' better by now.'

I forced out a calm voice. 'I thought you wanted them after the oatmeal. Here's a glass of water.'

She made a big production out of swallowing a Tylenol capsule. 'I don't know why you can't give me apple sauce. My mouth's awful dry.'

Oh God, I'd forgotten she took her pills on a spoon, with apple sauce or yoghurt. I was such a crap carer. 'Sorry,' I said as I went to the fridge. When I returned to the table with the apple sauce, she asked in a worried voice, 'Where's the morphine pill?'

The tiny disc was not there. 'Didn't you take it?'

'No.'

'It must have fallen on the floor, then.' I looked, but couldn't see it.

'Get the flashlight,' she commanded. 'It's in the garage. Get the little blue one, not that big red one.'

I located the required torch, and searched on my hands and knees under the table, but the pill was not in evidence. 'I'll get you another one,' I said. I put it on a spoon with a dab of apple sauce, and she swallowed it. Then she said, horror on her face, 'Maybe I did take that other one.'

'Don't worry. Ten extra grains of morphine won't hurt you.'

'How would you know?' she demanded. She still had plenty of energy in her voice. 'You better call the hospital.'

I didn't want to bother them. I tried to distract her by letting her know we wouldn't be unfreezing any expensive TV dinners that night because I was going to cook, like she wanted me to. I told her what I planned to make for supper. I said I'd fix enough for Linda and Anna and we could all eat together.

Dad was sitting across the table from Mother. His deafness prevented him from following our conversation word for word, but he could read the look on his wife's face. 'What's the matter?' he asked her.

'What do you *think*'s the matter?' She was about to cry. 'I'm dying and all Mary Kay cares about is salmon loaf!'

Chapter 8

Anna was really getting into life as an American high-schooler. She loved being on the track team. Though she didn't win any blue ribbons as an athlete, she thought it was great riding the yellow bus after school to interschool competitions around the district. There were boys as well as girls on board! When she and Linda would stop by the Baxter house, Anna was always chirpy and smiley.

For me, when Linda and Anna were at their respective schools or out on the farm, the monotonous days crawled by, with Mother sleeping a lot and Dad watching TV with the volume turned up so loudly I had to wear earplugs. Though I wanted so much for these last weeks with Mother to brim with meaning, I felt like my mind was atrophying from boredom. I missed John a lot more than I thought I would. My body must have been rejoicing at some level, to go so long without alcohol, but my soul longed to look forward to that glass of wine after work, when I'd sit and chat and laugh with my husband out on our front deck, or in cooler weather in our big kitchen full of light.

John and I exchanged emails in which I tried to make my experiences with Mother into entertaining tales. Sometimes I called home. If Katie was there, hearing her voice would make me miss her intensely. I'd be standing at the wall-mounted phone in Mother and Dad's living room, and Katie's voice would be like a jolt of life zinging across the Pacific. Having adjusted to the slow cadence of my relatives' speech, I found it amazing how loud and fast and brightly Katie talked. How un-Iowan she sounded.

Then, one boring morning, Mother's pain suddenly increased dramatically. She was moaning horribly, declaring that the agony was worse than childbirth. I called our nurse and it only took her a few minutes to get to our place. Mother begged the nurse not to send her to the hospital. 'If you take me down there, I'll never come home again!' But the nurse knew that Mother needed more intensive care. She summoned an ambulance.

Within half an hour the paramedics clomped in with a rolling bed; two big men wearing heavy boots and sweet smiles. They were proud of their brand-new ambulance, a boxy vehicle in fire-engine red, like something out of *Thomas the Tank Engine*.

Mother clutched my hand. 'Can my daughter ride with me?'

'Of course.'

My soul lit up. Despite my shortcomings, my mother wanted me by her side. I left a message with Linda's school to tell her we were on our way to the hospital, and asked her to let Joan and Anna know. I was ashamed of the flutter of excitement I felt at getting to ride in the cartoonish ambulance.

The men were very gentle with my grouchy mother. One of them drove while the other tended to her in the back of the ambulance. He sat on one side of her bed, while I sat on the other. We each held one of her hands.

We drove east to Newton, up the blacktop, then turned south onto Highway 14. Newton was our county seat, the once bustling little city where my dad worked at the Maytag washing-machine factory for nearly thirty years, after he had to admit that he couldn't provide for his family by relying solely on the farm. The route we took in the ambulance was the same one Mother had driven hundreds of times, with me in the passenger seat, when I was growing up. Most often it would be on a Saturday afternoon. First we would go to the Hy-Vee for groceries, and then she would take me to the most magical place of my childhood and teenage years: the Jasper County Library.

'How many hours do you reckon we spent at the library?' I asked her. 'If you added them all up . . . maybe a year?'

She couldn't answer. The jarring of the ambulance was making her pain worse. She gripped my hand and cried, 'Oh! Oh!' She meant '*Fuck!*' but she'd never sworn in her life.

The ambulance officer soothed, 'I know, Lela, I know. We'll be there soon and we can get you some proper relief.'

He spoke to her the way you would to a beloved baby. The sound of his rich, deep Iowan voice made me want to love her like that, too. I wanted to gather her up and hold her on my lap, to make her understand how precious this gift was that she had given me, the irreplaceable present of books.

Mother was right: she never came home. By the end of that day, she'd been 'made comfortable'; in other words, pumped full of morphine, at the hospice in Newton.

Mother had her own spacious room at the hospice. It included easychairs for visitors, and a couch that pulled out into a bed so a family member could stay overnight. There was even a little kitchen with a bar fridge and a microwave, and that indispensable part of every Iowan home, a coffee maker. Mother lay at the centre of all this, with a catheter inserted so she'd never have to get out of bed again. Near her right hand, resting on the starched sheet, was a button connected to a morphine pump. Her doctor assured us that she couldn't overdose, that he'd carefully calculated the amount of morphine that she needed to keep from hurting. 'But she'll still be alert,' he told me. 'Now that we've got her pain managed, she'll be able to enjoy these last days with you and the rest of the family.'

The doctor stepped into the room, went over to my mother and patted her shoulder. 'Now, Lela,' he said gently, but with reassuring authority, 'if you even begin to feel any breakthrough pain at all, you press that button right away.'

My mother smiled up at him. 'Thanks, Doctor.'

Now that she was on her comfy deathbed, I somehow believed my mother was going to be a sweet old lady, like in the movies, handing me golden nuggets of end-of-life wisdom that I could carry with me until the end of my days. But as soon as the doctor was out of earshot, she turned to me and demanded, in a voice entirely devoid of sugar, 'Where's my watch?'

I flinched. Just like when I was ten years old, a harsh tone from her made my stomach clench and my heart thump. What could I do, what could I say to stop her being angry, to make her like me again? 'We must have left your watch at home. I'll bring it in tomorrow. I'll make a list of all the stuff you need . . .'

'No, we didn't leave it! I had it right on my wrist when we came in here. That nurse took it.'

'What? A nurse wouldn't do that.'

'I know which one it was. That one who took down all the *details*,' Mother said scathingly. 'She liked it and took it right off my wrist.'

My mother could be so kind and patient. When I was six years old, Grandma and Grandpa, my dad's parents, still lived on the farm a couple of miles up the road from us. This was the year that Evelyn, my uncle's pretty young wife, lay on the couch in Grandma's living room. No one told me why Evelyn didn't stand up and get busy like all the other adults I knew. She smelled funny, and when her two tiny kids clambered up to be with her, she'd tell them to lie still and be quiet. She had to go to the hospital in Marshalltown for quite a while. When she returned to the house, this time to lie in the dark little bedroom off the living room, her right leg was gone. Again, nobody thought it was a good idea to explain to me what had happened, but I overheard Grandma talking to one of my aunts about 'stopping the spread of cancer'.

When Evelyn died, her little girl and boy, Lou Ann and Dougie, came to stay with us. They slept in my room; Dougie in a cot and Lou Ann in my bed with me. I loved the sound of their breathing in the darkness and I longed to keep them, for them to be my own little brother and sister. Dougie was still a toddler and Lou Ann was four. In the middle of the night she would wake up sobbing, begging for her mommy. I was a sound sleeper in those days and would only be half aware of what was happening, but I'd feel relief when my mother would appear, whisper to Lou Ann and lead her out of the room. As I slipped back into delicious oblivion, I knew Mother would be sitting in the big chair in the living room, with Lou Ann on her lap, speaking to her soothingly and rocking her back to sleep.

My little cousins didn't turn into my brother and sister. Their dad came and picked them up one day and they went back to being his. But through the years I witnessed many times like this when my mother lavished on others her gift of nurturing. She could take a dozen day-old chicks and look after them so well she didn't lose a single one, raising them all to be productive hens. When it came time to kill one, she would do it herself, pluck out its feathers, butcher it and transform it into the crispiest, most delicious fried chicken anyone ever tasted. She would make that chicken as perfect as possible for her family, serving it up with mashed potatoes and sweet corn from her garden. But she wouldn't eat a bit of it herself.

This was my mother: a relentlessly hard-working farm woman, who would uncomplainingly give up her sleep to comfort a grieving child; who couldn't bring herself to devour an animal she had raised by hand; who, after she had retired and with hands increasingly crippled by arthritis, would take the trouble to buy, parcel up and send beautiful dresses and babydolls to her little granddaughters across the sea.

This was also my mother: someone you could never relax with, because at any second she might turn on you. And when she did, she aimed to hurt. She was smart and insightful enough to know just what to say to skewer your soul.

Mother lay in that hospice bed for three weeks, and during that time I observed something that took me years to get my head around: she hated that nasty part of herself perhaps even more than we did. With the help of professional counselling, I now understand she desperately wanted to be good; she strove every day to win God's approval. But there was something inside her that hurt so badly, it burst out in snarling rages to bite and diminish those who meant everything to her. She didn't know how to control it. And, at least in those days when she knew she was facing death, she was terrified of it.

She was afraid it would send her to hell.

Anna only visited Mother two or three times at the hospice, mostly because she was busy with school and track. And it wasn't as if Mother was short of visitors. Five of Dad's sisters were still alive then, and two of them had partners, old guys they had acquired after their husbands died. Some combination of these seven was usually around, along with visits by folks from the Maxwell church. My sister Joan had also returned and was staying at the farm with Linda. But these weren't the main reasons I didn't encourage Anna to frequent the hospice more regularly. The real reason was that Mother's death was a terrible thing to witness. She wasn't in physical pain; her devoted doctor and the endlessly patient hospice nurses made sure of that. But mentally, emotionally, her agony was brutal. Perhaps the opiates that kept her physically comfortable contributed to her terror, to her unshakable belief that God was reviewing a ledger of every good and bad thing she had ever done or said or thought, and as the day of her death drew ever nearer, the tally was tipping her into flames, where she would burn for the rest of eternity.

The pastor from the church in Maxwell would often come to stand beside Mother's deathbed and pray with her. She never wanted him to leave. She would ask him, in a raspy and desperate voice, if he was sure that as long as a person repented from their sins, Jesus would forgive them. When the pastor couldn't be there, Mother would command Dad and my sisters and aunts (whom she'd never before cared to be friends with) to form a circle around her bed, hold hands and implore God to admit her to heaven. We reassured her a thousand times that she wasn't going to hell. We reminded her of the scene in the Gospels when Jesus told the thief on the cross next to him that since he had repented, they would be together that night in paradise.

My poor mother. Despite her fog of morphine and fear, she saw through us. She knew that we would, as we always had, tell her whatever she wanted to hear. And there was another voice that raged in her brain and would not be silenced as the tumour spread its cells. It was that of her father, whom she hated with a passion I have not witnessed in anybody else. She had been the only child of his born with the guts to stand up to him and try to defend her cherished mother against his tongue and fists. He could not make her respect him, no matter how much he beat her. This man, at ninety, was featured on the front page of the local paper because he had not missed a single Sunday at church for seventy years. There was no mention of him bellowing a curse at his young daughter that would follow her to her grave: 'God damn your soul to hell!'

I wasn't with my mother when she died. Dad said he couldn't stand to see her take her last breath, so I stayed home with him. My sisters were at her side, along with three of my aunts. One of them was Aunt La Von, who had worked at the local nursing home for decades and witnessed many old souls depart this earth. She said of Mother's last moments: 'I never saw anything like it. I never knew anybody could be that afraid to die.'

For Mother's funeral, on a late spring morning, the Maxwell church that she had loved so much was packed. Before the service began, as was the custom in Iowa, the immediate family waited in the church basement till everyone else was seated. Cassandra, whom I call my little sister, was with us. She was the girl we knew as Stormy, and she'd driven over from her home in central Kansas. Stormy was another child my mother helped, taking her in to live with us for a time after her mother, one of our neighbours, died. Stormy loved my mother with a love more clear and fierce than I could feel. It was colder than I'd anticipated in the church. Seeing me shivering with church-basement chill and nerves, Stormy came over to me and, without saying anything, took off her own jacket and draped it across my shoulders.

When all the other mourners had been seated, a young usher, who had taken the morning off from his farmwork, showed Mother's husband, children and grandchildren to the pew at the front of the church. I gave my mother's eulogy, which I'd spent many hours preparing. I tried to portray her life as more than the list of dates when she was born, married and had children. Without saying too much that she might have yelled at me for revealing, I wanted to give the listeners in that church a real picture of this glitteringly intelligent, wounded woman. I knew I couldn't get through it without my voice breaking. But I also knew that as a professional writer, it was one last gift I owed my mother.

Chapter 9

Anna and I stayed on in Iowa for a month after Mother died. School was finished for the summer, but Anna remained cheerful. I spent most of my time with Dad. He didn't enjoy going out to the farm much. It was difficult for him to get around out there with his wobbly walking, and I think it was just too hard to be on the land he had loved so passionately and not be able to get his hands in the dirt and grow something. As a result, we usually stayed in town.

Of course, Dad grieved. Several times a day he would say to me, 'I wish I could just have one more hour with your mother.' But he also made an effort to join in the life my sisters and I wanted to help establish for him. We encouraged him to buy a motorised mobility scooter, so he could ride along the sidewalks of Baxter to visit his sisters, two of whom had retired from their farms and moved to town. Some of our old neighbours had also done that. We talked Dad into getting tested and fitted for hearing aids. It was then much easier to have a conversation with him, so he and I did a lot of chatting. I felt like, for the first time, I was really getting to know my father, the man who'd stood in the shadow of my mother all my life.

As for Anna, she liked life on the farm more than ever now that Linda didn't have to drive off to work early in the morning and return home tired. They got along great, picking cherries together while complaining about the state of the world.

I think Anna found it a relief to be with someone who wasn't always telling her to look on the positive side. And there were horses to ride, new kittens born in the hay loft, dogs to play with, and Cookie the rabbit, who submitted to Anna giving him cuddles for hours in front of the TV, wearing a stoic look between his long floppy ears.

When it came time to leave Iowa, I was uneasy to be taking Anna away from a place where she was happy. No, it was more than that. It felt wrong. I remember lying in bed the night before we flew out and hearing a voice inside my head telling me with great force, 'Leave her here! For God's sake. Don't take her back there.' Whose voice was it? If I'd listened to it, perhaps we could have dodged all the pain that was to come. But how could I have heeded it? She was fourteen years old. As fond as Linda was of Anna, she certainly hadn't volunteered to adopt her. I needed to head back to my life in Australia, and I couldn't go without my girl.

I also had a plan for us and once I've made a plan, it takes something drastic to make me change it. Our travel agent had managed to re-route our round-the-world tickets, but they still required a stopover in Europe. So we flew to Madrid, just the two of us. We were to have two and a half weeks in Spain, then go on to England.

Spain was glorious, and I was pleased with myself for successfully getting us around using my rusty university Spanish. But even though I kept pointing out reasons to be cheerful, the smiley Anna of Iowa had begun to frown full time. Looking back at us plodding through the hottest summer that Europe had ever experienced, I'm exasperated at the depth of my denial. I told myself that the constant, dull pain deep in my guts was caused by the change in water I drank, that the ulcers lining my mouth resulted from all those crusty loaves of white bread. What my mind refused to acknowledge, my body had to deal with.

As for my daughter, my tall, gorgeous girl who should have been peeping eagerly through the doorway into womanhood . . . it was during that northern hemisphere summer that she began to stop eating.

Looking back now, even before we left for our trip, I can see there were signs. John and I had always marvelled at Anna's skin. We called it baby skin, because all through her childhood it retained the sheen and delicacy of a newborn's, without a single mole or freckle anywhere. Maybe that's why she hated her first pimples with such intense ferocity. She scrutinised them in the mirror, she attacked them with expensive ointments, and finally she decided to give up fatty junk food.

This forgoing of fat didn't seem such an outlandish idea. At the time, I subscribed to the commonly held view that fat consumption contributed to pimples. And what parent is going to admonish her sullen teenager for deciding to cast aside her childhood passion for Reese's Peanut Butter Cups and dinosaur-shaped doughnuts? Plus, it took a while for her food rules to become ironclad. While we were in Iowa, she munched her way through more than one corn dog, that delicious Midwestern delicacy – a wiener on a stick, dipped in cornmeal dough and deep fried. And she loved my aunts' culinary offerings: Mary Lou's apple dumplings, La Von's coconut cream pie, Doris's gooey chocolate chip bars.

In Spain, Anna was still eating but, in hindsight, not nearly enough for a growing girl. She consumed less than I did, and I'm far from being a big eater.

Anna and I both felt better once we got to England. We stayed with Gill, my dear friend and Anna's godmother, in a village which till then had only been a quaint name to us – Swaffham Bulbeck. Now it sprang to life and became our home for five weeks. Gill was living there to be near her own aging and ailing father. Her wealthy and generous sister had bought an old stable, which had been converted into a comfortable house. She'd done this so that anyone wanting to visit their dad would have a place to stay near his supported accommodation. She even provided a car, a Volkswagen Polo. Anna and I each had a room to ourselves. There was a village green where Anna could run. Yes, the track team had given her the running bug. It didn't occur to me to think of her insistence on exercising for at least two hours every day as obsessive.

When I look back on that English summer, wondering how I could have been so blind to the signs of impending anorexia, one particular incident comes to mind. Gill, Anna and I were spending the afternoon at a nearby village fair. We stepped into the cool of the church hall for a cup of tea, and presented there on a trestle table was a delicious array of homemade goodies.

'Come on,' I urged Anna, 'have something. The sponge cake looks really good.' It did. The cream was obviously fresh, and I knew Anna loved strawberries. For once, she couldn't resist. In fact, she enjoyed the cake so much she had a second slice.

Later, when we were driving back to Swaffham, Anna had a conniption in the back seat: 'Why did you tell me to do that? You shouldn't have let me eat two pieces. I didn't even want one! You *made* me eat it! You're a bad mother!'

My mistake was to agree with her, because I knew exactly how she felt. How many thousands of times had I yelled at myself for scoffing down too much cake? I felt she was justified in angrily claiming her right to make her own choices about food. I promised my seriously underweight daughter that I would never again tempt her with cream sponge.

Chapter 10

'This is *disgusting*.' I poked at the dry and stringy piece of fish on the tray table in front of me. All through the sleepless airplane night I'd been looking forward to breakfast, and this was what I got. It was the 14th of August and we were on our way back to Australia.

'Why'd you insist on getting low fat?' I growled.

'You didn't have to just 'cause I did,' Anna pointed out, pretty snarly, as she cracked open her hard, cold bread roll.

'The omelettes look good,' I whined, eyeing off the meals of the sensible passengers in our row. 'I didn't think they'd give me fish,' I muttered.

I peeled the top off my no-fat yoghurt (strawberry, my least favourite flavour), downed a slug of the awful coffee and told myself to stop complaining. I switched my voice to non-cranky and said to Anna, 'If this is the worst thing that happens to me today, I'll be lucky.'

She gave a little *humph* in response. It wasn't the first time she'd heard that line. But it cheered me up to say it. By the time I'd had my second cup of coffee, accompanied by the tiny Time Out bar that had somehow made it onto my tray of deprivation, I was feeling the wonderful mix of joy and nerves that jumps around inside you when you're about to descend from the sky and taxi into the arms of people who love you most.

Anna was in the window seat and I grasped her arm as we landed. 'Look at the light coming through the gum trees,' I enthused. 'It's so different from Iowa.' She appeared to be profoundly uninterested in eucalypts.

We made it through the slog of immigration and customs and quarantine, then the silver doors of the Tullamarine arrivals hall slid open.

When I think of that homecoming moment, I see Katie, slender and seventeen, detaching herself from the waiting crowd and rushing up to hug us. She was alight with smiles, coming a little too far into the roped-off area where only disembarking passengers were supposed to be. She was so beautiful, with the luminous eyes I never tired of looking at when she was a babe in my arms. And now, as then, she didn't need to speak for me to hear her bubbling over with the noise of life.

She grabbed Anna and me in a group hug and screeched, 'You're both so *skinny*.' I took that as a compliment. We'd passed through a land where a salad might well contain bacon bits and baby marshmallows, then another land where fat chips could be served with a baked potato, and we hadn't got fat.

John was waiting further back. My husband took me in his arms and said, 'Four months was too long.'

It felt good, and safe, to be enfolded in his strong warmth. I decided never to leave happy hour with hubby for such an extended time again.

When we arrived home the cold house was a bit of a shock, as summer in England that year had been hot. But John fired up the gas heater in the lounge room and pulled my favourite rocker close to it. He sat in the old-fashioned easychair he'd hauled home from the local op shop a few years previously. We both gazed out through the french doors, between the bare branches of the liquidambar and out over the valley. Although I hadn't missed it consciously, it felt so right to see that view again.

As I prattled on to John with some of the stories I'd been saving up for him, our cat claimed he didn't know who I was. He sat right next to my chair but with his ginger back to me, pretending he couldn't hear me when I crooned his name.

'Come on, Basil,' I said. 'You can't fool me.' At the sound of my voice I could see his ear give the tiniest twitch. Finally he gave in and jumped into my lap; and with him snuggled there, in my house on the hill, I felt wrapped in layers of love.

John reminded me I'd better call Dad to let him know we'd arrived safely. I did that, but the phone on the wall in the Baxter house rang out. I pictured Dad on his scooter, rolling along the sidewalk to visit his youngest sister, Mary Lou, then maybe stopping to have a cup of coffee with our old farm neighbour, Cap Dee. Later, I checked my emails and there was one from Joan. Dad had a bladder infection. They'd admitted him to a Des Moines hospital to put him on an antibiotic drip but it wasn't too serious. He should be home by the end of the week.

We had arrived home on a Friday. That weekend I desperately tried to get Anna ready to face the psychological challenge of school on Monday. I attempted to arm her with words. *Think of the confidence you've built up . . . Remember the track team . . . Our book has reprinted again . . . Smile!*

On the Saturday night, I drove her over to see Ellie. I was so scared for Anna, sitting there in the passenger seat beside me, looking pleased for the first time since we'd returned home. What if Ellie had made new friends? Maybe she'd only agreed to see my girl out of politeness.

But when we pulled into her driveway, Ellie came boun-
cing out to the car to give Anna a big hug. She seemed genuinely
glad to see her. Perhaps it would be okay, my soul begged.
I knew it wasn't necessary to have a whole swag of pals. Just
one true friend could make all the difference, and I was so
grateful that I'd always had at least that. When I was a child
and never really clicked with any of the girls in my class, my
soulmate was my cousin Rhita, who was a year younger than
me. She only lived a mile's walk up the gravel road from our
farm, but this happened to be beyond the dividing line for the
Baxter school district, so she went to Mingo instead. We spent
as many weekends and nights together as we could, and then,
whether we were climbing around in a stifling hay loft, or skat-
ing on the frozen pond over in the east timber, or challenging
ourselves to stay awake all night and talk, we were safe inside
our own world.

As an adult, I still didn't have a heap of girlfriends, but
the ones I did have were very close, and I cherished them. On
my first Monday back, after Margie finished work, we met at
Lygon Court to see a movie at the Nova, a rabbit warren of an
arthouse cinema that is one of my favourite places. But what
I looked forward to even more than the movie was the talk
that followed, over a carafe of house red and an excellent
pizza at the original La Porchetta's, where the walls and even
the ceiling were covered with photographs of the owner chum-
ming up with various figures from show business, politics and
the underworld.

When I got home, the first thing I did was pop into the
study where Anna was doing her homework. 'How was
school?' I asked her. 'Were they glad to see you?'

'I don't know.'

I wanted to scream at that passive, colourless voice.

'Well, did you smile and say hello?' I prodded. I was hoping she would have taken my advice.

She sighed deeply, staring into the computer. 'I've got heaps of homework.'

That's what she would tell us, again and again, over the weeks to come. Unlike Katie, who put off any homework till it was critically necessary and then zipped through it as fast as she could, Anna laboured through hers every night, thoroughly and slowly. Now, she told us, she had so much to catch up on that she needed to spend hours every evening at the computer in the study.

The day after Anna started back at school, Katie didn't have morning classes, so she and I headed to Highpoint shopping centre, with her driving on L-plates, to shop for her year 12 formal. Between us, we called it the prom, because ever since she was a toddler she had loved the photo of me in my mint-green dress at my senior prom, standing next to a guy in my class who was someone else's boyfriend. Because he and I had been pals since the sixth grade, he did me a favour by being my date.

After travelling with Anna for so long, it was such a contrast being with my other daughter, inside her field of fizzy happiness. She already had her dress, a short and tight little red number with a black beaded fringe at the hem. We plodded around to various shoe stores till she spotted exactly what she wanted: a pair of Italian leather ankle boots reduced from $250 to $75.

I was less ecstatic than she was. 'You're going to wear boots to the prom?' I queried.

'Yes, Mum. They're fashionable!'

Next, we went to Priceline for make-up, something Katie, with her perfect creamy skin, had never really used. A kind older woman seemed thrilled to have the chance to give advice on just the right shade of foundation. We splurged on some liquid eyeliner and two tiny tubs of eye shadow in beige and bronze. Aglow with post-purchase satisfaction, we took ourselves to the food court for lunch.

We shared a plate of Chinese, the three-dish special with steamed rice, and I don't have to consult my journal to remember exactly where we were sitting. We were at a table halfway between the frozen yoghurt stall and the fountain. I was gazing over the heads of the midday crowd to the espresso bar, debating whether it was too late in the day to have a long black, when my phone rang. It was John. He was off shift that day, so he was calling from home. He said, 'Your dad's gone.'

'What?' A stupid, desperate image popped into my head of Dad taking off down the blacktop on his scooter, like that old guy they made a movie about, who crossed Iowa on his ride-on lawnmower to reunite with his estranged brother.

'Joan called on the landline,' John clarified. 'Your dad's passed away. I'm sorry.'

I was flooded with a profound sense of unfairness. I thought I had more time to get to know him! Almost immediately, I censored myself. It's what he wanted. Though he went along with the scooter and the hearing aids, he'd also said to me several times a day, 'I just want to go and be with your mother.'

That's what I hung on to. *Don't feel sorry for yourself. Be glad that neither of your parents had to lose their dignity by ending up in a nursing home.* Yet after Dad died, the ache in my stomach got worse. My GP scheduled several tests, including a pelvic ultrasound. All the tests came back normal. But my intestines refused to settle. My teeth hurt as well, and my mouth was full of ulcers. I had to pee every twenty minutes. It was all I could do to make myself sit down at the computer and write for half an hour. Before Anna and I went on our trip, I'd been doing some emergency teaching at the local high school, but there was no way I could return to that gig, which required an intense mix of energy and concentration, not to mention seventy-five minutes between toilet breaks.

And through those weeks, while my mind was glazed with a grief I was trying not to feel, Anna was eating less and less. It's one of my great guilts that it took me such a long time to realise this. She said she had so much schoolwork to catch up on, she needed to spend all evening in the study. She refused to come out for dinner because she wanted to eat alone, in front of the TV, after we had gone to bed.

John protested about this. But Anna dug in her heels. And I supported her. I understood how she might want to set herself a goal for the evening, then reward herself with dinner after it was done and she could relax. Plus, it was the same old story . . . I just wanted to make her happy.

Anna used to love me making her scrambled eggs for breakfast, because she felt the protein would help make her the tallest girl in our extended family. Now she shunned scrambled eggs, because she only liked them with a heap of grated cheese stirred in, and the high fat content meant cheese had been relegated to Anna's no-eat list months before. In fact, she didn't eat anything for breakfast, but would grab a muesli bar and apple on her way out the door. 'I'll eat 'em on the way to school,' she would say.

Looking back, I can see ample clues to signpost anorexia. She started by asking me to switch from buying low-fat milk to no-fat. We kept a shopping list in the kitchen where we all noted what we needed in the next big shop. Before Anna became fat phobic, she used to write hopeful suggestions on the list, such as 'Tim Tams' and 'Doritos'. Later these morphed into 'natural Jalna, no fat'. Now she requested watermelon, Pepsi Max and passionfruit.

Should I have questioned these choices? Would it have made any difference? At the time, I was much more concerned about her relationship with her peers.

I found it very frustrating that she didn't contribute more to her own happiness.

Why wouldn't she value and act on any opportunities for friendship that came her way? At her karate class there was a girl her age, Rebecca, who went to the school where I did emergency teaching. Rebecca was a lovely person, smart and compassionate, and she was always asking questions about how Anna and I wrote books together. When I dropped Anna off for her first karate lesson after returning from the States, I noted in my journal: 'Rebecca ran over and hugged Anna ecstatically. Anna just stood there stiffly, looking confused.'

On the 2nd of September, a Tuesday, I noted in my journal: 'This morning when she got up, Anna collapsed on the kitchen floor, wailing, claiming she'd only had two hours sleep and that she had to stay home from school. I ended up yelling at her, so the day did not begin well. But she has to learn to cope with our society's hours!'

The school holidays started on the 22nd of September. Anna and I were supposed to be starting work on the second book in our trilogy about Kaitlin, but Anna was too pre-occupied to contribute much. She had been such a help with the first one. 'What's wrong with you?' I asked.

She told me she felt like her friendship with Ellie was too one-sided, that she was the one who had to initiate any inter-action. She'd decided not to contact Ellie, so she could see how long it would take Ellie to ring her.

Great, I thought grimly.

The second Tuesday of those school holidays is the first journal entry where I have noted John and I discussing our worries about Anna's eating. John thought that her lack of appetite might be a symptom of grieving for her grandmother. It was true that now we were back home, Anna missed the weekly epistle of affirmation landing in the letterbox. We had always been careful with our grocery shopping, only buying occasional treats for the girls, but now John had come up with an idea. To cheer Anna up, he told her to walk up to Coles and choose anything she wanted, whether it be Tim Tams or Doritos or ingredients for her favourite recipes. 'Call me when you're ready to check out,' he said. 'I'll come up and pay.'

Anna was ecstatic. 'You mean I can choose literally anything?'

'Yes, as long as it's food.'

She was happy that day, looking through our cook-book collection, making a list, then choosing $112 worth of groceries. She decided she'd cook dinner for the four of us. She said to John and me, 'How about you two go up to the Pacco and have a pre-dinner drink and when you get back I'll have it all ready?'

That sounded like a nice idea. So John and I walked to the Pascoe Vale pub, along the ridge beside the railway line. From a couple of high points, we could see the jagged outline of the CBD against the late afternoon horizon. At the pub, we sat across from each other at a little table and, ignoring the clanging of the poker machines in the adjacent room, got involved in yet another chat. How many conversations can the same two people have? In our first years together, I wondered if John and I would eventually run out of things to say to each other. But we'd been a couple for one year short of a quarter of a century and it hadn't happened yet. That evening, among discussions of the debate over live animal exports and the rising prospects of the Collingwood Football Club, John entertained me with tales from the quarantine line at the airport. On his last shift, a Vietnamese granny had vigorously denied bringing food into the country, even though her case was packed with sticky rice balls and fermented fish.

We returned home around 6.30 to a very messy kitchen and Anna constructing little filo pastry triangles filled with an elaborate meat mixture. She had just begun the second triangle. Katie was complaining that she was starving and that she couldn't wait forever as she had to learn the whole of post-war Italian history by the next morning.

We ate around nine o'clock. The triangles were delicious, served with tomatoes she had stuffed with a tasty filling. Anna watched us closely. 'Are they good? Are they done enough?'

'Why aren't you eating?' John asked her.

She said that she had stolen so many bites while cooking that she was already full.

Friday arrived and Ellie still hadn't called. Anna and I had planned to go to the library in Broadmeadows to write. My journal states: 'Anna would hardly eat anything for breakfast, and wouldn't take food for lunch. All she had while out was a skinny capp with no sugar.' I also noted: 'I couldn't get her to contribute much. It was like she was in a zombie state.'

After the school holidays, Anna started to get even more weird about food. Once she got very upset because she couldn't find a certain plate. She was searching through the cupboard, nearly in tears. 'Where's the plate with the yellow roses?'

'I don't know. Use a different one.'

'No! That's the one I visualise when I'm doing my home-work.' Her tone was tragic, as if this was a terrible loss.

It was a bread and butter plate, about 12 centimetres across.

A day or two later, she was in despair. 'I can't eat anything tonight.'

'Why?'

'Because when I got home from school I ate a whole tomato!'

Chapter 11

Finally, I took Anna to a paediatrician with an excellent reputation, in a nearby suburb. The girls had been to see him two or three times before, but they were hardly ever sick enough to need specialist attention, so usually we visited the local bulk-billing clinic. We had taken Anna to this doctor in grade 4 when she complained over several weeks of headaches. He had diagnosed her with what he termed 'good girl syndrome', after gently ascertaining that even though she herself never did anything to cause the teacher to raise her voice, Anna became anxious when anyone else was chastised.

As he weighed my daughter, a dark look crossed his face. Anna, at 167 centimetres, weighed 37 kilos. The doctor said he would refer her to a specialist at the Royal Children's Hospital.

I wasn't as alarmed as I should have been. I saw the doctor's concern as confirmation that Anna really should be eating more. Now that I was armed with a trusted professional's opinion, I would take her home and make her see reason. I figured the referral to the Children's Hospital wouldn't come through for weeks, and by that time she would be eating normally.

It seems odd to John, Katie and me now, but before then, none of us had uttered the word 'anorexia' as a possible explanation for Anna's weight loss. For me, at least, this was because mental images are hard to dislodge, and I had a firm picture of anorexia: it happened to plump girls who went on diets and couldn't stop losing weight because when they looked in the mirror they still saw a fat girl. Anna hadn't been plump since her adorable toddler tummy melted some time before her third birthday. She hadn't been a slim kid, she was downright skinny. It was difficult to buy clothes for her because any skirt or pair of jeans that fitted around the waist was always way too short. And unlike her sister, who from the age of two could not pass any mirror without looking into it intently, Anna had barely seemed to notice she had a body.

As soon as we returned home from the paediatrician's clinic, Anna headed for the study. She had karate practice later that evening, but first she had to do her homework. John was off shift that night, and Katie was home as well. When I told John I was going to insist Anna have dinner with us, he was massively relieved. He had never approved when I allowed her to eat whenever she chose. Katie volunteered to help out by making her version of chilli con carne, a dish she knew Anna used to love. Katie was passionate about food and cooking, and had been since she was tiny. While other toddlers constructed rudimentary castles at the beach, she would declare her pile of patted-down sand to be 'Paghetti car-nara!'

Now, with Katie's simmering meal emitting the most delicious aroma, I went to the study to fetch Anna.

'C'mon,' I coaxed. 'You can spare half an hour. You don't have to stay and chat. Just have dinner with us. You need to start eating more. You heard what the doctor said.'

She stared at the screen, which was full of numbers. It seemed as if she was not going to answer. But finally she said, 'What are we having?'

'Katie's chilli. She put fresh basil in it. That's how you like it.'

'Did she fry the onions in oil?' Anna's tone was tragic.

'Just a little. Olive oil's good for you.'

'You know I can't eat oil! Or beans. She always puts *beans* in chilli.' The way she enunciated 'beans' made them sound as though they were something pale and wriggling that Bear Grylls would pluck from underneath a loose bit of bark and pop into his mouth in order to survive in a South American jungle.

'Since when don't you eat beans?'

'They're full of *carbs*.'

Without glancing away from the computer and frowning at her maths homework as though it was nearly as distasteful as beans, she poked at a couple of number keys.

I resorted to pleading and bribing. 'Please? Your dad's been working so hard. He just wants you to have a meal with us and not make a fuss. Come on, if you come out to the kitchen I'll think about ringing Joanne.'

Joanne was a local and prize-winning guinea-pig breeder. We had bought Anna's first two treasured, furry babies from her and Joanne had recently rung to say she had a new litter of unusually attractive blonde newborns available.

My strategy worked. At least partially. 'All right,' Anna conceded. 'I'll come out. But I'm not eating chilli.'

She sat at the end of the kitchen table with her back to the oven, the spot she had occupied since she was old enough to sit in a highchair. While John and I made exaggerated claims as to the deliciousness of Katie's dish, hoping to tempt Anna, she rose to get herself a slice of watermelon from the fridge. She proceeded to cut it up into small chunks and drop them into a glass of Pepsi Max.

'What are you *doing*?' John asked. I didn't like his shocked tone. Just as when I was a child, ever vigilant in case my mother's mood darkened, a fist began to close around my heart at the slightest hint of conflict.

I tried to lighten the mood. 'How come parents always ask that, when it's totally obvious what their kid is doing?'

'Tastes good,' Anna explained, spooning a bit of caffeine-soaked melon into her mouth.

'That's your idea of a meal?' John asked.

Anna shrugged, as if her father's question was too stupid to answer.

It was karate practice night, which John now reminded her about. 'You can't do karate if that's all you eat,' he told her, too forcibly for my liking. 'You need protein!'

She looked as if the mere mention of that life-giving substance made her want to throw up.

'Katie went to a lot of trouble to make chilli just the way you like it,' John informed Anna sternly.

'Come on,' Katie coaxed, 'just have a little bowl.'

'I don't *want* any!' Anna was about to cry. Inside me, the fist closed tighter as I realised it wasn't going to be as easy as I had imagined to convince her to eat well. We were going to have to think of a different approach, but right now I was out of ideas. I just wanted to get out of there before a real argument erupted between Anna and John.

'Let's go to karate!' I snatched a couple of muesli bars out of the cupboard and an apple from the fruit bowl. 'You'll eat these on the way, won't you?'

She flounced out of the kitchen, returning in record time in her white martial arts outfit. I realise now she must have been wearing some layers underneath, because even though the orange belt was cinched tight around her tiny waist, you couldn't tell how skinny she really was.

It was already dark as she buckled her seatbelt and I dropped the muesli bars into her lap. As I began to back down the drive, she picked up a bar and squinted at the wrapper, trying to make out the nutritional details.

'Oh, for heaven's sake,' I hissed. 'It doesn't matter how much fat there is in it. You can't do karate on an empty stomach.'

My concentration was fragmented, to say the least, peering into the rear-view mirror as I backed down the drive. One of the reasons John and I had fallen in love with our house was because it was perched at the top of a hill. This meant the driveway was steep, and it wasn't all that wide, so it required a certain mindfulness to back successfully down between the retaining walls. On this particular night, my mind was zinging full of tension rather than attention. I'd also just downed a rather large glass of wine – or was it two? – without eating much of the chilli. By my side was my emaciated child, pointing out plaintively that the muesli bar was unpalatable because it had passionfruit yoghurt topping.

'You like passionfruit,' I reminded her, a tad forcibly perhaps.

'Yeah, I like real passionfruit, not this chemical crap sitting on top of a pile of carbs.'

'I should know,' I muttered. 'You insist on me buying the bloody things, even when they cost two dollars each.'

By the time she tossed the bars onto the back seat, we had reached the bottom of the drive. She then threw the apple back there as well. I heard it clunk onto the floor as she stated casually, 'I could tell by the feel it wasn't crunchy enough.'

'You spoiled little brat!' It wasn't my finest parental moment, but yelling was the only method I could think of to deal with a growing desperation.

Having cleared the drive, I put my foot on the accelerator too hard and didn't turn sharply enough, shooting backwards across the street. *Bang.* I'd forgotten that's where John parked his midnight-blue Sigma. In the dark I hadn't seen it and reversed straight into it.

Chapter 12

John was surprisingly sanguine about me running into his car. The damage to both vehicles turned out to be minor and, looking back, he was probably relieved to turn his attention to something that could be fixed by a trip to a panelbeater.

In fact, crashing into John's car may have saved Anna's life, because we never made it to karate. I found out the next morning why this was important. I got a call from the adolescent unit of the Children's Hospital, asking me to bring Anna in that very afternoon for a consultation.

She was examined by a specialist called Dr Richardson, with me at her side. The doctor was such a kind man, but Anna hated him looking at her body. She frowned her signature frown at him and when he asked if her periods had stopped, she refused to answer. It was me who informed Dr Richardson that even though she had recently turned fifteen, Anna's periods had never started. I was a little miffed at the hateful look she flashed in my direction for daring to refer to something so intimate. But Dr Richardson continued to speak to her gently and warmly, as if she was beaming at him in the sunniest of ways. He ordered blood tests. And he called her Sweetheart.

The next morning, the kind doctor rang me. 'We've got Anna's blood tests back. I'm sorry to tell you . . . she needs to be admitted.'

'What?'

I couldn't get it through my head that Anna was actually sick, not just going through a sad and stubborn phase. Beds in the Children's Hospital were precious. They were meant for really ill or broken kids: leukaemia, head trauma, debilitating genetic disorders that no one's ever heard of. I'd feel like a fraud if we accepted one of those beds for Anna. I said to the doctor, 'Maybe I can think of some way to convince her to have dinner tonight.'

'No!' I was startled by the alarm in his voice. 'She can't just start eating again. Her body couldn't take the shock. We've learned that from starvation cases in the developing world.'

Starvation cases? My brain could not comprehend how these words connected to my child.

'She needs careful refeeding. She has to be monitored.'

My concentration was fading. Dr Richardson was explaining what they'd found in her blood. A lack of this, too much of that. Usually I'd have grabbed a pen and jotted down the technical terms to discuss later with John. But that day, the doctor's words had jolted me into a place beyond jotting. I stared out the window, across our suburban valley to the train as it chugged through the spring morning to Broadmeadows. Yes, we lived on the Broady line, at the time reputed to be the most dangerous in Melbourne. Yet I had been travelling on it for years and had never been bothered by even a whiff of trouble.

'Mary?' Dr Richardson was demanding my attention. 'I asked you where Anna is right now.'

'She's at school. Why?'

'Does she normally walk home?'

'Yes. It's not far, less than a kilometre.'

'I don't want her doing any exercise. You should go and pick her up now. I'll arrange for her to be admitted tomorrow.'

'You mean it isn't safe for her to even walk?'

'Not with these results. Combined with her blood pressure and heart rate . . . they're both dangerously low.'

He was a thoughtful man. He didn't say, 'I'm surprised you haven't noticed that every day lately, your daughter has been edging closer to death.' What he said was, 'Her body is shutting down.'

John's shiftwork at the airport did not accommodate weekends or holidays. All through the year, he worked four days on and four days off. He was home that day, so we went to the school together. The year 9 coordinator, Miss Baxter, welcomed us into her office. We told her we needed to pick up Anna, so she sent a student who was assigned to help her for the day to collect our daughter from her classroom.

While we waited, I explained to Miss Baxter that Anna had lost a lot of weight and needed to be in hospital. Then added, 'We're having kind of a tough year.'

Was there a hint of disapproval in the look she gave me? She said, 'We thought Anna was getting too thin. A couple of the teachers mentioned it.'

'No one mentioned it to me,' I offered in my defence.

Miss Baxter didn't comment. Instead she asked, 'How long will Anna be in hospital?'

'We're not sure. The doctor said a few weeks at least.'

She did not look pleased. 'She's missed so much school already.'

'I know,' I agreed. 'I'm sorry . . .'

Why did I say that? Despite our plans not working out as I'd intended, I still believed taking Anna overseas for four months had been an excellent idea. But I've been like that all my life: toss a teeny bit of criticism at me and I crumble. I have to be really angry, there has to be adrenaline bubbling in my blood, before I'll stand up for myself. That day, adrenaline was in short supply. Unfortunately, as usual, whatever chemical produces tears was abundantly available.

John, sensing an imminent meltdown, stepped in. 'Anna's always been very close to her grandmother. It was important for her to spend that time with her.'

Miss Baxter said, 'Yes, I heard she wrote a very moving personal piece about that. But the important thing now is Anna gets better. I'll put an item in the staff newsletter saying she'll be absent for an indefinite time.'

Still feeling disapproval hovering in the air, I was glad to have it dissipated by a knock on the door. 'Come in,' Miss Baxter commanded.

The door opened and there was the student helper, a hefty girl in a headscarf. 'I got her, Miss,' she announced proudly. 'Here she is.' She gave Anna a little push into the room. Compared to that healthy girl, our daughter looked like a pale collection of sticks inside her school uniform. 'Thanks, Asmahan,' Miss Baxter said. 'You can read outside while I finish here.'

I thought Anna might be angry at us turning up like this, but at the sight of us she actually smiled a little half-smile. She headed straight for her dad, saying, 'I'm cold. I wanna sit on your lap.'

I expected John to discourage this childish behaviour, but he let her plonk into his lap and he held her close, as if with his arms tight around her, he could keep her alive.

The teacher seemed a little embarrassed. She didn't look directly at Anna but shuffled some papers as she said to her,

'Your parents need to take you home now. We'll see you when you're feeling better.'

Was Miss Baxter really looking at me as if this situation could have been avoided if only I'd tried hard enough?

'I'm sorry,' I murmured.

Why did I do that, apologise again? Because really, I was sorry. Not because Anna would be missing out on a chunk of the year 9 curriculum. I knew that wouldn't do her any long-term damage. I was sorry it was her sister who first noticed just how thin Anna had become.

'Mum,' Katie had asked me one morning about two weeks earlier. 'Have you seen Anna with her clothes off lately?'

'Are you kidding?' It had been years since either of my daughters had allowed me to look at them naked.

'I saw her when she was getting out of the shower,' Katie said. 'She's way too skinny. It's scary.'

I felt a deep and genuine sorrow that my daughter seemed to be heading down a similar crazy path to one I had taken. It took decades for me to recognise my own terrible relationship with food as an eating disorder. It has never been diagnosed, so I don't know its name. I do know it swallowed a huge helping of my adolescence and early adulthood.

When I was ten or eleven, Dad bought himself a good camera and from then on, he was always taking pictures. But they were slides, and it had been ages since anyone had bothered with the tedious business of setting up a projector and screen to look at them. Then, when I was visiting Linda on the farm in 2010, she fished the big box of slides out of her attic. We took a selection down to the Newton Walmart and had them transferred to a CD so we could look at them on the computer. So I saw myself at thirteen, and I was shocked.

Was that really me? It was at that age I started to feel hopelessly big and awkward compared to Rhita, my fine-boned and blonde cousin, the soulmate of my childhood years. But the girl in the picture didn't even look plump. She had a sweet little pubescent figure. I wanted to pull her out of the computer and hug her tight, pat her back, tell her she didn't really need to go through what was about to begin.

The year I was thirteen, several things happened that made me acutely aware of my body. Before then I hadn't thought much about it, but suddenly I found it horrible. My breasts began to swell, I had to wear a mattress between my legs, and my stomach started to pooch out. My parents found all this at least as disgusting as I did. So I went on a diet. I lost a few pounds and was heartily congratulated. I wanted to keep dieting. I longed to lose more. But I loved food so much.

In our family, we didn't snack between meals. The meals themselves were a treat. My mother was a superb cook, in a down-home, Midwestern style. When you stepped into the warmth of our farmhouse at supper time, out of the brittle cold of a February evening, the smell of her meatloaf and scalloped corn in the oven nearly made you swoon. Her pork chops were browned to a perfect crispiness while somehow remaining succulent inside. In late September she would bring in the squash from her garden. These were dark green and ridged, about the size of a cantaloupe. She would split them, scoop out the seeds and roast them, the hollow filled with butter and brown sugar. This for me was the ultimate comfort food, tasting like the warm colours of autumn leaves.

Then there were the desserts. My mother provided a homemade sweet after every main meal. Before puberty struck, I used to look forward to this for hours. I didn't obsess, I would just occasionally think about it as I was moving through my daily activities. As I was, say, sitting at my grade 6 desk memorising the names of the ninety-nine counties of Iowa, it was nice to have something lovely to anticipate at the end of the day, just as I now look forward to a glass of wine with John. And believe me, Mother's desserts were something to look forward to. Coffee cake with burnt sugar swirled through it, served warm, drenched in thick cream. Apple crisp, made from the tart jonathans that Dad grew down by the horse pasture, also served warm, with vanilla ice cream and a sprinkle of cinnamon. Or my favourite, gooey sour cream chocolate cake with fudge frosting.

I would eat whatever portion Mother served up, enjoy it thoroughly and not even think about seconds. All this ended when I condemned myself to dieting. I needed to lose weight, therefore I could not have desserts. Ever.

I missed them like crazy. Then I received, from someone I respected, the single worst piece of advice I was ever given. It was an airless August day and I was over at my aunt's farm, hanging out with Rhita, as I so often did. I suggested we walk to visit our Aunt Jean, another of Dad's sisters, who lived over on the blacktop. Rhita pointed out that this would be a long, hot and sticky walk. She thought we should instead sneak off to some shady place with a couple of her mother's special magazines. Rhita had recently discovered the stash under Mary Lou's bed, volumes of luridly illustrated short stories, the likes of which we'd never guessed existed. Men in these stories fell hopelessly in love with women. The women dreamed of these same men and eventually they were united in a passionate kiss. Sometimes they even put their hands inside each other's clothes.

I knew it was wrong to read that stuff. I was afraid of the feelings it generated in my body. Most of all, I wanted to burn calories. 'Come on,' I prodded Rhita, 'don't be lazy.'

So off we went. Aunt Jean, a skinny smoker, was thrilled to see that I had lost weight. 'Mary Kay! Look at you!' She ran her hand admiringly along the side of my shorts. 'I can feel your hipbone,' she marvelled, as if I had achieved a great triumph.

Before then I'd been barely aware that I had a hipbone. For years afterwards, the first thing I did when I got into bed was to search for it, despising myself if my fingers found a covering of soft flesh where only bone should be.

Apart from that, there was Jean's advice. She said to me, 'I've been dieting all my life and I can tell you one thing, Mary Kay. You're gonna get cravings. When that happens, you gotta figure out exactly what it is you want and then eat it till you can't hold no more. That way the craving won't come back for a long time.'

I tried out Jean's method that very night. Mother had made sour cream chocolate cake and, as usual, I refused it. But later, when we were watching TV together, I decided the cake was exactly what I craved. So I went into the kitchen, cut a chunk from the pan and shoved it into my mouth. After depriving them of sweetness for so long, my tastebuds sang with joy. More, they cried. More! More! I cut chunk after chunk from the pan and ate till I could hold no more, or at least as much as I thought I could get away with – I wanted to avoid Mother having a fit when she saw most of the cake was gone.

The funny thing was, when I woke up the next morning my craving had not disappeared. In years past I would have happily munched through a bowl of cornflakes and then got on with things, because I adored the school-free days of summer on the farm. Now all I could think of was cake.

God, how I hated myself. My little breasts, shapely as twin scoops of ice cream, each with a cherry on top, appalled me utterly. If a surgeon had offered to restore my flat chest by slicing them off, I'd have agreed in a heartbeat.

Stupid, flabby, undisciplined pig, I yelled at myself. Today you will diet properly! For many years to come, on every single morning, that would be my first waking thought. It would be decades before my eating began to resemble anything close to normal.

Chapter 13

After returning home from school the day we collected Anna early, she headed straight for the lounge-room heater, switched it on and sat on the floor in front of it, her knees hugged to her chest. 'I can't get warm,' she murmured, apparently speaking to the carpet.

The day before, when Dr Richardson had examined her, he'd pointed out the fine fuzz that covered her arms and legs. Later, when he'd sent her out of the room, he explained to me, 'That's her body making a last-ditch effort to keep her alive. It's trying to conserve heat any way it can.'

Each of these details felt like a bright and very sharp drawing-pin being stuck into my heart. Why hadn't I noticed that new crop of tiny blonde hairs? Looking back, I realised it was because she'd been wearing layers of winter clothes since we'd returned to Australia.

I pulled over my favourite wooden rocker, one of my best op shop treasures. John had gone out to the garage to attend to one of his projects: he was always fixing or improving something essential to our domestic life. On the way home from Miss Baxter's office, John and I had told Anna she'd be going to hospital the next day. I'd been expecting her to start protesting, to say there was no way she was going to be shut up in a room where she couldn't do her running or go to karate, not to mention eat exactly what she chose. Now I asked her, 'What do you think about going into hospital?'

It appeared she was not going to answer, or even indicate that she'd registered my voice. Ever since she was tiny, it had often been difficult to attract Anna's attention. Of late, this annoying characteristic had become even more exaggerated. I'd speak to her and she just wouldn't respond. If it was important, I'd repeat it firmly, but half the time it didn't seem worth the effort and I'd walk away in a huff.

Dr Richardson had taken a different approach. He asked her questions in his gentle manner, and simply waited until she replied. After he'd sent her from the room and told me about the protective fluff, he also said, 'Have you noticed how long it takes for her brain to process what you've said to her?' He tapped his own head. 'That's because there's not enough glucose up there to send the messages around smoothly.'

Armed with my new knowledge of mental sugar, I sat in the rocker and waited for Anna to answer. Finally, she said, 'I'd better go to hospital. I don't think I can do it on my own.'

I was so glad that she was willing to accept help, and grateful it had been offered.

That night, before Anna went into hospital, she joined us for dinner. We told her she could have whatever she wanted; there would be no nagging. She chose some watermelon and two spoonfuls of no-fat yoghurt in a tiny bowl.

Katie whipped up her favourite pasta for the rest of us, rich with caramelised onions and fresh tomatoes. It was a dish she learned to cook in an Umbrian family kitchen on her year 10 trip to Italy. She dished me up a small portion, which I ate slowly, putting my fork down between each bite, as I'd learned to do during the long and painful process of combating my cycles of binging and starving.

We all watched Anna. I could see that it caused her father physical pain to see her make that amount of yoghurt last for minutes, but he said nothing. I looked at her and saw back through all the years that she had sat in that spot, back to when she was a toddler in her yellow highchair. I heard echoes of all the stories we four had told each other around this table.

The first time Anna told us a story about her day was dinner time on her second birthday. She had raised her plump little arms in the air and shouted, 'Pip, pip, ray!' Since at that age she usually used cat noises to communicate rather than words, she had our attention immediately. 'Pip, pip, ray!' she repeated, grinning. It was John, always good at filling in blanks, who figured out she was telling us what had occurred at day care, with the kids and staff singing happy birthday to her.

Where had that delighted and vibrant child gone? She'd been replaced by someone so quiet and thin she was barely there. Katie, as always, attempted to cheer us up with her chirpy chatter.

When Anna was on her way to bed that night, I asked if she wanted me to sit with her for a while, as I had done so often when she was nine and ten years old, after Katie moved out to the bungalow and Anna found it hard to get to sleep. She shrugged and said 'Okay', which at that point in her life was quite an enthusiastic response.

So I sat beside her bed. I didn't try to talk to her. I just looked at her lying there in the pale light coming in from the street, as if by watching her breathe I could hold off the terrible possibility inside the specialist's words: *Her body is shutting down.*

I remembered putting her into her cradle when she was four and six and eight weeks old. She was warm from her bedtime breastfeed, yet my thoughts on lying her down would always be of cot death. I prayed that she would sail through till her next feed and wake unharmed. Now a sultry teenager, she was still just as precious to me. And, it seemed, even more fragile.

John and I took Anna into the Royal Children's Hospital the next morning. Dr Richardson was there to admit her. She would be in a general ward because, he told us, they had learned it was better not to put the anorexics together. 'They swap tips with each other, and compete to see who can keep their weight the lowest.'

For a second I thought it was rather a shame that Anna wouldn't get the chance to experience this contest, where she might actually do better than her peers. But then I remembered what winning that competition could lead to, and agreed that a general ward was good.

Anna was assigned a bed, and while she was shoving her clothes into the drawers of her bedside cabinet, I sneaked a look at the other patients. Across from her was a little boy of perhaps six, being treated for pneumonia. But he wasn't just sick; he was so disabled he couldn't sit up or talk. His mother hovered around him, reassuring him, giving him drinks from a sippy cup. He was propped up with pillows, and his eyes looked bright. He responded to his mother and the nurses with smiles and gurgles.

Next to Anna was a tiny girl, maybe eighteen months old, cradled in the arms of her young father, where she would always be when I saw her in the weeks to come. She, too, appeared to be too disabled to walk. She couldn't even eat. Her dad carefully poured formula straight into her stomach, through a little surgically constructed opening. As he fed her he would murmur to her, and later read to her, and show her toys. He was so absorbed in his daughter that he rarely spoke to us, but he did tell us he was from the country, and that the baby's mother had left them.

Dr Richardson outlined the rules for Anna's stay, and when he'd said she wouldn't be allowed to do anything, he wasn't kidding. Until she gained the required amount of weight, she couldn't even walk to the toilet. A commode would be provided for her beside her bed. I assumed this was to make sure she didn't disappear into the bathroom to vomit, although I couldn't imagine her doing that.

Anna would be carefully fed, building up to the consumption of three full meals and two snacks a day. A nurse would sit beside her every time she ate and for thirty minutes afterwards, to watch for any anorexic tricks. Dr Richardson also said that if she did not begin to eat within twenty-four hours, a nasogastric tube would be inserted so nutrition could be forced down her throat.

I found this thought thoroughly disgusting, but Anna merely frowned.

Although the parents of Anna's young roommates seemed to live at the hospital, Anna would only be allowed visitors for one hour a day, and not at meal or snack time. The purpose of her stay was to get her to eat, the doctor reminded us, and adolescent anorexics were experts at manipulating their families. Anna needed to direct her energy elsewhere.

Chapter 14

The day Anna was admitted to hospital, Dr Richardson said we should stay until the dietitian came by to go over her food plan. So we waited.

It was warm in the ward and Anna wore only a hospital gown. She would need to earn the right to wear her own clothes. She wasn't allowed to leave the bed but refused to lie down. Through the loose gown I could see all the knobs of her spine, leading up her neck.

John and I sat on chairs on either side of the bed. Anna hardly talked at that stage so we just sat there, while the busyness of medical professionals concentrating on their jobs surrounded us.

Anna was mumbling to herself. Had she gone crazy as well?

'What are you doing?' John finally asked her.

She frowned and kept on mumbling. I leaned closer and was able to make out, 'Nine nines are eighty-one . . .'

She was an expert on how many kilojoules were burned up by various activities. She knew the brain used more fuel than any other organ.

'Stop burning calories with mental exercise,' I told her.

'Let me give you a massage, then,' she countered.

I couldn't resist that. Her bony little fingers got in just the right spots.

Eventually, in the late afternoon, a pale man of about thirty appeared beside the bed, holding a clipboard. 'Hi, I'm Ken, Anna's dietitian.' He wasn't exactly fat, but he was certainly well padded. Somehow, I'd expected a dietitian to be a woman. And slim.

Ken showed us what he had on the clipboard. It was a sheet listing all the food that Anna, once she was safely through the refeeding period, would be expected to eat in a day. Eggs, cheese, cereal. Three meals, each of them topped off with a tub of yoghurt. Plus milkshakes or smoothies for morning and afternoon tea. I couldn't imagine Anna making her way through all that. Even when she was eating normally, she'd never had a big appetite. She was staring at the words as if they were worms.

'There's a heavy emphasis on dairy,' Ken explained, speaking to Anna. 'We need to get your calcium levels up as soon as possible. You've only just turned fifteen, so if you work at it, you should be able to minimise the development of osteoporosis. You won't be drinking water or anything else with your meals, because we don't want liquid taking up valuable stomach space.'

Ken was speaking in a manner I admired, kindly but firmly. Anna wouldn't look at him. She glared at his sheet as if she hated what was printed there. *Banana. Porridge. Omelette with fetta.* Her deep distaste for these things seemed to seep out and form a kind of force field around the bed.

'Remember,' Ken said, 'if you don't start on the refeeding program by tomorrow afternoon, we'll be putting the nasogastric tube into place.' It made me want to gag, the image of a tube being forced down my girl's gullet. It was hard to say how she felt about it, because her expression remained the same.

The dietitian shook my hand, then John's, and wished us luck. It was time for us to go. We kissed our daughter's frowning face and left her there, alone in a hospital bed, not allowed even a magazine or a screen for company.

The next day, Anna announced that she would not have a tube stuck down her throat. She was going to eat whatever was required. My soul jumped around in childish ecstasy. My daughter had chosen life! Years later, when she was finally able to talk about her anorexia, she would tell me that it had nothing to do with body image. Starving had been a kind of prolonged suicide attempt. 'I just wanted to disappear,' she explained.

Thank goodness they only let us visit the hospital for an hour a day. Once Anna started to eat, she became more annoying than ever. I went in every day, sometimes with John or Katie in tow. We would arrive at her bedside and she wouldn't greet us, wouldn't even smile. She'd launch straight into moaning about how much her stomach hurt, overloaded with the ridiculous amount of food she had to stuff into it. This daily update would be followed by a complaint about the quality of the menu and the appalling ineptitude of the staff. On one visit, she uttered to us in a tone of contempt and dismay, 'They didn't put my milkshake in the freezer. I *told* them to put it in at 2.30 so it would be ready by three. But they forgot. I had to drink it warm!'

I glanced around, hoping none of the overworked nurses had heard her. 'I'm sure it wasn't actually warm.'

'I like it slushy,' she sulked.

Yes, I'd heard that before. The milkshake needed to be just this side of frozen. I was amazed at how patient the nurses were, having to sit beside my picky daughter and watch every morsel that went in her mouth. Usually they ensured her food was as close to her liking as possible.

'Maybe they're short-staffed today,' I suggested.

She didn't care to discuss staffing levels. 'They ran out of vanilla yoghurt. They didn't even have raspberry. I had to eat *banana*.' She made it sound like squashed insect flavour would have been more acceptable.

I looked across to Robbie, the little boy with the chest infection. He had to have pillows propped on either side of him in order to sit up in bed. I watched his mother, who was allowed to spend all day and night with him, gently tilt a sippy cup to his lips. When she lowered it, he gave her a big happy grin.

Anna frowned deeply. 'They forced me to have porridge for breakfast. *And* toast. Talk about a carbohydrate avalanche!'

I attempted to remind her there was a world out there, beyond the window at the far end of the ward, but she refused to even peep in its direction. However, she did say one interesting thing, sandwiched between moaning about the disgustingness of the hospital's steak and the stinkiness of their overcooked broccoli. 'Grandmother's really worried about me,' she told me.

It was a comfort to hear Anna mention her grandmother in the present tense. I liked to imagine Mother at last able to relax, sipping coffee at her polished wooden table in heaven. With the terror of judgement behind her, she could think of us again. Of course she would be worrying about Anna.

Whether or not it was due to Mother's urging, Anna continued the grim task of feeding herself. Despite all the energy she used on complaining, by the end of her first week in hospital, nutrition had begun to work its magic. Her gaunt little face became pretty again and, below the scowl, her blue eyes regained their shine. The pelt of fuzz disappeared and the top of her spine no longer resembled a row of avant-garde doorknobs.

Every few grams she gained earned her a privilege, such as being allowed to wear her own clothes. She actually smiled a little the day she announced that she was now allowed to walk to the bathroom.

By the end of the second week she'd chomped and slurped her way through more calories than she'd consumed in the previous six months, so she could now spend an hour a day in the group activities room. This is where she burned a CD for me, called 'Baroque at Bathtime', for which she painted a beautiful cover. It's also where she was allowed to mingle with girls who were trapped in full-blown anorexia nervosa. Many of them had not been able to force themselves to eat and Anna reported that she could see the end of the green tubes poking out of their noses. She called them, not without some disdain, the Garden Hose Girls.

Like a premmie baby, when Anna reached a weight compatible with life outside hospital, she came home. She was supposed to keep seeing Dr Richardson once a week as an outpatient, but she loathed discussing her body with a man. So, just as they had tried to accommodate her by freezing her milkshakes, the Children's Hospital found Anna a female doctor. Dr Debra Wilson, based at the Broadmeadows Health Service, would become our devoted Dr Deb. She is still the doctor I trust most in all the world. When Anna was a stick-thin fifteen-year-old, Deb was young and beautiful; Anna adored her, at a time when she found most humans wanting in major ways. Until she turned eighteen I took Anna to Broady Health to see Dr Deb, at first every week and later once a fortnight.

Deb was always running at least forty-five minutes late, and often more. But I never begrudged the time spent in that dim waiting room, because once Dr Deb came out to fetch Anna, she kept her for a full hour. It was Deb's role to look after Anna's physical health and I'm sure she did that with aplomb, weighing and measuring and monitoring. How long would that have taken? Maybe ten minutes? What made Deb an exceptional doctor in my eyes was the other fifty minutes she spent with Anna. I'm not sure what they discussed during that time, but I know it was a highlight of Anna's week.

Anna also received psychiatric help once a week with a social worker at the Children's Hospital. Anna didn't click with Christine the way she did with Dr Deb, but most weeks she agreed to go, and Christine felt she was making progress.

Christine certainly was a lifeline for John and me. When things got tough, we could always call Christine, who knew Anna and cared about her, and she would give us impartial and professional advice.

Sometimes I think about all that the Australian public health system did for Anna when she was a teenager. Apart from the initial appointment with the paediatrician, we paid no money for the help Anna received. I look back at that team of professionals – Dr Richardson and Dr Deb, Christine, the nurses at the Children's Hospital bearing their slushy milkshakes – and it still amazes me how much care they put into saving that one little soul, how hard they worked to launch her into a productive adulthood.

Chapter 15

When Anna returned home from the Children's Hospital, Katie, John and I watched her anxiously. As long as she put food into her mouth and swallowed it, that's all we expected of her. We didn't care if she didn't tidy her room or help around the house. We didn't even expect her to be nice. Did that mean we were spoiling her rotten? Probably. But we just wanted her to live.

It would be years before Anna would discuss her anorexia. Just like the running-away incident when she was six, no one was allowed to mention it. If anyone said anything about her body, such as a friend or relative commenting, 'Anna, you're looking terrific since you've put on weight,' she would fix them with her glare and stomp out of the room.

But in other ways, the time just after Anna's anorexia, while not exactly easy, held plenty of fun and promise. Even though John still felt that the girls' school was the best for her, he agreed that if she really wanted to, she could apply to attend a senior secondary college for her last two years of high school. I encouraged her to apply for the senior campus of a well-respected school in Essendon.

Against my predictions and fears, Anna's friendship with Ellie did not splutter out. This was partly because Anna had her own bank account. Once a year she received what was, for a teenager, a substantial injection of funds from the

Public and Educational Lending Rights schemes, payment for the books we had written together. Whatever little treat Ellie asked for, Anna was happy to provide: McDonald's, a CD, bling . . . I held back on the 'Don't buy friends' warning because Anna needed Ellie so much, and Ellie seemed to genuinely enjoy Anna's company. They could be so funny together. I can still picture them standing side by side in our kitchen, tall blonde Anna and tiny dark Ellie, ad-libbing lines for a comedy duo they'd invented, Bruce and Beryl. In their sketches, Bruce and Beryl spent a lot of time 'heading down to the servo for Winnies' and doing things like 'washing the baby on the gentle cycle'.

Gill, my good pal and Anna's godmother, had returned from England by then and was back living on her acreage, forty-five minutes outside Melbourne. I'd often take Anna and Ellie out to Gill's for weekends, for horse rides, hikes and dinners by the open fire. I loved having the two girls near me out there, clowning around. It was when they were out of sight in the city that I worried trouble might entangle them.

One sunny afternoon, in the summer before Anna would begin year 10, she had gone to Glenroy, about a kilometre up the road from our place, to hang out with Ellie. A couple of hours after she'd left, John and I were startled by a loud, commanding knock on our front door. John opened the door and there on our front steps stood a brawny police officer with our skinny daughter by his side. She was crying. 'Are you gonna put me in jail?' she whimpered to him.

'We don't put kids in adult jails,' he answered gruffly, though not unkindly. He informed us that Anna had kicked in the plate-glass window of an estate agent on Pascoe Vale Road. *What?* We figured she might sneak a smoke behind

Coles, but to inflict major damage on someone's property? The officer explained that we'd need to take Anna into the Coburg police station for a formal reprimand, which we duly did. Her offence was officially recorded but the officer at the station told her that as long as she kept out of trouble, her record would be expunged when she turned eighteen.

She got a bill from the estate agent for $2500 but, in the end, didn't need to pay it since Christine, her counsellor at the Children's Hospital, wrote a letter explaining that her client was a young person who had been hospitalised for a mental illness and still struggled with impulse issues. Should we have made Anna take more responsibility for what she'd done? She still had some money in her account; she hadn't yet spent it all on Ellie. But we didn't feel like insisting she pay up to save an insurance company money.

The main thing I wanted to know was why.

'I was mad at Ellie,' Anna said. 'She picked up some boy at KFC, and all she wanted to do was talk to *him*.' I did give her a lecture then. The old 'it's dangerous to only have one friend' refrain.

Anna wrote an exceptionally well-worded letter of apology to the estate agent. She promised she'd never do such a terrible thing again. And I believed her. For so many more years, I believed in the power of words.

Anna's 'impulse issues' were evident in a few more incidents during her teenage years. The most frightening manifestation was when she decided to impress Ellie by train-surfing, resulting in another call from the police. We grounded her for that, with the unqualified blessing of Christine. In her opinion, Anna was 'actually asking to be tightly contained'. This was the summer before Anna began year 11. She was sixteen but Christine said we should treat her like a much younger girl and 'set firm boundaries'.

So, after the train-surfing incident, and following further discussions with Christine, we set up a bunch of rules that Anna would be expected to follow. I don't remember now precisely what all the rules were, but they had to do with carefully monitoring our daughter's coming and going. John and I were meant to keep her in our sight whenever possible. If we went away for a night or even for just a few hours, say, to visit friends, we were supposed to take her with us. I do recall the regulation John was especially keen on: the going-to-bed-at-a-decent-time rule. Even though it was the summer school holidays, he hated how late she stayed up. Sometimes she'd spend virtually the whole night in the lounge room watching DVDs, or in the study writing reams of obscure fiction for the internet. (She didn't yet have a TV or a laptop in her bedroom.)

Such harsh restrictions didn't feel good to me. I thought a sixteen-year-old should have the right to make basic decisions about her own life, such as when to go to bed. But Christine was an adolescent expert, and John felt strongly that she was right, so I went along with them. I wasn't looking forward to the objections I was anticipating from Anna. So on the first evening of the new rule regime, I was relieved when Anna announced blithely at around 9 p.m., 'Well, I'm off to bed. I'll just listen to some music till I get sleepy. Is that okay?'

'Of course.' John was always in favour of listening to music.

This music, which we could clearly hear through Anna's closed door, didn't sound like any of the CDs she usually listened to. It was the radio – Triple J – and it went on and on. As 11 p.m. ticked over, Anna hadn't come out to use the toilet or raid the chocolate stash. (She'd decided she never wanted to go back to hospital, so had rediscovered the joys of junk food.) There was something strange about Anna's silence. I tapped on her door. 'Want some ice cream?' I offered as an excuse, knowing she'd hate me checking up on her. No answer. So I inched the door open. Still no response . . . because she wasn't there. In her bed there was merely the cliché of a rolled-up blanket meant to resemble a human form. Her window was wide open, while the radio sang on to no one. My little girl was gone, vanished into the darkness she used to be so afraid of.

Chapter 16

As soon as I discovered the lifeless blanket roll where my daughter should have been, I wanted to ring the police. But John said we should wait till the next morning, because there was a good chance she would reappear at any moment. I didn't think so. Just like the time she disappeared when she was six, in my mind, if she hadn't already been snatched up by some unspeakable epitome of evil, she soon would be. John, as always, was my voice of reason. He told me to settle down and go to sleep, so I tried to do that.

At 3 a.m., John was lying on the couch in the lounge room. If Anna tried to sneak in through the front door, he was ready to confront her. I huddled under the doona in our bed. I'd rung her phone half a dozen times but it just went to voicemail. I'd texted her, begging her to let us know if she was safe. But my phone just lay on my bedside table, a silent and lifeless rectangle of black.

I don't recall trying to ring Ellie. Not all kids had phones then. I'm pretty sure Ellie, who was a year younger than Anna and had no money, didn't. It seems obvious to me now, as I sit at a table at the back of Brunetti's sipping a long macchiato and wishing I'd had only two scoops of their excellent gelato instead of three, that of course Anna would have cooked up something with Ellie before she absconded. Why didn't I contact Ellie's mother, even if it did mean jarring her out of sleep, even though I knew Ellie had had a falling out with her and was living with her dad in a suburb across the river?

I'm not sure. What I do remember is the horrible, powerless feeling of having no idea where my child was. As I lay in bed bedside my deaf and dumb phone, I realised how enclosed and protected I had always felt in the many hundreds of nights I'd slept in this room. There were so many things on the outside of that weatherboard wall, but I had barely noticed them. Now, that wall had turned into the thinnest membrane. I could clearly hear the rustle of the breeze in the camellia and azalea bushes outside our window . . . the swish of a car passing in our street . . . a dog yapping somewhere in the distance . . . the constant hum of traffic on Pascoe Vale Road. What was I listening so hard for? I didn't know. I only knew I wanted the night, which had suddenly seeped into my home, to give back my daughter.

Dawn eventually arrived, as it always does, and even though my brain was an exhausted mush of worry, it brightened a bit to see light come in around the curtains. It was morning! I could ring the police. I hoped that the amicable officer we met at Coburg police station after Anna kicked in the estate agent's window would be on duty, and he was. But he told me we'd have to wait a few days before the police could do anything. Unlike six-year-olds, teenagers ran away from home all the time, and 99 per cent of them either returned home quickly or turned up at a friend's house.

As soon as I figured it wasn't too early to wake Ellie's mum, I rang her. It was a relief to hear her no-nonsense voice. Of course she was concerned but her default response, unlike mine, was not panic. She was sure the girls would be together, and she thought she knew where. She gave me her ex-husband's number. I was about to ring him when a text arrived. I saw the name of the sender on the screen, and my soul lit up with relief. Anna's message was brief: 'I'm okay. I'm moving out.'

She still refused to answer her phone, but in a series of texts over the next couple of days, she angrily informed me that the firm boundaries we'd worked out with her counsellor were in fact draconian restrictions she wasn't going to put up with. She claimed that Ellie's dad totally understood and was happy for both Ellie and Anna to live with him. In fact, he was going to get Anna a job at the supermarket where he was the manager. She texted, 'I'm not gonna do year 11. I'm gonna take a year off and have some fun.'

What? After we'd agreed to let her leave the girls' school? After all the forms we'd filled out, and interviews I'd taken her to, and the smile that lit up her face when she found out she'd been accepted at the senior secondary college in Essendon? We'd even enrolled her in a gym across the street from the school and paid for a semester, so she could keep up with the kickboxing that was her current preferred form of martial art.

This was January 2005; up till then I hadn't done much texting. Now I gained plenty of practice as I fired off a few hundred words, telling her she'd better come home. Part of me was glad Anna was capable of rebelling, no longer the passive sylph lying in a hospital bed. But a bigger part of me desperately wanted her not to throw away her future. I spoke to Ellie's dad a few times. At first he was all for Anna and Ellie staying with him, but somehow the promised job at his supermarket didn't work out, and after a couple of weeks, he began to agree with me that Anna should return home to do her VCE. In the end, that's what she did. And once she was back home, we did not attempt to enforce the strict rules that had driven her to run away. It's easy now to see the pattern: if we tried too hard to control her, lectured too much about what she should do, she would threaten to blow her life – and by extension ours – apart. But how can you discern a pattern when you're enmeshed in the beginning of it?

When Anna was a teenager, John, Katie and I believed that she was heading towards a satisfying adulthood – maturing more slowly than most, doing it her own quirky way, but growing up nonetheless. And in many ways, she did seem to be growing up. She sailed through the academic requirements for VCE, even doing year 12 psychology when she was in year 11. She got a job at the local Coles deli and earned her learner's permit – with her dad's tutelage, she had no trouble negotiating the gears of our manual Corolla.

Best of all (pop the champagne corks!), at her new school she found a group of friends. There was a lovely Korean girl whose family had sent her to Melbourne to study and live at a homestay; a gentle boy from the new housing development on the other side of Moonee Ponds creek; and Rachel who, like Anna, had been bullied in primary school and was growing up more slowly than most of her peers.

Katie, John and I never tired of talking about Anna. She could be a pain, because she never noticed anything that needed doing around the house, instead leaving a mess of lolly wrappers, tissues, dirty dishes and discarded clothes in any spot she'd occupied for more than five minutes. But, at that stage, we didn't mind too much. We were so glad she was no longer the sad little girl who never smiled. We reminded ourselves that as each year passed, she was getting better. We hardly noticed that she still didn't engage in an actual two-way conversation with us. We just savoured the enthusiasm in her voice when she informed us at length about her latest findings on the psychology of serial killers. What did it matter if she didn't ask our opinions, or enquire how our day had gone?

As a storyteller, Anna was very entertaining. She told us about a middle-aged guy who came to the Coles deli every Saturday night at 9.30 and always ordered the same thing: six slices of leg ham, cut thin. At that hour the store was quiet, and after his purchase, he would linger at the counter, telling Anna about his plans. 'I think I'll watch *The Sound of Music* again tonight,' he might say. 'I've got every musical ever made on DVD.' Anna had a remarkable gift for impersonation; she made this lonely guy who cruised the empty aisles on a Saturday night come alive in our kitchen. And she wasn't making fun of him. She liked him. If a Sunday passed without her mentioning him, John, Katie or I would prompt, 'How's Mr Six Slices of Ham?' And unless she was in a terrible mood, she would be more than pleased to tell us.

Chapter 17

Anna seemed to enjoy her time at her new school. Her group of friends there appreciated her sense of humour, and her teachers were impressed with her intelligent originality. Her English teacher, especially, loved having such a talented writer in her class. All this brought out the best in Anna, and we saw her wonderful smile nearly every day.

These were good years for Katie as well. When Anna began year 11, Katie was nineteen and had finished high school the year before. She decided to pursue her passion for food and wine, so enrolled in a hospitality management course at William Angliss Institute, arguably Australia's best tertiary institution for fledgling foodies.

During her time there, Katie got together with a local boy who was doing a surveying apprenticeship. Matt was very quiet: we used to joke that Katie talked enough for both of them. In turn, she teased me about being in love with Matt's sweet smile and dark curls. Anna had a major crush on him and sat on his lap whenever she got the chance. Matt treated her like a kid sister he occasionally found irritating, but was basically very fond of. He called her Annabelle. Matt and Katie divided their time between our place and his parents', who lived a couple of kilometres from us.

For a while, it seemed like both of our girls were sailing smoothly towards rewarding adult lives. At twenty-one, Katie was managing the breakfast shift at the Botanical, a fine-dining restaurant at the edge of the spectacular gardens that lie at the heart of Melbourne. By this time, she and Matt had moved into their own apartment in Abbotsford, but she would come home to have dinner with us at least once a week, and she and I talked on the phone nearly every day.

Anna was eighteen years old. She finished her VCE, earning the same university entrance score as Katie, and began studying psychology at Swinburne University. Her dream was to become a forensic psychologist. Anna did well in her university classes, especially during the first year. She would ask John and me not to offer her a glass of wine with dinner because, she said, 'I don't want to wake up feeling like crap.' Sometime during her second year, she began to feel like crap a lot of the time anyway. We watched in growing dismay as the happy mood that coloured her final two years at secondary school faded. Her friends from high school never contacted her, she complained. If she wanted to see them, she had to beg for 'a fucking appointment'. She had quit her job at Coles to look for a better part-time position, but now that she wasn't on junior wages, no one wanted to hire her. She'd tried online dating, and several of the guys seemed great at first. She told me that when they met her they'd all say, 'Wow, you're beautiful', but then they would either stop contacting her, or she'd work out how stupid they really were. She informed us that the stuff they made her study at university was 'useless'. *Fucking statistics!* All the girls she met in class were up themselves, and the boys were boring losers. We'd hear about how excruciating it was getting up every morning and dragging herself to Hawthorn by train. But would VicRoads let her have a driver's licence? Not a chance.

They kept finding ways to make her fail the test! It was all too hard. She was going to drop out of uni.

Nooooo! John and I cried. *Please just stick it out: you'll be so glad later you've got a degree. You don't need a part-time job; we're happy to support you. We won't even expect you to help around the house. All you have to do is study.* John made a deal with her: if she would finish uni and get her degree, he would never again nag her to do anything. So she plodded on through the months, making herself get on that train, wearing a furrow in the middle of her forehead that caused my heart to hurt.

Despite all this, Anna could be generous and joyous. She loved, as we all did, little Charlotte who came into our lives around this time, thanks to Katie's best friend from primary school, the other half of 'the Kates'. We called 'the other Kate' Katie Rose, using her middle name to differentiate her from our own daughter, and she meant far more to John and me than being simply Katie's friend. She was like our third daughter. We'd known her since they were both two, when she and our Katie met at daycare. Katie Rose's parents split up before she was three, and she stayed with her dad. Her mother, who had gone to live in a country town, worked long hours as a nurse and could only see Katie Rose on weekends. We became good friends with Katie Rose's dad, and were happy to help him out by looking after Katie Rose till he got home from work. She was at our house so often, she really was part of our family. Especially when 'the Kates' were in early primary school, before I went back to work full time, I used to pick them up after school with Anna in tow, and take all three to swimming or Irish dancing lessons, or bring them home to run around our big garden, climb trees and squabble. Even when Katie Rose went to live with her mum during high school and came to visit her dad on weekends, she would spend most Saturdays with us. She called Anna her little sister and would greet me with a big hug and a hearty 'Mummy!'

Katie Rose was always fascinated with babies and couldn't wait to have some of her own. At twenty, she got started on that project. The October that Anna turned seventeen, Charlotte Rose was born, twelve weeks early. My girls and I went to visit her when she was two days old. Such a teeny scrap of a human, enclosed in her big plastic box, yet already – somehow – she buzzed with life. Thanks again to our public health system, and to the devoted care of her young mother, tiny Charlotte progressed with astonishing alacrity. She had her first sleepover at our house when she was a few months old. As she grew, her stays with us increased in frequency and duration. When she was with us, Anna would spend hours playing with her: building cubbyhouses, colouring in pictures, taking her to the park, creating cool dance costumes out of Anna's extensive collection of clothes. Katie was fairly besotted with Charlotte as well, but she was living away from home and working long hours, so it was Anna who spent the most time playing with Charlotte. As a result, Charlotte loved Anna – and still loves her – with a searing loyalty.

Anna had that side to her, that capacity to enjoy a moment, especially when it involved small children or furry animals. Yet it seemed she lacked a solid internal bedrock of . . . what would you call it? Well-being? Resilience? It's something vital to a good life, and I so wanted to hand it to my daughter.

One night I dreamed that she and I were in a doctor's office and the doctor calmly told Anna she only had a few months left to live. Then he turned back to his computer, dismissing us. 'Wait!' I pleaded. 'I'll give her my years . . . all the rest I have left to live . . . she can have them!'

When I woke up, I wondered if I would really make that bargain. It felt like I would, if the doctor could guarantee that Anna would be happy.

I remember hearing in my late teens a definition of happiness that I still believe to be excellent: someone to love, something to do and something to look forward to. I kept trying to persuade Anna that she possessed the first two components, and I was always attempting to provide her with the third. In the middle of her second year at uni, when she was struggling to slog through the semesters, I suggested she plan a trip to Iowa for the long summer break. Her uncle in Sydney, John's sister's husband who had sadly died of bowel cancer way too young, had left all of his nieces and nephews money, specifically for international travel. We'd been keeping this in a special account for Anna. John and I thought, and Anna agreed, that a holiday in Iowa would be a good way to use it.

Looking back, I shake my head at us, holding so tight to the controls of our daughter's life. But at the time, as we strolled away from the international departure lounge, we high-fived with relief. Phew! We'd got her through two years of university!

Chapter 18

Anna returned from her Iowa holiday in February 2009. That was a terrible month in Victoria. We'd had years of drought and water restrictions. In sunny city parks, where droplets used to dance from sprinklers, grass that once glowed emerald was now yellow and crunchy, if it was there at all. Out in the bush, trees parched through too many seasons had turned into hectares of bone-dry fuel. On the 7th of February, the temperature rose to 46 degrees Celsius and ruthless winds roaring down from the desert reached 100 kilometres per hour. Old-timers said they had never seen fires like the ones that raged on what we soon came to call Black Saturday. On farms and in little towns close to Melbourne, 173 people died in the most horrible circumstances.

Yet, as can happen after a tragedy, February 2009 was also a wonderful month. Fellow Victorians and other Aussies reached out to the bushfire survivors, offering them comfort, shelter and clothes, and donating millions of dollars. A farming couple came up with the idea for BlazeAid, a charity that would send out volunteers to rebuild burnt-out fences. Across the state, life continued. Rescued animals were lovingly tended. Babies were born. And Anna met Andrew.

I've never been a romantic. In high school, I felt awkward and unnatural when the cool girls fantasised about their weddings and honeymoons. I didn't trust my own dreams enough to admit that what I longed for was not a lacy dress and a handsome husband, but international travel. By the time my daughters came along, I had matured enough not to feel guilty when I didn't dream of their future weddings. Katie subscribed to this attitude very early. She was perhaps ten years old when she opined over dinner, 'Fancy weddings are a waste of money. If I ever get married, I'm gonna walk up the aisle in my trackie dacks.'

I have never believed that meeting the 'right man' would be a solution to Anna's problems. Yet when I watched her and Andrew during their first year together, my heart filled with light. I had never seen, in real life, a couple more in love than they were. They didn't meet online, a fact that Anna was especially proud of. Rachel, the one friend from high school who Anna still saw on a regular basis, had invited Anna to a pool party hosted by a pal of hers over by Chadstone shopping centre. Andrew was there, and he was impressed by the sight of Anna in a bikini. She must have been in one of her sparkling moods, bubbling over with jokes and wry observations. He was smitten.

Anna still lived with us during her final year at uni, but she spent a lot of time with Andrew. He was often at our house. They looked so cute together: he was three years older than her, about the same height, dark-haired and a bit stocky, with the sweetest face. He had a degree in information technology and, at that stage, was still living at his mother's big house in East Malvern, helping her with her business. Heather, Andrew's mother, owned a highly successful company in the medical information technology field. She was always jetting off overseas, to attend conferences and meetings. When she was home, she'd work all day in her study, then whip up a

gourmet dinner of crispy duck and stuffed portobello mush-
rooms. She found such cooking relaxing! I would have
expected to find someone like her pretty intimidating, but
she is one of the most warm-hearted people I've ever met. She
was endlessly generous with her money and her judgements.
Heather welcomed Anna into her life with a big hug, announcing, 'She's the daughter I've always wanted.'

It felt to me like a delicious miracle, that something this
good had finally happened to Anna. I can picture Anna and
Andy in our kitchen during their first year together. She's sitting at her usual place at the table and he's standing behind
her, fiddling with her hair as he chats to John about the footy,
or a car he is thinking of buying. In those days, he was always
touching her. She looks up at him and smiles. For months after
she met him, it seemed, she hardly stopped smiling. If she did
get grumpy, Andy didn't hold it against her. He was better at
handling her moods than John, Katie or I had ever been. 'She's
just hungry,' he might explain to us with a shrug. And then
he'd say to her, 'How about I get you something to eat?'

Anna had taken over the bungalow by this time, after Katie
moved out with Matthew. She and Andrew would hang out in
the bungalow on weekends, playing PlayStation or watching
DVDs of *Father Ted*. They could recite every word that Father
Jack ever said, and sing all the lyrics of 'My Lovely Horse',
from the episode in which Ted and Dougal dream of making it
to Eurovision.

Andrew was so proud of Anna at her twenty-first and when
she earned her degree. We were proud of her too, but it was the
pride shining in Andrew's eyes that brought tears to my own.
After she finished her degree, Anna went to live at Andy's with
him, his mother and brother. There was plenty of room, and

Heather kept saying how great it was to have another female in the house. Anna said that after the giant effort of completing her degree, she needed a break before she looked for work. Meanwhile, she helped Heather out by doing housework.

As Anna's break stretched into months, John and I became a little concerned, but we honoured our promise not to nag her. The main thing, we reminded ourselves, was that psychologically she seemed to be in the safest place that she'd been in since before she started kinder. I wasn't afraid of Andrew's power over her: I knew he would never betray her. Numerous weeks went by when we didn't see her during these years, from when she was twenty-one till she turned twenty-four. It seems strange now, considering the amount of brain space she later commandeered in us, that we actually managed to spend large amounts of time not thinking about her. What a lovely, unrecognised freedom that was, to not hear the constant background buzz of dread.

Katie, earning a good wage at the Botanical, saved for that Aussie rite of passage: a backpacking trip around Europe. When she returned from that adventure, she broke up with Matthew. John, Anna and I were sad to see him leave our family, but accepted Katie's need for change. It was at this time she made another big change: she decided hospitality was not for her after all. She took up studying for an arts degree at Melbourne University, majoring in anthropology.

Not long after Katie broke up with Matt, she reconnected on Facebook with a guy she'd known as a child. This was Tom, the son of an old friend of John's. For a few years, from when Katie was about ten, we'd spent a lot of time with that family. But then the couple's marriage failed and we drifted apart. When they rediscovered each other a decade later on Facebook, both Katie and Tom remembered the fun they used to have together. So they arranged to meet up . . . and started having fun again.

Too quickly for my liking, Katie and Tom moved in together into a share house in Brunswick, an edgy suburb of inner Melbourne where Italian widows growing tomatoes in their front gardens live alongside artists and hipsters. Katie and Tom had casual jobs in hospitality to pay the rent, and while they both loved the community of their street in 'Brunnie', they shared a common vision for a future away from the city. Somewhere in the Victorian countryside, they wanted to create a sustainable oasis of peace where they could grow veggies and produce ethical meat. This meant raising sheep, goats and cattle that would live as naturally as possible and be killed quickly right there in the only home they had known, sparing the animals the trauma of a miserable trip to the slaughterhouse.

As for my working life, it had been ten years since I had resigned from the Education Department. In that time I'd produced eight novels. Some of them sold quite well, but none as well as I'd hoped, so I was becoming discouraged with writing for children. I hired a guy to set up a website for me and experimented with a blog and articles for adults. Meanwhile, John took long service leave and embarked on an extensive camping trip to Far North Queensland. After a couple of months, I flew up to meet him and slept in a tent for the first time in decades. At least I had an air-mattress! When I returned from that trip I decided I'd had enough of emergency teaching. It had provided me with many golden moments and I believe I helped a lot of kids at our local high school, but it was a tough job and getting tougher. Although I still wanted to use my skills to contribute to the upcoming generation, I was thoroughly sick of crowd control.

A lovely friend of mine coordinated teachers of chronically ill children. When she heard I'd decided to stop emergency teaching, she wondered if I'd be interested in a position with the Ronald McDonald Learning Program. I definitely would! That's how I became a tutor of seriously ill or injured kids who had been or were being treated at the Royal Children's Hospital, and needed help returning to school. I also acquired a few private students through an agency I joined.

So, John, Katie and I lived our lives on the northern side of the Yarra, while Anna got on with hers in the south. It makes me go cold with sadness to think of the love and support she had there, the opportunities she was offered but could not embrace. Heather tried to interest her in helping with the business, asking her to start by doing some paperwork. Somehow, that did not work out, but Heather did not hold that against her. Because of all her international travel, Heather was awash with frequent flyer points. Towards the end of 2010, Anna's first year out of uni, she shouted Anna and Andrew a month-long holiday in England and Scotland. Soon after they returned, Andrew gained a position in a city firm, negotiating a sizable salary. During the following year, 2011, he upgraded his car and started looking to buy a house.

If only Anna could have grown up a bit too and started being an adult with Andrew. She did manage to find and hold a job in a call centre for a few months. I put the best possible spin on it when telling people about it: *She isn't selling things. She's doing research on water consumption in Western Australia.* What's more important in Australia than conserving water? But we all knew the job was far below what Anna was capable of. This was not what Andrew had expected when he had gazed with such pride at his freshly graduated girl-friend. When the water research at the call centre ended and Anna was assigned to a different project regarding banking habits, she couldn't get people to answer her questions, and suddenly she was no longer offered any shifts. And yet Andrew still loved her.

During the Christmas holidays of 2011, two years after Anna finished uni, Andrew still liked to smooth Anna's soft hair and touch her flawless skin. When she was in a good mood, maybe after lunch when her morning grumpiness had worn off, she savoured lying on a couch with her head on his lap. That Christmas, one of John's nephews from Sydney (a son of the lovely man who left his nieces and nephews money for travel) rented a ritzy house in Sorrento on the Mornington Peninsula for a week. John's extended family gathered there. The kids frolicked in the pool while the adults sipped bubbly. Sometimes we all went down to the back beach to paddle in the rock pools, then returned to the house to crack open fresh prawns and play Scrabble. When I look back at that holiday, I know how fortunate I am to have experienced that kind of privilege. I can acknowledge without hesitation the generosity of John's nephew and his wife. But what I feel is a terrible loss. Because it was there, on one particular morning in that luxury house, that I began to truly grieve for my darling blonde baby, my haunted child, my gorgeous girl.

In that house, the living area was on the first floor to take advantage of the views, while the bedrooms were on the ground floor. John and I were sharing a big bedroom with Anna and Andrew. We had one set of bunk beds and they had the other. On one morning that still hurts to remember, it was about 7.30, and above our heads we could hear the sounds of little kids beginning their day: lots of running around, a bit of whining, some character on *Sesame Street* grandly chanting, 'The letter of the day . . . the letter of the day . . . the letter of the day is J!'

It was way too early for Anna to be woken up, and she was making this very clear to Andrew. She was lying on the top bunk and he was standing next to her trying to appease her. It wasn't so much what Anna was saying that gave my heart a sudden icy injection of fear. It was the snarly tone she used and the hateful way she looked at Andrew, as if he wasn't doing his job well at all, and that job (obviously!) was to smooth out the environment for her so she could bloody well go back to sleep. It was his tone, too, that terrified me, and the way he looked at her. He was calm, he didn't raise his voice like she did, but for the first time I could hear and see that he was becoming fed up with her behaviour.

I wanted to drag her down from that bunk and shake some sense into her, as my mother used to say. *How much longer do you expect him to put up with that sort of treatment*, I wanted to scream at her. *Can't you cope with your bad moods in some way that doesn't involve pushing away the best thing that has ever happened to you?*

I didn't say anything then, because I knew it would just make her complain even more viciously. I did try to talk with her later, when she and I were alone, and she was in a good mood – just like they advised in self-help books on healthy communication. Like so many times before, I tried to ward off disaster with words.

Chapter 19

When I look back to that time, when I knew that Anna's relationship with Andy would end – because I could see there was something inside her that would not let her grow into the successful adult we had hoped to meet – I feel sliced through with pain. This was when the real hurt began, even though Anna and Andrew were still together.

A month or so before the Christmas in that ritzy beach property, Andrew had bought a little house in the southeastern suburb of Chadstone. He and Anna moved in there in February 2012. Just because you feel something, just because you know it in your heart, doesn't mean you can admit it. I so wanted Andrew's house to be Anna's happy home. How could I make it work for her? I copied out her favourite dishes, including step-by-step instructions, that she could cook for Andrew: scalloped corn, meatloaf, chocolate chip cookies. Maybe if she welcomed him home each evening with a tasty dinner and home-baked treats he would overlook her lack of career. I went to Officeworks and bought a packet of overpriced index cards and a fancy box to keep them in. As if I could hold my daughter's life together with recipe cards stacked neatly in a plastic container.

She thanked me for the gift, hugged me, put it on the kitchen bench, and never used it. In the little house that could have been her home, she spent way too many hours alone. When she was living with Andrew at his mum's place, there were always people around: when Heather wasn't overseas, she worked at home, and Andrew's younger brother usually had uni friends over.

Now, as the long, quiet days crawled past, Anna had only herself for company. She was lonely. And she was angry. She was angry at potential employers because they wouldn't give her a job. She was angry at Andrew, because even if she curled her hair with the curling iron, did her make-up extra carefully and slipped on a sexy dress, he hardly ever took her out at night. 'He says he's too *tired*,' she snarled. When I pointed out to her that this was understandable as he worked long hours, she got mad at me.

She was especially white-hot angry at Andrew's father. He and Heather hadn't lived together in quite a while, but he frequently visited his sons. He was fond of Anna, but he didn't coddle her. Now she was living as Andrew's de facto, he had asked her confronting questions. What did she plan to do with her degree, with her life? Why was she always demanding Andrew drive her here or there? Why didn't she get her own driver's licence?

That was a good question. If someone asks me why I'm so sure Anna's brain was always wired differently, this is the example I give: she couldn't learn to drive. It wasn't that she couldn't ace the written test, or master the mechanics. Our trusty Corolla only had to splutter a few times before she got the hang of changing the gears smoothly. The problem was, she wasn't able to internalise and integrate the many tasks that become automatic to most drivers. She was required to log one hundred hours of practice with an experienced driver by her side, but she racked up many more than that . . . with me, with John, with Katie and with her godmother Gill, who used to take her out on the country roads in her four-wheel drive. We also paid for lessons with a professional instructor. Despite countless kilometres of practice, whoever was sitting beside her had to be on high alert to remind her of everything: *watch your speed*; *look out for that bike*; *there's a parked car*; *you'd better put your blinker on now because you are going to have to merge right, remember?* No, she never did remember that northbound on Pascoe Vale Road, just before the Red Rooster, the three lanes merged into two, even though she had been regularly travelling that route since she was born.

It was amazing to compare Anna's ability to orient herself in space to Charlotte's. Charlotte – the little girl born to our 'third daughter' Katie Rose – was, at two and a half (I kid you not), more interested in where she was in the physical world and better at memorising routes than Anna was at twenty. Charlotte was tiny for her age but was an early talker. I remember driving south down Pascoe Vale Road one day, with her perched in her baby seat in the back. For some reason I wasn't going straight home, so didn't turn right at the street I usually did. Charlotte immediately started pointing and chirped urgently, 'Mawy, your house is dat way!'

There was something drastically wonky about Anna's sense of direction. Not only did you have to remind her of every turn needed to get to a place we'd been to a hundred times before, if an intersection was at all complicated she would often get disoriented as she turned and not know which lane she should be in. More than once I had to yell, to keep her from driving into oncoming traffic. I told Anna I wouldn't take her to sit her driver's test till she could at least navigate the 5 kilometres from our place to the Airport West shopping centre on her own and remember to slow down for pedestrian crossings. She never became completely, reliable with either of these requirements, but eventually, when she was twenty, John thought she was ready to have a go. So I dropped her and the freshly washed Corolla off at VicRoads and waited at the nearby library until she called. 'They failed me,' was the plaintive result.

Reading the examiner's report gave me the heebie-jeebies. It explained that when turning from Dimboola Road into Pascoe Vale Road, drivers were permitted to turn right from the left lane. This was what the examiner had instructed Anna to do, but she became confused about which lane she should end up in. The report stated that 'other drivers were forced to take evasive action'. I'm glad I didn't have to witness that.

A couple of months later, Anna resat the test. This time she concentrated hard on being in the correct lane but forgot to look at the speedo and exceeded the limit by so much, the test was terminated within two minutes. After that, she didn't try again and I didn't encourage her. I couldn't see how she would ever be safe on the roads alone. John recommended leaving it until her brain matured a bit more.

Anna wouldn't have been able to articulate all this to Andrew's father, or even to herself. Living there in Andrew's little house, she was just angry, resentful and lonely. But one day when she rang me, her voice was full of light. 'Guess what?'

Hope sprang up in my heart. *She's got a job!*

'I got a pair of guinea pigs!'

Andrew, who liked pretty much everything, deeply disliked these creatures. I don't think it was the guinea pigs themselves he resented, but what they represented: his beautiful girlfriend just could not grow up.

On the other hand, she had begun to employ more adult means to soothe her pain. I didn't realise, during that year she lived in Andrew's house, that she was drinking more and more. But there was someone who did notice – a schoolfriend of Andrew's named Dan, who had grown very fond of Anna. Too fond, I thought; but Anna insisted he was just a good friend. Dan worked in his father's business, so his hours were fairly flexible, and he began spending a lot of time with Anna.

Looking back, I know Dan genuinely cared about Anna, and like so many others, he tried to help her. He told me later that during her last months with Andrew, he might drop by their place midmorning and find her sitting at the kitchen table, and she'd have in front of her the mug with the cartoon cat on it that I'd given her. But instead of coffee, the mug contained red wine. Dan said that as the day progressed and the mug got refilled too many times, Anna would become increasingly anxious and irritable; one wrong word from him or Andrew could tip her into angry raving.

So Dan made a suggestion, which he considered sensible and kind: Anna would probably feel better if she switched from drinking to smoking weed. He got her some weed, and they smoked it together; she loved it.

How much did the introduction of weed to Anna's daily life contribute to her mental decline? I don't think anyone can answer that. I could only watch, with an increasingly aching heart, as her relationship with Andrew disintegrated. Anna left his house and moved in with Dan. To celebrate, they went to Chadstone shopping centre and bought a baby guinea pig they called Mowgwai.

Anna lasted a couple of months at Dan's. He soon decided that though she was his best mate, actually living with her was putting too much strain on their friendship.

Chapter 20

Towards the end of 2012, Anna returned to us. She brought the three guinea pigs with her in a big plastic storage box, which she plonked in the corner of the kitchen. She had managed to make it to the age of twenty-four without ever having paid a cent in rent or contributing towards domestic bills. I suggested to John that, as it seemed she was going to be living with us for the foreseeable future, perhaps she could use some of her Centrelink payments to contribute towards her room and board.

'What?' he responded crossly. 'You want to make money from our own daughter?'

What I actually wanted to do was introduce her to the idea of being an adult, but I didn't labour the point. There's no use pretending that John and I always agreed on the best way to handle Anna. I would usually give in. I hated fighting with him, and I knew he loved our girl as much as I did, though he had different ways of expressing it.

When I think of that first summer Anna was back with us, two images dominate: one is of Anna under the three-storey-high pine tree in our backyard, smoking a bong. I might go out to the yard in the midafternoon to hang out a load of washing; by that time she would have roused herself out of bed, and there she would be, bonging away. A few hours later I'd go out again, perhaps to water my veggie garden, which I still had a lot of hope for at that stage, and she'd be in the same position, fiddling with her phone, maybe smoking a cigarette instead of the bong. I couldn't get my head around how long she could sit in one place like that, on a green plastic lawn chair, with our small, round metal table quietly rusting beside her.

I didn't yell at her, because that would upset John. I often wonder how I would have reacted to her taking up residence under the pine tree if I hadn't had my husband to put a brake on my behaviour. Tired or in a bad mood, would I have marched over to her and screamed that she was being a lazy little shit? Probably. Would that have done any good? I don't think so. I'm very grateful that I didn't have to deal with Anna on my own. In online forums, I would read desperate posts from mothers who regularly had huge fights with their addicted offspring. Arguing with or trying to reason with young people whose brains were addled by drugs invariably led to hurtful words being hurled by both sides, and too often ended in physical violence.

Not that I didn't have meltdowns on occasion. It had been high summer when Anna returned to us, along with her trio of guinea pigs. The plastic storage container she brought them home in was pretty big, but it wasn't much of a life for animals to stay cooped up in there. From under the house, John retrieved the large wire cage without a bottom that we'd used for Anna's former generation of guinea pigs. She'd loved them a lot when she was a teenager. The idea was that the current crop of pigs, as we referred to them, would spend the nights inside in the safety of their container. Then each morning, Anna would move the cage to a new position in the yard so the pigs could spend the day out in the fresh air, grazing on couch grass.

The main fault with this plan was that Anna rarely made it out of bed before early afternoon. In the mornings I had to choose between facing her grumpiness if I managed to wake her up, or putting the pigs out to pasture myself. The second alternative was easier. In the evenings Anna would be up and relatively cheerful, so at least she would help by bringing her furry critters back into the house.

On the January afternoon that simmers in my memory, it was very hot, and it had been like that many days in a row. Anna had gone to Dan's to stay for a few days. This gave me a welcome break from watching her smoke dope, but it left me entirely in charge of her pets. John thought I fussed over them too much, but when I have responsibility for an animal, I think I ought to make sure it has the best life I can possibly provide. So on days when the temperature was in the high thirties, I felt the pigs shouldn't be put outside to swelter in a cage, but left in the house with us. And of course they didn't deserve to be condemned to pass their days in a plastic storage crate. I had gone to Bunnings and raided their supply of free cardboard boxes. I'd lined up half a dozen of the boxes, upside down, along the kitchen wall. Each of these little houses had a tiny door cut in it, so a frightened pig could scuttle in. Otherwise, they were free to wander around.

Usually I didn't mind looking after the latest of Anna's creatures. I liked getting to know their individual rodent personalities, and I admired the acuity of their hearing: they quickly learned the significance of the various plastics in our kitchen. They would squeak with mild interest at the sound of a sandwich bag being pulled from its box, but squeal wildly if someone opened a packet of salad mix. Sometimes I even had fun with them. During the heatwave, Charlotte came to spend a few days and we turned the kitchen into a rodent playground, creating obstacles and steps the pigs had to climb to get to their very favourite treats, red capsicum and kiwifruit skins. I explained to Charlotte that pets needed to exercise their minds as well as their bodies, and I didn't want any guinea pig in my care getting dementia.

This particularly hot afternoon, when Charlotte had returned home to get ready for the new school year and Anna was still at Dan's, any fun I found in Anna's pigs was swallowed up by a big, sweaty lump of resentment. Her bloody rodents were capable of producing a seemingly endless number of poo pellets on the floor. I spread out fresh newspaper every morning for them to scamper around on, but plenty of droppings made their way underneath the news sheets, and then they'd be trodden into the lino, the original vintage flooring from when the house was built in the late sixties.

The only way I could get the embedded shit out of the pocked and fading surface of the lino was to scrape it off with an old kitchen knife. So there I was, on my hands and knees on the kitchen floor, prying up scat while John sat at the table reading *The Age*. Suddenly, I hated that I had to do this. 'I've got students I should be getting lessons ready for!' I was crying, even as I kept on scraping. I was hot and my back hurt and I was thoroughly sick of cleaning up Anna's messes. 'I feel like a slave looking after another bunch of her fucking *pets*!'

John did not look pleased at my outburst. He needed peace before a long night's work at the airport. I hated him not being happy with me. An annoyed look from him, just like from my mother before him, stabbed a cold little hole in my heart. But how was it possible to keep him and myself and Anna and her animals content all at the same time? There were days when I just couldn't.

It fascinates me, how memory works. Before I started writing this book, 2013 looked like this in my mind: at the beginning were the endless bongs and the hot frustration of the pooping pigs, then it zoomed right to the end when we had to face some really nasty stuff, when for the first time John and I were afraid not just for Anna's safety but for our own. As for the months in the middle, they were a muddle of memories with no vivid images that stood out. But as luck would have it, (more precisely, as my compulsive nature would have it) in my study there is a record of every single day. I don't often dip into my old journals, let alone read them through an entire year, but in researching this book, I thought I should.

This was not an entirely painful business, reading through 2013. It gave me a chance to recall movies I'd been to with friends, the week that John and I spent at Lakes Entrance, the funny or touching things kids said to me when I was tutoring them. Even the many references to Anna weren't all negative. Especially during the first half of the year, she helped me a lot with preparing lessons. We were both pretty excited about the laminator I bought. Too many hours when I should have been writing, she and I would be fiddling around creating slick little coloured cards for the elaborate games we invented to introduce my students to wonders like metaphors and onomatopoeia.

But it was also sad, reading through that year, because as I turned the pages I could see my daughter deteriorating. During the first couple of months, she was drinking heavily and smoking a lot of bongs, but at least it was actual marijuana she was ingesting. I'm not sure where she got the dope, but there is a reference in my diary that reads, 'I "lent" Anna $150 to pay her dealer.' Then she made a discovery that I believe led to a catastrophic decline in her mental health: she found out she didn't need a dealer. At the sex shop across from Moonee Ponds station, she could legally purchase synthetic weed.

On top of the alcohol and weed, Anna had developed a great love for Seroquel, which was prescribed to her by a psychiatrist she saw during her last months with Andrew. She told me the doctor had instructed her to take it on an 'as-needed' basis, when she was having trouble sleeping. I didn't question this, and along with so many other things, I ask myself why I didn't, until I recall how snarly she became if I tried to talk to her about anything she put in her mouth. I have since learned that Seroquel is one of the brand names for a drug called quetiapine, and it is mainly used as an antipsychotic. If you google this medication, on almost all sites the first sentence includes the phrase 'used for the treatment of schizophrenia'. So I now doubt that the psychiatrist who first prescribed Seroquel to Anna intended it to be used as simply a sleeping pill. And I'm sure he would have meant for her to take it regularly as part of a monitored medication regime, rather than popping one in when she was desperate for unconsciousness.

I didn't have to consult medical sites to understand that this drug was a powerful sedative. When she took one of those pills, on top of half a bottle of vodka and a few bongs, you couldn't wake her up until it wore off. I worried, just as I had when she was a six-week-old infant, that she would stop breathing while she slept. One cold night I tried extra hard to wake her up. But even when I shook her arm and prodded her in the side, she remained in a virtual coma. So I got under the doona with her and cuddled up to her lovely warm back, as if by force of will and wanting, I could keep her alive.

And there was another addiction, which I hadn't really identified till I read back through all the days of 2013. Anna had become addicted to dating. In my journal there are a dizzying number of male names recorded: 'Sam picked Anna up and they went off to the city . . .'; 'Alex was here for a barbie and Anna went home with him . . .'; 'Anna stayed at George's place all weekend . . .' and many, many more. A face floats up in my memory when I read some of these names. But for most there is no image attached; they are just names on a page. I recorded where she met each one: online, on the train, in the street, through a meet-up group she was in for a while, at a short bartending course that the dole office sent her to.

Anna wasn't a sex addict. Just after I finished reading 2013, I would have said that she was an affection addict, that she was trying to fill the aching hole in her life where a trusted girlfriend should have been. (Rachel, her one friend left from high school, had gone to New York to study acting, and when she returned, Anna barely saw her.) But now I've had time to mull it over, I'd say Anna was more of an admiration addict. She loved getting dressed up, doing her hair, putting on make-up, then having whichever boy or man showed up tell her how beautiful she looked. She craved that rush, I can now see, as much as she did dope, alcohol and nicotine.

Chapter 21

I think Anna's slide into debilitating mental illness and addiction began in October of 2013, when she made one last and, for her, mammoth effort to join mainstream society. With the help of Break Thru, an organisation that assists people to get off the dole, she undertook a five-week course in hair and beauty. This would lead, hopefully, to an apprenticeship in hairdressing.

Back when Anna was in high school, acing exams and winning public-speaking awards, we might have considered that profession far below her capabilities. Now, if she were able to achieve success in that field, we would rejoice like crazy. John was already congratulating her, reassuring her that this was the job for her, seeing how skilful she was with her own hair and make-up. Katie and I weren't so sure: didn't hairdressing require more people skills than Anna possessed?

Still, we couldn't have been more pleased that she was trying to take charge of her future. Since moving back home, the only real initiative she'd shown on the professional front was when she took herself up to the local St Vincent de Paul's and volunteered to do a shift a week. They offered Saturday afternoons, and she managed to get to almost every one, no matter how hungover she was, or which man she'd been out with the night before. Only once was she sent home, for wearing something the older lady in charge deemed inappropriate – a lacy white mini dress that barely covered her bottom.

The hair and beauty course was being conducted on the other side of the city, near where her pal Dan lived. So she arranged to stay with him for the duration (and I transferred $80 a week into his account to help with food and utility expenses). The first four and a half weeks went pretty well. Alarm bells only clanged in my head a few times, for example, when after about three days she was posting ecstatic messages on Facebook: 'I've made some fantastic friends at TAFE!' Two weeks later she informed me, though thankfully didn't post, that these friends had turned into 'useless bogans'. Halfway through week four she posted on Facebook, in capital letters to denote screaming, 'I'M IN PAIN!' I called her about that and she actually answered, telling me I had to help her because she'd run out of prescriptions for her meds. This plea irritated me somewhat, as she had more than once sharply pointed out that it was not my business to monitor her scripts, or even inquire as to exactly what she was taking. She'd told me about the Seroquel, and because I'd been in the room with her at the time, I also knew that Dr Deb had rather reluctantly prescribed antidepressants. Figuring this was not the time to question anything that might assist Anna to get through the hairdressing course, I spoke to Dan. He came to her rescue, taking her to a doctor where she managed to procure repeat scripts, and I put money into her account so she could pay for the meds.

So with at least some of Anna's usual drugs back in her system, things were going okay . . . until midnight on the Wednesday of week five, two days before she was due to finish the course. That when my ringtone jerked me out of sleep. It was Dan, who informed me grimly, 'She's called the police on me.'

'What?'

'She claims I abused her.'

I found out later she'd had a practice exam that afternoon on applying make-up and she'd failed. She'd arrived back at Dan's in despair, and when he got home from work she demanded to smoke some of the dope she knew he had. He'd said no, so they'd quarrelled all evening, culminating in a physical struggle when she tried to get to his stash. She claimed he pushed her, and she fell against the wall. That's when she screamed at him for assaulting her, and called the police.

By the time Dan called me, she'd begun to settle down. I could hear her, on her phone, talking to the police again. 'It's all right. You don't have to come. I'm not really hurt.'

But it wasn't that easy to reverse a domestic violence callout. The police had to investigate. A few minutes later one of the officers rang me from Dan's place. I didn't record what he told me, but I do remember what I said to him: 'Can you just put her in a taxi? I'll pay when it gets here.' He sounded relieved at the suggestion. So, as I recorded on Thursday the 24th of October: 'Got to bed at two o'clock after paying for Anna's taxi ($60) and talking to her . . . up at 6.45 to make her coffee, pack her lunch, dry her make-up brushes and apron (she got caught in the rain yesterday) and see her off to the train.' On Friday my journal says: 'Up again at 6.45 to make lunch for Anna, take her a Red Bull and encourage her to get to the train.'

That Friday, Anna was allowed to resit the failed practice exam, and this time she passed. She earned a certificate for the course, and even scored interviews at two salons for apprenticeships. She made it to the first interview, but it went badly and she didn't get the job. This sapped her confidence so much she refused to try for the second one.

Still, we did have something to look forward to. I'd bought an excellent present for her birthday: tickets for her and me to go to a special screening of *The Exorcist* at the Nova. It was the scariest movie I'd ever seen and Anna loved it. But the really great thing was that Linda Blair was going to be there, speaking and signing autographs. This was the actress who, forty years earlier had played Regan, the little girl so thoroughly possessed by the devil that her head could turn 360 degrees.

It turned out to be a terrible night. Not because of Linda Blair. She was lovely: tiny and sincere, standing up in front of the screen, telling us how thrilled her mother was when Linda was awarded the part of a girl who swore at and spewed fluorescent vomit all over a priest. I felt sorry for her, because it still hurt her, that at twelve she was vilified by the evangelical Christians of America for masturbating with a crucifix. 'I had no idea what I was doing,' she protested.

The night was excruciating for me because I realised just how hopelessly addicted Anna was. She'd had 'a few puffs' in the backyard, along with a couple of glasses of wine before we left, then when we got to Carlton she insisted I buy her two four-packs of Vodka Cruisers.

'I don't know if we should take those into the cinema,' I said.

'Mum!' she growled. 'I wanna have a good night!'

She stowed the cans in her backpack. As soon as we were settled into our seats, she sucked one down at astonishing speed, then pulled out another. This one, thank goodness, she sipped slowly.

Linda Blair was very late arriving for her Q&A appearance, but the Nova staff assured us she was definitely coming, so we waited. Sitting on the other side of Anna was an interesting looking young woman, on her own, in the seat between Anna and the aisle. She was comfortably curvy, with pink spiky hair and several facial piercings. She was writing something in a large hardback notebook balanced on her lap. Anna turned to her and said, 'I just want to tell you I think you're really beautiful.'

Oh, God. No doubt the girl could smell the alcohol on Anna's breath. She leaned away from Anna, but picking up on social cues such as body language was not Anna's strong point. She persisted. 'Most people can't carry off a ring between their nostrils,' she opined in slightly slurred tones. 'With a lot of people it makes them look like a pig, but on you it looks really good.'

'Uh . . . thanks.'

'Are you a film student?' Anna gestured towards the notebook on the girl's lap.

'Sort of,' she admitted. 'I do reviews online.'

'Oh, wow!' Anna enthused. 'I write online too. Do you wanna take my number and we could get together some time?'

The girl thought for a couple of seconds about Anna's invitation and then answered, 'No, I don't think so.'

'Why not? I'm really cool!'

Mercifully, at last, Linda appeared. And then we watched the film, during which Anna drank her way through three more Cruisers. Afterwards, we waited in line for Linda's autograph. By this time, Anna was swaying unsteadily and was beginning to slur her words. It was nearly midnight. 'Let's just go home,' I begged. 'I've got students tomorrow.'

'No way! I've been waiting weeks for this!' The line was moving slowly. Everyone wanted to talk to Linda, to hug her, to have a selfie with her. Anna plonked her backpack on the floor and pulled out her last Cruiser. The houselights were on. 'Don't have that now! Everyone can see you,' I said. Tired, cross and mortified, I tried to snatch the can out of her hand.

'Mum!' Her eyes, her beautiful blue eyes, blazed too much like the possessed Regan's. 'Stop trying to control me!'

And then she said something that haunts me to this day. Her tone was hard and angry, but behind it I could hear a pleading little girl. 'Mum, I don't want to hate you.'

Chapter 22

In the months after the horror movie night, after Anna failed to become a hairdresser, her life became truly chaotic. She often slept all day, and was sometimes up all night. Her coordination became wonky; she dropped and broke quite a few of our glasses and plates. She spilled wine on her bed, and a can of vodka and cola into the netbook Andrew had given her for her twenty-first. One evening she convinced Scott, a guy from her friendship group at high school, to come over. John and I were glad to see him: he had the same gentle nature he'd possessed at eighteen. He sat at the kitchen table with us, sipping a light beer and chatting about his job at the Botanic Gardens. Inwardly I winced, while, as my journal attests: 'Anna slurped down glass after glass of cask red.' She started to rave on about some conspiracy theory she'd discovered on the internet, then she began to slur, and finally she staggered out to the lounge room, collapsed on the couch and passed out. Scott finished his beer and bade us a polite goodbye.

We didn't see him again for quite a while, but now Anna had a boyfriend. This was Billy, whom she met through an online dating site. She told me she had specified in her profile that she only wanted to meet stoners, so apparently he was one of those, but he was a high-functioning one – a plumber who worked long hours and had an air of nuggetty fitness about him. Anna actually went out with him long enough for us to get to know him, and we liked him a lot. John especially enjoyed chatting with him. They had similar tastes in music, and John didn't mind a good chat about plumbing.

I wondered what Billy was getting out of his relationship with Anna, because by this stage she basically existed in three states:

1 Flying high, babbling about some idea she was nurturing, such as the gruesome methods that should be used to torture elephant poachers to death.

2 In a grumpy half-stupor, in which she would stumble over anything in her path and abuse you if you got in her way.

3 In one of her virtual comas. She seemed increasingly unable to manage a 24-hour sleep–wake cycle, but instead would drug and drink herself into unconsciousness whenever or wherever she could.

Often on Saturday or Sunday, during the last few months of 2013, Billy would have dinner with us and then take Anna home with him. He lived a 45-minute drive away, in a suburb on the west side of Port Phillip Bay. Anna found it too much trouble to get the train back from there, so she'd stay at his place till he had time to drive her home. As a result, she might be at Billy's for several days, and in a way this was a welcome break for me. I didn't have to clean up after her, or get woken up in the middle of the night by the clanging she would make in the kitchen as she pottered around creating more mess. I especially appreciated not needing to pretend to listen to her loud and wild opinions, when all I really wanted to do was yell at her to shut up and turn her mind to something useful.

Yes, with Anna away, my world was certainly more peaceful, but it was also coated with a grey film of worry. Gradually, over decades, I had managed to give up my main method of dealing with anxiety: stuffing myself with so much fat and sugar that all I could think about was the next day, when I would starve away the self-loathing. Along the way I had gathered a few other tools, from self-help books, and Radio National shows, and friends. I'd found it was possible to change the default setting of my brain, to direct my thoughts away from darkness towards pathways of light. But knowing this didn't mean it was easy to do. When I realised that Anna's relationship with Andrew was unravelling, when I had to let my dreams for her diminish by the day, I finally admitted that to cope with all this loss I needed more help than books and broadcasts could provide. I did what I should have done when I was in my twenties, and sought professional support. I asked Dr Deb to refer me to a good psychologist, and that's how I met Margot. She was lovely, around my own age, slim with a neat white bob. I respected her spicy intelligence and her advice.

I told Margot how my worries over Anna seeped into every nook and cranny of my day. She suggested that I allocate one hour out of every twenty-four for worrying about my daughter. After some deliberation I chose the dull and sleepy sixty minutes I liked least: three to four in the afternoon. Often, if I asked them politely, I could persuade my disastrous thoughts to go away for a while, reassuring them I would give them my attention at 3 p.m. But this didn't always work. The longer Anna stayed away from home, the harder it was to quarantine my concern.

I really feared for her, alone in an empty house for hours while Billy was at work. Who knew how much dope she had access to, on top of her seemingly endless supply of Seroquel? What if she stopped breathing at, say, eleven in the morning? Billy wouldn't be home till six, at the earliest. I yelled at my mind, ordering it not to create these terrible images of my beautiful girl. If only I could hear her voice, but she never answered her phone any more. Sometimes, after seven or eight missed calls from me, she'd fire off an impatient text: 'Yes, I'm alive!'

Once in a while she'd be in a good mood and send me a jokey message.

'Hey Mummy,' she texted once, 'why wasn't Cinderella good at football?'

'Does it have something to do with her wearing glass slippers?' I guessed.

'No!' came the answer. 'It's because her coach was a pumpkin. Lol.'

Other times, hours would pass with no text. I'd check Facebook every thirty minutes or so, hoping to see that she'd posted one of her raves or just shared a picture of a tattooed woman or a pair of luscious boobs. She was fairly obsessed with breasts at the time, having declared herself to be bi-curious.

Anna's devoted godmother, Gill, told me she was considering unfriending Anna because she was sick of seeing tattoos and boobs come up on her newsfeed, but changed her mind when I explained how these images reassured me that her goddaughter was still breathing.

During this time I was very grateful to have my tutoring. It was the best tool in my psychological first aid kit. When I turned my thoughts from Anna to my students, I could feel my brain lightening from a mad mess of muddy colours to clear, clean pastels.

I liked searching for resources to help my charges attain the best results they could. It was a special treat to go into Campion Books on Pascoe Vale Road. In the middle of a school day, it was so peaceful there. Often I'd be the only customer, just me and the nice sales lady and walls of textbooks quietly waiting to divulge their civilised secrets. One day I chose a large, colourful paperback, which cost nearly as much as I'd be paid for a lesson, but its blurb promised to set out exactly how I could guide a young person to achieve an excellent result in VCE English. I already had enough books like this to open a small shop of my own, but just like my succulents and the teapots to grow them in, it gave me a blessed moment of joy to buy a new one. And I had a young person in mind to try the textbook out on, a sweet and ambitious year 12 girl with chronic, life-threatening asthma.

It gave me another flash of happiness to open the shiny new book for her. Her cute, round face, made plump by steroids, lit up. During the hour I was with her, in a quiet corner of her school library, using all my conscious brain cells to squeeze as much personalised teaching as I could into our allocated sixty minutes, everything else in the world dropped away. This girl, and her mother and teacher, were so grateful for my help. I took on too many students, so that I had virtually no time to write, but being with those kids felt so good. It seemed that in one hour a week of concentrated attention, I could make a difference in a young person's life. I could assist a boy who'd suffered a stroke at sixteen to understand how Stan Grant and Barack Obama and the advertisers of Nike used language to persuade. While back in the murky reality of my life, where no textbook existed to guide me, I couldn't find the right words to persuade my own child to stop self-destructing.

But I tried. How I tried to save her with words!

After days at Billy's house, he would bring her back home . . . dishevelled and depressed, but alive. I would suggest brightly that if she would only eat some fruit every day, she would feel better. And exercise . . . she could go for a walk with me, or on a run or a bike ride with her dad. I'd enthusiastically describe the study I'd heard about that listed the most effective tools to help with depression. Guess what was number one? Not medication, not counselling . . . it was exercise!

I advised her not to tackle all her problems at once, but to make gradual improvements, like getting out of bed before midday. But for Anna, it was perfection or nothing.

My entry for Saturday the 7th of December reads: 'Anna was up at 6 a.m. That was scary. She did a bunch of jobs, including vacuuming and picking caterpillars off the nasturtiums. She had a coffee with John and then went for a WALK with him. She told me she's gonna give up dope, then cigarettes, then grog, and run a marathon.'

This is the entry for the next day, Sunday: 'I must learn not to hope . . . Anna drank nearly a whole bottle of vodka last night, went to sleep in her clothes, and she must have dropped her netbook. She went off to "shop" at nine in the morning. She sent me an angry text saying "All you ever do is nag and criticise me and tear me down".'

That's what she thought of my carefully phrased suggestions. That's how they made her feel.

Chapter 23

Anna didn't come home that Sunday after her trip to the shop. She did text me late in the afternoon, to say she'd spent the day with Rachel, her girlfriend from VCE, who was back from her acting course in New York. Anna said she'd been invited to have dinner at Rachel's, and afterwards she was going to Billy's for the night. Of course I wondered how she was getting there . . . but I didn't want to risk an outraged reply, so I just requested that she text to let me know when she got there. I didn't hear from her again that night.

By 9.30 the next morning, that nasty little rat of worry was gnawing at the edges of my heart. Anna wasn't answering her phone, so I texted Billy. I imagined him elbow deep in some unpleasant plumbing business, but it wasn't long before he texted me back. He and Anna hadn't made plans to see each other over the weekend and she hadn't come to his place.

I texted Rachel. 'She wasn't here,' Rachel answered, 'I haven't heard from her in ages.'

I was shocked, then baffled, then angry. She'd never lied to me outright before. I called Katie to debrief with her, as I often did, and noted later in my journal: 'It's strange, but . . . it feels like we're heading *somewhere*.'

Anna's lies had pushed me to a place where I could no longer pretend that her life was anything but a shambles. Up till then I hadn't wanted to admit how far she had sunk. I had led my sisters, who only had my word for it, to believe that Anna was basically okay. I simply told them about the positive things she'd done, and edited out the unsavoury bits. Now, the unsavoury bits were pretty much all that was left. I wrote my sisters an email that began, 'We're having a terrible time with Anna.' I told them how I had come to suspect that the anorexia of her teenage years had been just one manifestation of a serious underlying mental illness. I wonder now why it took me so long to put this into words, but I remember the profound relief I felt when I wrote that to my sisters. When I said 'Anna has a mental illness', I was pointing out to them and to myself that Anna's situation was not entirely the result of our parenting. *You wouldn't condemn John and me if I told you she had diabetes, would you?* Although I didn't come right out and say it, that was my plea. I also confessed in the email that Anna was 'self-medicating'. That's how I let my teetotal, churchgoing family know that my daughter was an addict.

It felt good to press send. But Anna was still missing. Having gone AWOL on Sunday morning, she still hadn't turned up by Wednesday night. She had texted me a couple of times to say she was alive, so even though I didn't know where she was, I knew there was no point in calling the police. At ten on Wednesday evening, with John at work and me in the lounge room, dividing my attention between a TV show and worry, Anna burst through the front door. 'I think he's followed me!' Her voice was a hoarse, frightened whisper, and her hair, usually so lovingly cared for, was tangled and matted.

'Who's followed you?'

'The psycho I've been staying with! I tried to get away but I think he was on the same train as me. Look what he did!'

She held out her arm, and there on her pale skin were the round marks of cigarette burns. 'I think he's out there . . . can you hear him? Don't open the door . . . Mum!' She was truly scared.

And so was I, of her wild eyes and the 'psycho' who had hurt my girl. 'Who is he?'

'His name's Lance. I met him on the train. He seemed really nice!'

My phone rang. Unknown, the screen announced. I answered, 'Hello?'

'Mary?' said an unfamiliar male voice. 'Don't worry. I'm heading back to the train now. I just wanted to make sure your daughter got home safe.'

I glared at Anna. 'Why'd you give him my number?'

'I don't know!'

Maybe he hadn't really followed her. He could be bluffing. But this thought was dismissed from my mind as wishful thinking with his next comment: 'Oh, by the way, I really like the roses beside your mailbox. I noticed the blooms are nearly finished. You'd better pick one and put it in a vase before it's too late.'

That was the first night I didn't feel safe inside the house I'd loved for nearly three decades. That was the night John decided, when he got home, that we should keep the doors locked all the time.

The next day, the weather was beautiful. Katie and Tom came over for a barbecue lunch in the backyard. I only had fruit and frozen yoghurt because, later that evening, I was planning to go to a dinner I'd been looking forward to for months. Anna slept till midafternoon. I'd gone into the house to make coffee, and when I was walking across the back deck with it, on my way to the garden, Anna emerged from the bungalow. She was fully dressed, with her hair brushed and her backpack on. 'Where are you going?' I asked her.

'Lance wants me back,' she announced lightly.

'You're kidding! After what he did to you?'

'He's been talking to me for ages,' Anna said. 'He's really sorry.'

I plonked the tray of coffee and chocolates down on the wonky table we kept on the deck and I walked towards her, screeching. 'You can't go to his place!'

She stepped backwards, into the doorway of the bungalow. John groaned as he registered the tone in my voice. 'What's wrong *now*?'

'She wants to go back to that psycho! We can't let her!'

Katie appeared at my side, helping to block the doorway. I begged Anna to stay with us. I promised I'd bake her a batch of extra squishy brownies right then.

'This has gone beyond a joke,' Katie told her. 'You're killing Mum and Dad. You need to go to rehab!'

'I'm going to Lance's!' she shouted, pushing past us.

'Tom!' Katie yelled. 'Come and help!'

We wanted Tom to help us corral her before she managed to unlatch the back gate. But before he got to her, Anna's phone rang and she stopped to answer it. She retreated back into the messy murk of the bungalow. A couple of minutes later she came out, with Lance on the line. 'He says you can't keep me from leaving. He says if you touch me it's assault and —'

'Let me talk to him!' Before Anna could stop me, I snatched her phone out of her hand and marched to the end of the yard. 'Lance? This is Mary —'

'Listen,' he cut in, 'you can trust me. I won't let any harm come to Anna. I have connections in every police department in Australia, and across the world for that matter.'

'Do you realise Anna —'

'She's beautiful, your daughter! I can understand why you're protective of her, but I can certainly take care of her. You don't have to worry about that, Mary. I know her very well now!'

It wasn't just what he said that was scary, but the way his sentences came out so fast, tumbling against each other in their urgency to be heard, combined with an utterly confident tone.

I tried again to make him see reason. 'I don't think you know how immature Anna is —'

'Ha!' he snorted. 'I think I do know what her capabilities are. Anna's probably told you I'm a major player in the . . . well, I hesitate to say the name of the organisation . . . but it has tentacles all over the globe.'

I kept attempting to inform him, patiently but passionately, that Anna was mentally unstable and he shouldn't encourage her to come to his place. I can still clearly see myself that day, up by the back fence where the agapanthus grew, trying to combat madness with words.

'Do you know what I think I should do?' He asked me loudly, with great authority. 'I think I should marry your daughter!'

By this time Anna, with Katie close behind her, had followed me and was standing beside me. 'Let me talk to my boyfriend!'

I held the phone behind my back and whispered to Katie, 'He's insane!'

'I'll talk to him.' She took the phone and walked back towards the bungalow. Lance must have continued blathering because I couldn't hear Katie say much and, believe me, you can hear her over the length of any backyard in the northern suburbs.

Anna started after her, and that's when I began to cry. She hesitated.

'Please!' I begged her. 'He's known you for four days. We've loved you your whole life!'

That, on top of Katie's assertion that she was killing her dad and me, must have got to her. I could see, inside the big brave runaway, the little girl who needed her mother. I reminded her what Dr Deb had told her, that any time she was ready for rehab, Deb would give her a referral. 'You need help,' I pleaded, 'like you did when you had anorexia.'

There was that frown, the vertical crease between her eyes that the maternal and child health nurse had chuckled at when she was a week old.

Katie joined us, but was no longer carrying Anna's phone. 'He's a meth head,' was her conclusion. That may well have been the main reason Anna wanted to return to Lance: a free supply of ice.

For some time, Katie had believed that Anna was using ice when she could get it, but this was the first time I was convinced that she was sampling the substance that Dr Deb had described as 'the most evil drug I've come across in my twenty years of practice'.

'Where's my phone?' Anna asked Katie.

'Dad's got it. He's talking to Lance inside the house.'

'Anna's thinking of going to rehab,' I said to Katie.

'Really?'

'Yep.' It was the frown, and the fact that she wasn't having a fit about John commandeering her phone, that let me know she was, at last, considering it.

'If I go tomorrow, can I have as much as I want to drink tonight?'

'Of course!'

'No nagging?'

'No way!'

We were flying high. We had snatched our darling back from a madman. But she had one more stipulation. 'If I can't stay at Lance's tonight, then I wanna go to Billy's.'

Oh, God. We knew that if we were to actually get Anna to Dr Deb for a referral and then on to rehab, we couldn't let her out of our sight. 'I can't drive you there!' I said miserably, knowing that I would, if it was the only way she would agree to rehab. I'd have to give up the dinner I'd been looking forward to for so long, a reunion of the funny and energetic people I used to work with at the kids' magazines. It was the only time I got to see them, once a year.

Katie saw my disappointment. She sighed. She said to Anna, 'Okay, I'll drive you to Billy's. But I'm taking charge of your phone. And I'm staying there with you all night. And I'm taking you to Dr Deb in the morning.'

Katie looked at me. 'We'll meet you at Deb's, okay?'

I was beyond grateful. What would I have done without Katie? It's a question I still ask myself, and don't want to imagine the answer.

Chapter 24

It seems kind of amazing to me now, reading over my journal, that I was able to continue living my life among all that emotional chaos. But with Anna safe in Katie's hands, I took myself off to the wayzgoose. This is a centuries' old word for a summer entertainment or outing provided by a printing house for its employees. Back when I was working on the kids' magazines published by the Education Department, it was the name we gave to our end-of-year bash. Now it was an annual reunion for anyone who'd ever worked in the publications branch. That year it was held at a pub in Abbotsford.

I enjoyed the evening, noting in my journal which of my former, much-loved colleagues had been the most fun to chat with. Since our long-ago days of smoking and laughing and flirting in those windowless offices on Queensberry Street, several had gone on to be more successful than me in writing, illustrating and publishing. I was proud of them, and tried to fight off the sickening slash of jealousy. I recorded that by the time I made it to the bar to order dinner, the lamb shanks had finished, so I just had mash and veggies, which were very tasty. What I didn't mention, but remember clearly, is a friend I'd been especially close to asking me if I had any books on the go, or if I was planning any overseas trips. Not really, I told him, then blurted out what was most important to me:

'I'm taking my daughter to rehab tomorrow.' He looked alarmed and didn't know what to say.

The next day, Friday the 13th of December, I wrote: 'Began the day with hope. Looking forward to meeting my daughters for brekkie . . .' We had arranged to meet down the street from Dr Deb's, so we could arm ourselves with coffee before fronting up at the clinic when it opened. My girls arrived on time, Katie looking exhausted and Anna bleary eyed and dishevelled. While we waited for our coffee, with Anna outside smoking, Katie filled me in on the previous night. After I'd gone out, Anna had persuaded John to let her have some of his whiskey; with this on top of all the wine she had also consumed, she was so drunk she could barely climb into Katie's car. Yet when Katie stopped for petrol on the way to Billy's, Anna had managed to stagger into the servo with her and quickly collect chips, chocolate and Red Bull, which she plonked on the counter for Katie to buy. 'And I'll have a packet of Marlboro Red,' she'd slurred to the guy behind the register. Katie had learned, as we all had, to pick her battles. She put the junk food and cigarettes on her bank card. I thanked her, and told her I'd pay her back.

Katie went on to relate that when they arrived at Billy's, Anna headed straight for the couch and promptly passed out. 'It was really awkward!' Katie said. 'It was eleven by then and I had to sit there and think of things to chat about with Billy.'

But it was all worth it when Katie and I triumphantly escorted Anna through the doors of the Grantham Street clinic. Dr Deb wasn't available that day so we saw Dr Roberts; we hadn't met her before but she seemed equally concerned and efficient. I suspect Deb had briefed Dr Roberts about her long relationship with Anna, because she looked at Anna with genuine concern, and tried so hard to help us. It didn't take long for us to discover how incredibly naive we were. Dr Roberts had to explain to us that before she could go to any sort of rehab, Anna would first have to detox, preferably in a medical unit set up for that purpose.

We spent hours at the clinic that day: Dr Roberts parked us in an unoccupied office and kept popping in between patients to ring various organisations and institutions, invariably to be told they'd get back to her. Some did, some didn't. She explained that the most promising option was a facility in Heidelberg called Curran Place, which offered in-house detox. That sounded good! As we waited, Katie and I took turns to escort Anna out the front for a ciggie. We never let her out of our sight, because we had no faith she wouldn't do a runner back to Lance if she got the chance. Each time we took her outside her hands shook more: she was increasingly in need of a stronger drug than nicotine. Maybe three hours into our vigil at the clinic, the sun rose in my heart when Dr Roberts handed me her phone with a smile. 'It's ReGen. They're the people who run Curran Place.'

I held the phone to my ear, with hope in my soul. A woman's calm voice informed me, 'We can see your daughter for an assessment interview on the 23rd of December.' She sounded like I should be happy about that. Ten days from now! She could be *assessed*? I made a note of the appointment, but that woman might as well have blithely stated, 'We can see your daughter in ten years, no . . . make that a hundred. Have a nice afternoon!'

Dr Roberts must have been able to sense my heart sinking. She kept making calls, rushing off to see patients, then returning to us. She managed to arrange for Anna to be evaluated at home by people from the Crisis Assessment and Treatment Team, which we came to know as the CAT team. We were promised that members of this team would call around to our place the next morning.

Before we left, Dr Roberts did give us one other option: if John and I had between $20 000 and $30 000 available, we could send Anna to a private rehab. The doctor could recommend a good one, where Anna could detox and then undergo rehabilitation in the same facility.

I called John to ask him what he thought. His answer was instant, and I agreed with it: we weren't going to part with that kind of money when we had no guarantee that the treatment would work, or that she would even remain at the facility.

Was this the moment we went wrong? Was this the hour when we could have intervened and thrown off course the terrible train that would plough through a good man's life? If I could go back to that long day at the doctor's clinic and remake our decision, would it have made a difference?

I'm not certain, but I think Anna could have been admitted almost immediately. I do know she could have walked out any time the regime became too taxing. Who knows? Maybe she would have stayed. Perhaps a stint in private rehab would have been the start of a fresh, clean life for our girl. Maybe, by being unwilling to gamble a sizeable chunk of our life savings, we threw away our daughter's chances – and, more permanently, Johnnie's.

Looking back, having learned a lot more about addiction and mental illness, and about Anna herself, I don't think we made the wrong decision. But I can understand why people might think we did. And I would never question the choice of parents I've read about online who send their chronically relapsing children to private rehabs multiple times, spending hundreds of thousands of dollars and sometimes re-mortgaging or even losing their homes. When you're desperate to save your child, you do what you can live with.

John and I believed in the public health system. Coming from the United States, I was proud of living in a country where quality care was accessible to all. The system had certainly come through for us before. And we had the CAT team coming. That sounded pretty wonderful: a trio of professionals arriving at our door to fix our damaged daughter.

So, well into the afternoon, Katie trooped tiredly back to her car to go to her home, and I left the clinic with Anna and headed for ours. By that time, it had been nearly twenty-four hours since Anna had had any alcohol or drugs. My journal reads: 'Because she'd agreed to the CAT team, I fucking drove her to Club X and bought her a hundred dollars worth of synthetic. Had to go straight home so she could suck down bong after bong, and slurp down the cask wine.'

An angry tone had crept into my journal. Before, I might have griped about her but there was always an underlying layer of sympathy. In this entry I used expletives, later even referring to her as 'that little bitch', because after she consumed the synthetic weed and the wine, she did something that hurt me in a way none of her previous actions had.

While she was still busy bonging and drinking in the backyard, someone from the CAT team had called her to see how she was doing. I hovered around, curious to hear if she would make any plans for a drug-free future, but she waved me away, wanting to speak to them in private. I figured this was a reasonable request, so I retreated to the kitchen. Through the big window over the sink I could see her pacing around the yard, talking for ages. Eventually, she took her phone into the bungalow, where I assumed she was lying on her bed, still chatting with the CAT team. Relieved that she was engaging with people who knew how to help her, I started assembling a platter of raw veggies and dip as an entree for dinner. I took from the fridge celery, snow peas and Anna's favourite, red capsicum. I'd put our heavy wooden chopping board on the bench and was about to slice the capsicum when, out of the window on the other side of the kitchen, I spotted Anna walking briskly down the driveway. I dropped the knife and sprinted out the front door and down the steps. 'Where are you going?'

'For a walk!' She didn't sound pleased that I'd seen her. She knew that I knew she never just went for a walk. Maybe the CAT team had convinced her of what I had been trying to drill into her for months: exercise was excellent for warding off depression.

'I'll go with you,' I announced. 'I haven't been for a walk yet today.' John was at work. I remembered his security warnings, but I couldn't risk going back up the front steps to lock the front door, or even shut it. Anna frowned at me and walked so fast I had to practically sprint to keep up with her. At the corner of Pacco and Devon roads, at the McDonald's where Katie worked as a teenager, Anna said, 'I'm going in here.'

'That wasn't much of a walk,' I remarked as I followed her in. I wanted to persuade her to wait and eat the fresh food I was preparing at home, wholesome nourishment for her body and poor abused brain. But she was already at the counter ordering. 'I'll have two large Big Mac meals please, one with a chocolate thickshake and one with a frozen Coke.'

'Why are you ordering two?' I whined. 'I don't want any-thing.' She just turned and stared at me. *Pick your battles, Mary.* I paid for the two meals.

We sat across from each other on one of the smaller tables. Anna proceeded to unwrap both Big Macs, take off the top half of the buns and toss them aside, then push the meat, pickles, lettuce and sticky sauce off the bottom of the buns onto the table.

'What are you *doing*?' I couldn't quite take in what I was seeing.

She picked up the large packets of fries, one in each hand, turned them over and shook the contents out on top of the burger mess. Her eyes looking into my shocked ones were more than ever like Regan's from *The Exorcist*. 'I'm going out for a smoke,' she informed me.

So she left me there, doing what she knew I would, attempt-ing to restore order, shoving chips back into their cardboard receptacles. It took a minute or two to sink into my stub-bornly maternal mind that she had no intention of returning to eat any of this so-called food. I left the mess and rushed outside, but she wasn't out the front smoking, or around the side. It was useless to look out the back as that was where the drive-through was, but I had to look anyway. I saw only a car full of happy kids being handed their Happy Meals. And beyond that, the scrubby verge leading up to the railway line. She wasn't there. I wanted to cry. How could I leave this place without her? One hundred metres away, but unreachable and unstoppable, a city-bound train thundered past. My mind did not want to process the truth, that she was on that train on her way back to Lance, who would provide her with her chilling new three-letter love.

I called her phone. It went to voicemail. I texted, 'Where are you?' No answer. I just couldn't get it through my head that she could do this. If I kept standing there, in that desolate space behind McDonald's, surely she would appear. But she didn't.

What choice did I have, but to leave that place without her? I put one foot in front of the other and trudged back home. I was too shocked to be angry. But I had never felt so defeated. The thought of walking back into our house and being there alone felt horrible, like venturing into a black cave where wild snarling animals were ready to jump out of the darkness. I called Katie and told her that Anna was on the way back to Lance's. 'Are you kidding?' was her response. She said she would come over. She, too, needed to debrief.

I feel so incredibly sorry for mothers of addicts who don't have anyone to talk to. Many turn to God and I respect that, but when I am feeling overwhelmed, I need to be with someone I know is real. My journal says: 'Katie and I talked for hours. And then we went to Sandy's and talked some more.'

Sandy was our next-door neighbour, a couple of years younger than me. She was also our good friend, a chronic insomniac who welcomed Katie and me in that midnight with her husky smoker's laugh. Over the three decades I lived next to Sandy, how many hours did I spend at her kitchen table, drinking cups of tea and glasses of red wine and talking? Many, many hundreds. Sandy was the least sentimental of people. I can hear in my mind's ear her hearty scoff as I try to pay tribute to her. It pisses me off that her skinny little body and her lungs gave out before she could read this book. If only I'd known she wouldn't be alive as I type this, I'd have made her listen to me say how much I appreciated her being there beside me in my journey with Anna. On an autumn after-noon in 1988, I sat across from Sandy at her table and told her my sweet secret: I was pregnant. Twenty-seven years later, on the afternoon of Black Sunday, I sat at that same table and she talked me through some of the worst hours of my life.

Why didn't I thank her when I could, for the hours of solace she gave to Anna? Sandy watched my newborn grow into a chattery child, who then turned into a young woman so troubled she would knock on Sandy's door at two in the morning, her brain soaked in a soup of synthetic marijuana, Seroquel and vodka. And Sandy would take her in, give her cigarettes and tea and Tim Tams, then listen to her rave until she conked out on the kitchen floor. It was a great comfort to me to know that our good neighbour would slip a pillow under my girl's head and cover her with a blanket.

Chapter 25

The incident at McDonald's might not seem a big deal to parents who've been through much worse with their addicted children, but to me it felt horrible. It reduced me from being the mother that Anna loved and respected, to an inconvenience that needed to be dealt with, an obstacle to get out of the way, using the most effective and convenient method she could think of.

Anna didn't come home that night, and we didn't hear from her. My journal for Saturday the 14th of December reads: 'Didn't sleep long. Head full of shock: how could she betray/lie to/humiliate me like that, leaving me with food strewn around me that *I* had paid for, for *her*?' By that time I was incredibly mad at her. The CAT team was scheduled to come to our place early that afternoon, the same time I'd booked to attend a free movie preview I was entitled to see as a Nova Privilege member. So off I went to watch *Nebraska* with Marcelle.

John told me when I returned home that the CAT team had arrived as promised. He said he'd had a good chat with them, even though Anna wasn't there. Because she didn't show, the team recorded 'a failed visit'. If the CAT team arrived to find her missing a certain number of times in a row – I think it was perhaps three – then they would stop coming. On Sunday morning, we still didn't know where Anna was, and the anger I was feeling hadn't diminished. I took John a cup of tea in bed, as was our custom. I told him I'd decided not to give

Anna any more money. He agreed that was a good idea. But just because I was mad at her didn't mean that I didn't worry about her. The worry was always there, a dirty grey hum behind everything, a kind of psychological tinnitus. Yet I kept on making plans for each day. On Monday, I was going to wrap up all my end-of-term paperwork for my students from the Children's Hospital program (believe me, there was plenty of that). I needed to buy Christmas presents for my sisters and send them off, wanting to believe that the exorbitant airmail fee would get them there before Christmas. Also, in the afternoon, we had a family meeting scheduled with the CAT team at Merri Health in Coburg. John wasn't keen on going, which was not a surprise. In fact, I'd been amazed that he said he'd enjoyed his chat with the team when they came to our house. Normally he was almost comically wary of mental health professionals. Doing his job at the airport, if he saw the profession of 'psychologist' written on an incoming declaration card, he told us he would not make eye contact with that passenger. 'I don't want them sucking the thoughts out of my head,' he claimed. But Katie and I wanted to go to the family meeting, even if Anna didn't show up.

I woke up on Monday morning ready to tackle all my jobs. Here is my journal entry for that day:

What a way to start the day! Before I had my coffee, there was a call from Anna . . . frantic voice . . . 'Mum I got away from him! What should I do?' Suddenly she's not the 25-year-old who treated me like shit on Friday. She's my baby and I have to protect her! 'Just call a taxi and come home. I'll pay!' It cost $95 and all my plans for the day fell into pieces as I cared for her.

Katie came over, bless her, and Tom. John was desperate for us to get Anna to the family meeting with the CAT team, hoping it might do her some good, even though he wouldn't go himself. She agreed to go, if I would drive her to Club X for synthetic ($60). I did that, then brought her back home and counted the minutes to two o'clock, hoping she would stay in the backyard with her bong and not bolt . . . Such a sense of accomplishment getting her to the meeting! Doctor and social worker talked to her for an hour plus, then to Katie and me.

I don't know if Anna got anything out of that meeting, but I certainly did. An authoritative health worker instructed me in a very firm voice: 'Don't buy her drugs again ever, under any circumstances.' She said this in Anna's presence. Somehow, being told by this professional that I would only prolong my daughter's addiction by supplying her gave me permission to stop doing it.

The next day, Tuesday, the CAT team came to our house again. Anna was there and in a sober enough state to sit at the kitchen table with the three young women and me and discuss how we should 'move forward'. The team leader was very skilful at redirecting the conversation, again and again calmly suggesting that Anna and I not become 'emotional' with each other – that is, to stop snapping and sniping and making accusations. Instead, she wanted us to come up with a list of boundaries that we could both stick to. Anna's main point was, 'I want Mum to stop nagging me and dragging up shit I've done in the past.'

It irked me that she really didn't seem to notice all that John, Katie and I did for her. Did she not even register the endless goods and services we provided? To bring these to her attention, I decided to include a few samples in the list of boundaries I typed up after the team left (see rule number five). I also tried to incorporate the wishes that seemed most important to her, and to take heed of what the CAT team pointed out – that Anna was an adult responsible for her own safety, and that she shouldn't have to inform me of where she was going or when she'd be back.

Here is what I came up with:

1. I have finally realised I can't protect Anna. She has to do that herself.
2. John and I want to provide a refuge where Anna will feel safe.
3. I agree not to 'nag' about how much Anna drinks or smokes. I will not comment on her consumption of these substances.
4. I will cease to question where she is going or try to stop her leaving the house.
5. John and I do not expect Anna to make a monetary contribution towards food, wine, electricity, gas, rates, water or household items like toilet paper, tissues, soap, etc.
6. However, when she is staying here, Anna is expected to spend at least an hour a day doing jobs in the house, garden and/or home office.
7. John and I have decided not to 'lend' or give Anna any more money.
8. I will not nag Anna to get to appointments on time.
9. I will not nag Anna to take her meds.
10. I will not nag Anna to honour her commitments, such as returning forms to Centrelink.

11 I will still remind her of commitments, but only once.

12 I am happy to provide transport if it fits into my day. However, I will no longer 'drop everything' just to get Anna somewhere on time if she has neglected to budget her time.

13 I will try not to make Anna feel guilty for help provided in the past.

14 If Anna decides she wants help regarding her drug and alcohol use, or help with her mental health, John, Katie and I are more than willing to support her in this. We have established contacts in the community who will also support Anna if she chooses to reach out to them.

15 Although Anna is free to make her own decisions, if John, Katie or I feel unsafe because of actions Anna has taken or is thinking of taking, then we strongly feel we should discuss the situation and decide together the best way to proceed.

When I showed my carefully worded document to Anna, she grumped, 'This makes me sound like a big problem.' I didn't contradict her.

The next morning, I went to the city with a friend, but made sure I got home in time to take Anna to see Dr Deb, who had made some time in her schedule to see Anna. When I arrived home ready to take Anna to her appointment, she made up a story about Deb cancelling. Disgusted, I noted in my journal: 'Washed the car with mop. Watered all pots and veggie garden. Meanwhile, Anna got herself dolled up and headed out on the train . . .'

She made sure I saw her before she left. Standing before me as I worked in the veggie garden, it was as if she was daring me to question where she was going. I visualised point number four on the boundaries agreement, and asked nothing. She didn't say anything either, but something about the redness of the lipstick she wore and the way she flounced her shapely bottom made me think that even if she wasn't intending to go back to Lance, she was prepared to schmooze up to some other man on the train.

People always guessed Anna to be about ten years younger than she was. So, looking like a tarted-up teenager, off she disappeared into the summer night. When I got up the next morning, hoping she would have returned in the wee hours and be snoozing in the bungalow, she wasn't there. John and I had planned to drive to Lorne that morning for a three-day holiday. We'd been looking forward to it for ages. Months before, John had spotted an ad in the *Sunday Age* for a special luxury package at the gracious old Grand Pacific, and I'd booked and paid for a room with an ocean view. We decided we'd still go. My friend Marcelle was a bit of a gypsy. She was a sort of house-mother at a residential unit for adults with cognitive disabilities, so she spent most nights there. On her nights off she liked staying at different friends' houses. She had already agreed to stay at our place, to guard against any ice freaks that might turn up like Lance had. Now we asked her to welcome Anna back when she got around to returning.

Like all my close girlfriends, Marcelle loved Anna. To them she was a playful little girl, warm and affectionate, giving them hugs and making them laugh. She could be that way with me too, when she wasn't mad at me.

As John and I trundled down the Great Ocean Road, one of the most spectacular drives on the planet, I gazed out at the beauty of this incredible coastline that was in my very own state, two hours drive from my house. Back in Iowa, when we embarked on a family vacation, the only scenery we passed for two days was cornfields. I stopped myself from speculating out loud where Anna might be. We didn't believe she was at Lance's. She had now decided she hated him, referring to him as 'that abusive piece of shit', and she had blocked his number. That alone would not have convinced us she wouldn't go back to him. But we more or less knew his movements because he called John at least once a day. The first few times he called, he'd asked if he could speak with Anna to try to persuade her to like him again, but John would always say she wasn't home, whether she was or not. So Lance would yak on to John for forty-five minutes, or an hour. He no longer even asked if Anna was home; he just called to chat with John. John found him quite entertaining, but the real reason he listened was so he could get to know how Lance's mind worked.

The Grand Pacific experience in Lorne was pretty much as good as the ad had promised. When we walked into our room in the early afternoon, we were dazzled by not just one but two sea views, as we'd been given a corner room. There was a bottle of bubbly waiting for us in an ice bucket, resting in the bay window, along with two little packets of Ferrero Rochers.

After we drank two glasses of the bubbly, we made love in the sea light of our clean, quiet room. Later we walked along the curve of beach that the town was arranged around, and the next day I visited a peaceful, sandalwood-scented room, where I had a massage from a competent Chinese masseur, using the voucher that came with the holiday package.

It's lovely to recall those moments of crystal and gold, because before I revisited it in my journal, that holiday in Lorne was just a vague cloud of sea and sky floating in my mind. What I remember with harrowing clarity about those final weeks of 2013, and all of the next year, is the feeling of a terrible thing approaching. It was like a dull roar ringed around the edges of my consciousness.

There were some hours when I stopped listening to it, especially when I was with my students, but also if I was absorbed in a book or a movie or a conversation with a friend. But the sound of relentless dread was always waiting, ready for me when my concentration eased towards neutral.

When we got home on Sunday evening, the 22nd of December, Marcelle – who was by far the most evangelical Christian of my friends – was thrilled to tell us that Anna had showed up that day and went to church with her. But then she'd asked Marcelle for a lift to the train, and didn't say where she was going.

Anna didn't return that night, but I heeded boundary rule number eleven and only reminded her once, via text, that the next day was her appointment to be assessed for in-house detox. She didn't respond. Finally she got home, late on the night of the 23rd of December, many hours after her scheduled appointment had come and gone.

For the first time since I met John, we hadn't planned Christmas with his family. It was just too hard to face a celebration with Anna the way she was. We decided we'd have a quiet (no dramas, please!) barbie under the pine tree with Tom and Katie, and Anna, too, if she was home and conscious. I recorded in my journal the day before Christmas:

Weather was perfect . . . At two in the afternoon Anna still slept on and on in the gloom of the bungalow amid the rubbish. I'd asked her to do two jobs to help prepare for tomorrow: sweep the prunings from the steps up to the garden and vacuum. I asked her to get up and do them and she said yes, she would. So she got up, smoked a bong, messed up the kitchen making baked beans, then went back to bed. I rang Katie to ask if she'd come early and help tomorrow, since Anna refused to do anything. I was out on the back deck talking to Katie, so Anna heard. She suddenly stormed out of the bungalow and swept the garden steps while yelling at me. I said, 'We need family therapy.' She stomped off to use her remaining twenty dollars to buy Christmas presents.

On Christmas Day, Anna behaved well but after lunch took off 'to go to church'. It was extremely hard to stick to rule number four. What church had a service on Christmas afternoon? I desperately wanted to know where she was really going, to beg her to stay safe. This time she was away for a week.

The sound of dread throbbed loudly in my head. What if she hooked up with another guy like Lance? How many times could she chat up random men on the train, go home with them for affection and drugs, and not get badly hurt? She texted after a couple of days and said she was at Billy's. I stopped myself from calling him to see if that was true. Even if she really was there, he might not check on her often enough. I assumed he was on holiday, having a break from plumbing. But no doubt he'd want to spend time with his mates. What if he couldn't rouse Anna to go with him? She always smoked so much dope at his place, on top of the vodka and the Seroquel.

Anna celebrated her first birthday and Katie turned four on one of our trips to Iowa. My sister Joan, keeper of the family history, arranged this studio portrait to be taken at the time.

Ollie thinks it's funny when we tell him how much he looks like his mumma and his mummy when they were little.

Back when Anna was our happy little angel.

At this age, when she was in kinder, Anna was already being ostracised by other children and most likely beginning to hear voices. In hindsight, that's when we should have reached out for professional help.

Anna bringing the garden into the kitchen, where so much of our family life happened and our past was displayed on the cabinet doors.

Katie and Anna walking down our drive on Anna's first day of school. Little did we know how much Anna would need Katie by her side in the years to come.

Aged about nine, Anna knew no one would want to dance with her at the school social, so she made a paper man to take with her.

I believe my mother unconditionally loved only three people in her life: her own mother, Eleanor Roosevelt and Anna. This photo was taken on a trip to Iowa when Anna was eleven and Mother was still in relatively good health.

One of Iowa's great attractions for Anna was the endless supply of kittens on my sister Linda's farm.

My dad and me in 1990. He loved just about everybody.

Despite weighing only 37 kilos, Anna was still competing successfully in karate.

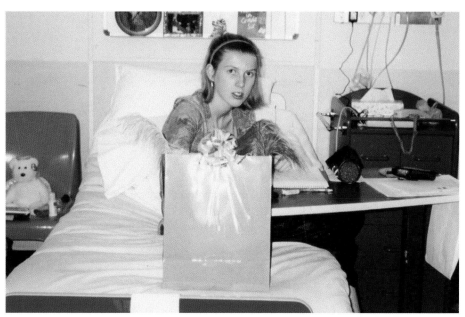

Anna was not allowed to leave this bed in the Royal Children's Hospital until she began to put on weight. At first, she had to sleep with a heart monitor in case she stopped breathing during the night.

Above: Anna's godmother Gill, pictured here on Anna's eighteenth birthday, first held her when Anna was an hour old. Now Gill visits her regularly in prison.

Right: How many hundreds of times did I advise her to smile more at school in order to make friends?

Below: It hurts me now to look at this picture of Anna with Andrew and think of what might have been.

Above: In her last years living with us, Anna spent endless hours on the lounge-room couch, virtually unconscious. At least Poppy would wake up when I spoke to her.

Left: A selfie taken after Anna had moved to Jim's place. She dyed her hair to disguise herself from the gang she imagined was pursuing her.

Right: This was taken when Anna still thought Daddy could protect her.

My favourite photo of me with Anna, taken on my birthday in 2012 just before she began to self-medicate.

I insisted on taking this picture of Katie and Tom by our side fence before they headed off for an evening out.

John and Ollie on our farm, where John has made one of his favourite jokes come true: he's now able to be out standing in his field!

And I wasn't even sure she was there. Comatose and alone in Billy's or someone else's bed, who would hold her close to make sure she continued to breathe?

Those were the questions wrapped up in the roar that rumbled in my head. Then one hot evening between Christmas and New Year, I said the words out loud. Katie was at our place, and she, John and I were in the kitchen with the air-conditioner on, the remains of a dinner of salad on the table.

I don't remember, and didn't record, what led to me expressing what I held in my heart: 'I'm afraid Anna's going to die.'

Katie started to cry.

'That's what I think too.' John didn't cry. He never cries. But the pain was there in his voice. 'If it happens,' he couldn't bring himself to say what 'it' might be, 'there's nothing we can do about it.'

Chapter 26

It was a relief when John, Katie and I brought into the open what had been gnawing inside us: the fear that Anna was going to die. Now we moved toward this as a trio united by honesty. But it was still a horrible thing to face.

Before she could sleep each night, Katie would pray for her sister, as she had when she was a child lying above Anna in the solid wood bunk beds their father had made for them. Only now, the prayer was more desperate. *If Anna has to die, please let it be quick, please don't let her suffer.*

Katie has told me about this many times. These days, when she and I are together, just the two of us, we do discuss other subjects apart from Anna. Katie is passionate about politics, and sustainability and the ethical raising of farm animals, which is why she wants to be a farmer as well as a writer. I like to fill her in on what I've learned from the latest *Health Report* on Radio National, or tell her about some new book or podcast I've become enamoured of. Still, as we walk the streets of the suburb where she grew up, or meander down the long, graceful drive of the farm where she now lives, we always end up talking about Anna. Over and over again we revisit key scenes in our personal drama, like the night when we addressed the elephant in the room and named it Death.

I believe many women who've experienced a tragedy need, as Katie and I do, to talk and talk and talk some more about what led up to it. It's our way of trying to wring some meaning from the unfathomable. Sometimes we raise subjects we've never talked about before. Just last weekend I said to Katie, 'Why didn't we try to find out more about synthetic weed? She smoked a shitload of that stuff and I never thought much about what it actually was.'

Katie, whom John claims has inherited his sensible genes, replied, 'We were in damage control, just trying to get through each day the best we could. Anyway, it's probably good we didn't know a lot about it. It's not like we could have stopped her smoking it.'

True, indeed. After I refused to buy it for her, Anna used her income from Centrelink and from the books we had written together to purchase it herself. Since John and I paid for her essentials, all she had to do was cut back on expensive hair products and make-up, forgo her weekly stack of celebrity gossip magazines and not buy too many DVDs from Cash Converters, and she'd have enough money to spend at Club X.

Although I didn't do it at the time, it's not hard to research synthetic marijuana. You only have to google it to discover the havoc it can wreak on fragile brains. We called it 'synthetic' but it's known by several other names: K2, Spice and Skunk are the most common, I believe. Whatever you choose to call it, according to the US government body the National Institute on Drug Abuse (NIDA), what Anna ingested on a more or less daily basis for close to two years were synthetic cannabinoids: man-made, mind-altering chemicals sprayed on dried, shredded plant matter. The website explains that these chemicals are called cannabinoids because they are related to chemicals found in the marijuana plant and are often marketed as safe, legal alternatives to that drug. In fact,

NIDA states, cannabinoids may affect the brain much more powerfully than marijuana; their actual effects can be unpredictable and, in some cases, severe or even life-threatening.

The NIDA website lists the possible effects of 'fake weed', beginning with elevated mood and ending with symptoms of psychosis. From the beginning of 2014, Anna's mental health deteriorated rapidly. Perhaps this would have happened to some extent anyway, but I'm sure the process was exacerbated by her heavy use of synthetic, as well as ice. Although I don't believe she ever sought out or purchased ice, she would take it from people who would give it to her.

From the reading I've done and people I've talked to, and particularly from observing Anna, it seems to me that mental illness and addiction are hopelessly intertwined. Anna was in emotional pain from the time she ran away when she was six, perhaps even earlier. Once she got to an age when she was expected to behave like an adult, and couldn't, the pain became overwhelming. Sometimes when I'm talking to someone who doesn't know Anna very well, they refer to her as having been 'in the drug scene'. But it wasn't like she had a bunch of friends she smoked with, who would hang out together and engage in fascinating stoned conversations, like I used to do in university. She didn't go to parties and have fun getting high or drunk. She used drugs to try to blot out hurt.

As 2014 arrived and the months of marinating her mind in manufactured chemicals plodded on, Anna began to hurt more than ever. One positive development was that she stopped going out on the train so much and cosying up to random guys. Lance went from ringing John daily to once a week, and then gradually we stopped hearing from him altogether. Anna spent more time at home, which was less stressful in a way because we could check on her to see whether she was alive or not. But dealing with visible Anna wasn't easy either. She'd always seemed to lack the control most of us develop to hide unpleasant emotions for the sake of politeness or peace. John and Katie and I used to chuckle at how instantly she could transform from being the smiling, jokey girl we called Good Anna to scowling, angry Bad Anna. Now she cycled through these phases faster than ever and it was ceasing to be funny even to us. One minute she'd be on her phone bitching about me to Katie, saying I was a tight-arse with money who criticised everything she did. The next thing I knew she'd be hugging me tight, telling me how she loved me more than anything.

One night she got into bed with her dad and me and cuddled up in between us like a frightened four-year-old. The ghosts that tormented her as a child had come back, the ones who jabbered outside her bedroom window and breathed in her ear. Only now they were louder and meaner. She sobbed that she couldn't sleep in her own bed because her room was full of spirits. A demon had attached itself to her. That night, I couldn't stick to the boundaries we'd drawn up with the CAT team. A sheet of A4 paper was way too flimsy a thing to hold between my daughter and a band of howling wraiths from the underworld. I said to Anna, 'Tomorrow I'm making you an appointment with a psychiatrist or a priest. You choose.'

She chose the priest. It might seem odd to some, that I would suggest turning to the church as an option. But religion had been a huge part of my life as a child and teenager, and though my beliefs evolved through the years, I had never totally disregarded the idea that human life might continue to exist in some form after death.

Though I no longer believe in the vengeful God of my childhood, I have attended one church or another for most of my adult life. Soon after we moved to Oak Park, before Katie was conceived, John and I joined our local Anglican church. Over the years we helped with the music, served on the vestry, planned stalls at the annual fete and took our turn running the youth group. When our babies were born, they were welcomed and cherished by our church family. John and I both thought it was important for our kids to know the stories, to hear the language and sing the hymns of Christianity. So, every Sunday, unless we were out of town, we attended the 9 a.m. service.

Unfortunately, as with many churches, our congregation was aging and dwindling. When Anna was in her mid-teens, our local church was closed and the land sold to developers. We never quite made the transition to the main parish church in Pascoe Vale. But we knew most of the people there very well and still kept in touch with some of them who lived in our neighbourhood.

So I was aware there was a new vicar, at least new to me. When I rang him he sounded friendly and pleased to hear from me. I explained to him that Anna felt the presence of evil spirits and asked if he'd be willing to meet with her.

'Do you believe these spirits are real?' Father Ron inquired.

'Probably not.' In conceding that, part of me felt I was betraying the vivid voices that had spoken to my sister and me through the ouija board when I was a teenager. But I was pretty sure those fascinating hours of spelled-out conversations had arisen from the same primal storehouse that produces dreams. I told Father Ron that Anna had mental health problems, so most likely the unseen presences had been conjured up by her ailing brain. But the demons were desperately real to her. I was hoping that by speaking to a priest, whom she believed had a connection to God, her distress would be eased.

Father Ron made it clear that he did not believe departed souls hung around to annoy or torture the living. However, he did like to bless people and the rooms they lived in, to remind them of the presence of God. He would be more than happy to try to bring some comfort to Anna by doing this.

Two days after I spoke to him, Father Ron appeared at our house, a guy in his mid-fifties, looking seriously priestly in his floor-length white robe and a crimson stole draped around his neck. He spoke kindly to Anna, and as I watched her relax with him in the house, it made me realise how tense she had become. Father Ron blessed Anna's room, swinging his silver ball of incense on a chain as he read a passage from his prayer book. Anna really liked it when he sprinkled holy water in the four corners of her messy abode. Back in the kitchen after a cup of tea, she also appreciated him praying with her.

This all made Anna feel better for a few days, but one by one the spirits crept back to surround her. And there were living jerks as well, according to Anna, who wanted to make her life a misery. When her back was turned, people snuck into her room and riffled through her DVD collection, stealing her favourite ones. One ferociously hot afternoon in late summer, they pinched most of the synthetic she'd slogged through the boiling streets to procure. Now she hardly had any left to get her through the evening. Her voice was drenched in disappointment when she told me, 'I was looking forward to a good night!'

Oh, God, I hated to see her sad. I wanted to give her something to look forward to that didn't come in a bright foil packet adorned with a name like Kronic or Kush Apple. I decided to tell her about the plan I was hatching. It involved the one person Anna always made an effort to be nice around, to stay sober for. That was Charlotte.

Earlier in the summer, when we were afraid that Lance or some other dangerous character might show up at our house, it broke my heart a little to have to tell Katie Rose that we couldn't have Charlotte stay with us for a week or so of the school holidays like we usually did. The reason was that we couldn't fully guarantee her safety. It was especially sad because I'd booked Charlotte in for a dance camp and she would have loved that. Katie Rose said that Charlotte was disappointed, but she understood.

Charlotte did understand Anna; she still understands her in a way I find amazing. She was eight years old then, in grade 3. Charlotte had never seen any of Anna's drug paraphernalia; Anna didn't even smoke cigarettes in front of her. Just as I had done with Katie and Anna, I spent countless hours of cubby-house time with Charlotte, sitting in the dark and chatting with her beside her bed. I'd explained to her that Anna's brain worked differently to most people's, that she was often in mental pain. This just seemed to make Charlotte more devoted to Anna than ever.

I'm making Charlotte sound disgustingly angelic, which she definitely is not. She can behave like a maddeningly screechy little brat, demanding Subway when I've planned to take her to a nice cafe, or sulking when I hesitate to buy her another hunk of plastic in the toy aisle at Coles. But she does love Anna. I remember once when Anna, uncharacteristically, lost her temper with Charlotte and made her cry. Later, Anna apologised to her and Charlotte answered calmly, 'That's all right. I know life's hard for you.'

So this was the idea I proposed to Anna, the night that the phantom thieves snuck in to steal her last shreds of synthetic: 'How about, later in the year, you and Katie and I take Charlotte to the theme parks on the Gold Coast?'

Chapter 27

Everybody thought that the Gold Coast holiday idea was an excellent one. I booked it for August: paying for our airfares, arranging a hire car and booking a cabin in a kid-friendly resort that sounded nearly as fun as the theme parks. That's how I tried to tint Anna's future with colour and light, while I was about to face the most taxing months of my life.

As soon as all the arrangements for our trip were made, Anna began to tell me that part of her wanted to die. She'd never actually spelled this out before. Previously, my fears for her had focused on someone taking advantage of her, or her accidentally overdosing. Now she seemed to be saying that she might actually want to participate in her own demise. This threat drove me to a place I'd never been before. I desperately wanted to find and hang on to the part of her that didn't want to die. The rules I'd drawn up for the CAT team were becoming harder to stick to. Why did there have to be boundaries between us? I wanted her to be my chubby baby again, lying naked on the change table. I'd walk my fingers up her body, starting from her toes, then on to her delicate little thighs, over her creamy, plump tummy to her chin . . . *one step, two step, tickly under there!* And she would giggle like anything. Then I'd scoop her up, squash her against my heart and keep her there forever.

But the human soul rarely contains only one desire. Clanging against my longing to protect my beloved baby was my growing anger at my adult daughter for doing so little to help herself. Plenty of cynics on the internet dismiss the premise that addiction is a disease. You can't prevent multiple sclerosis from stripping the protective coating from your nerves, they point out, but you sure as hell can stop sticking a needle in your arm or raising a glass to your lips. I knew it wasn't so easy. Hadn't I excoriated myself with that idea through the ripest years of my young womanhood? You stupid weak pig, I screeched at my body, it's your hand that shoves the food into your mouth. Just don't do it!

So I certainly didn't expect Anna to toss away her water pipe and her vodka bottle and her beloved ciggies, and dance away into a perfect future. Still, I saw a crucial difference between how I had handled my food addiction in my mid-twenties and how Anna was handling her addiction. No matter how full I felt on my eating days or how light-headed on my starving ones, I managed to have a life, and to maintain a career, a romantic relationship and friendships. Why couldn't she do any of this? Surely she was capable of replacing some hours of bonging and drinking with meaningful activity. Like, for example, a job!

In order to be paid by Centrelink, Anna had to apply for a certain number of jobs per fortnight. The way she did this looked like something out of the best situation comedies, where a flawed but loveable character does stuff that makes you really uncomfortable. She would talk about high-flying positions she intended to apply for, but in reality she'd come to the end of the first thirteen days of the fortnight with no actual applications lodged anywhere. On the eve of her appointment at the dole office, she'd crank up her laptop to begin looking at job-seeking sites, but those cat videos were so tempting, and there were lots of new photos of luscious women with their alluringly placed tattoos. Early on the morning of her appointment she'd be frantic, eyes red from lack of sleep, wildly tapping out applications, begging me to give her a lift because she didn't have time to make it by train.

Very infrequently, appearing like a minor miracle, one of the harried applications she'd spewed into cyberspace would actually attract some interest. One autumn day, she had an interview lined up for a hairdressing apprenticeship on the other side of the city. She had agreed to be there by 9 a.m. The night before, I might have overstepped boundary number eleven just a little, by suggesting that she consult a train time-table and work out what time she should leave home. Before heading off for bed at eleven o' clock, I stopped by the bunga-low to urge her to turn off the PlayStation and watch no more than one DVD because she really needed to get to sleep before 5 a.m. She snapped back that I'd agreed to only remind her once about commitments, pointing out that I'd already men-tioned this one to her like four times!

She did manage to stagger into the kitchen the next morn-ing, after I'd knocked on her bedroom door the allowable one time. She looked awful, still in the jeans and T-shirt she'd had on the day before, her hair greasy and tangled. 'I'll have to cancel that appointment,' she told me in a half sob. 'I didn't sleep at all. She's finally murdered him.'

'*What?*'

'The woman up the back. I heard the old guy moaning and crying, and then there was a crash and he just suddenly went quiet.'

The woman Anna referred to was Donna, who lived on the other side of our back fence, in the end unit of a group of three. She was an older lady, about my age but plumper than me, which softened her kind face and made her look younger. I wouldn't say we were friends, but I'd spoken to her a few times. I'd been around to Donna's place on two or three occasions to discuss practical things like the overhanging branches of our silky oak that John intended to chop back.

'Donna lives by herself,' I informed Anna. 'She told me.'

'She lied!' Anna protested. 'I said before I've heard that old guy moaning.'

'You never told me that.'

'Yes I did!' she whined miserably. 'And now he's dead and rotting. I went right up to the fence last night and I could smell him!'

It was then, on that beautiful blue-sky Melbourne morning, that I realised my daughter's mind had gone to a place where mine, even on its most self-loathsome days of binging, had never been close to. I knew that if the mere anticipation of a job interview had pushed her into this state, I was going to have to defy the CAT team. From that point on, I began to help her in any way I could. I put my writing on hold. I continued my tutoring, with all the preparation and paperwork and driving that that entailed, plus the professional development opportunities I had to track down in order to keep my teacher registration up to date. But with all the other available hours of every day, I attempted to access help for Anna and find her activities she might participate in.

To be honest, this decision was not entirely selfless. Deep in my heart, I didn't feel that I could keep her alive. I thought it was only a matter of time until, by being ridiculously reckless or through a deliberate act, she would kill herself. And when that happened, my life, too, might as well be over. I didn't

see how I could go on after that. But if I had to, for John and
Katie, then it would be absolutely vital to know that I'd done
everything I could to help her.

The first thing I did, after Anna told me about the murdered neighbour, was to insist that I take her to a doctor. She
didn't protest. Dr Deb was so popular you had to book weeks
in advance to see her, so I called our local bulk-billing clinic,
where I'd been going for years. My usual doctor wasn't available, but Dr Khoo could fit us in. I hadn't met him before but
I liked and trusted him immediately. Over the nightmarish
months to come, this positive first impression was reinforced.
He was a tall guy, who spoke like a homegrown Aussie but
looked as if he had a Southeast Asian background. I guessed
he was in his late thirties, and he had a shiny, perfectly bald
head. His brown eyes were big, and as he listened to Anna,
looking straight at her with intense concentration and concern, his eyes seemed to grow even larger. Dr Khoo spent
nearly an hour with me and my bedraggled daughter that day.
After I informed him of the various substances she was ingesting, I let her do most of the talking. I expected her to blurt out
her tale about the alleged murder, but she didn't mention it.
Instead, she told Dr Khoo she was suffering from a painful
condition of the jaw called TMJ, as well as roseola, migraines,
insomnia and most likely chronic fatigue syndrome. 'I need
Valium,' she concluded.

Dr Khoo didn't think this was a good idea. He talked to
her about the importance of good sleep hygiene and exercise.
This sounded great to me, but Anna wanted medication. He
prescribed something safer to help her sleep. I recorded in
my journal that he searched for a while on his computer for
a rehab that he could refer her to, then handed her a referral

for a facility in Footscray. I can't remember what happened to that, but I'm sure I would have followed it up. Like so many leads that lit little fires of hope in my heart, it came to nothing.

I vividly recall the next thing I did to help her. The following morning at 8.15, she and I were lined up outside the Broadmeadows Centrelink office. I knew from experience that if you fronted up even a bit later, like 9.30, you'd likely have to wait for a couple of hours to be seen. How had I pried Anna out of bed so early? I'm sorry to say I bribed her with a promise of driving her to Moonee Ponds for synthetic. I know, I know, I'm a bad, enabling mother. But I didn't yet understand how those harsh chemicals, lying atop what looked like mixed dried herbs from the pantry, fed her paranoia rather than relieved it. And I promise, it was the last time I ever did it.

There were about fifteen of us waiting outside the Centrelink office; most of the group were middle-aged men of Lebanese or Turkish appearance and like us they peered through the glass doors at the front of the building, waiting for someone to appear and unlock them. This happened at exactly 8.30. We all rushed past the man who'd let us in, eager to get to the gatekeeper with the iPad who would allocate us to one of the officers in the rows of desks beyond the barrier behind her. Before long, Anna and I were seated in front of one of these officers, a slim and serious woman of about forty who was studiously well groomed. Anna smelled of alcohol and the cigarette she'd just smoked outside the glass doors, and she looked like a caricature of a homeless person. This suited the purpose of our visit. 'Anna has . . . um . . . some problems with her mental health,' I began. 'Ever since she was fourteen —'

'So why are you here?' the officer interrupted my well-prepared explanation.

Because I want to save my daughter's life! I felt like scream-ing. But I knew this woman had hours of dealing with needy, often agitated clients ahead of her. I'd better make my story short. Some months before, I'd floated with Dr Deb the idea of getting Anna on the Disability Support Pension. She said they'd cracked down hard on the eligibility criteria and there was no way Anna would qualify. So I said to the carefully dressed Centrelink officer who appeared incapable of smiling, 'It's not that Anna doesn't want a job. She wants to contribute to society. Don't you?' I prodded my daughter, who was look-ing more dishevelled with every moment that passed in the presence of this immaculate woman.

Anna frowned and nodded. I continued, explaining that Anna applying for jobs through the normal channels was a joke, a waste of employers' time. 'Isn't there a scheme where she could get some help? Where she could do some kind of supervised work while she gets herself a bit healthier?'

The woman tapped something into her computer, then told us to try to get a short-term medical exemption from a doctor.

'Is that like paid sick leave from Centrelink?' I inquired.

She huffed, and from that I gathered it was.

We were able to see Dr Deb fairly quickly, thanks to a cancellation, and Deb agreed to give Anna a three-month exemption from applying for jobs. 'But I want you to use the time to work on your mental health,' she instructed. I can see the scene as clearly as a photo in my mind: this beauti-ful doctor with her springy, cinnamon-coloured hair, shaking her head at the young woman she'd looked after and cared about for over a decade. A few months before, when Deb had reluctantly prescribed antidepressants for Anna, she'd wist-fully wished that Anna would give up alcohol, dope, nicotine and even energy drinks so they would have 'a clean brain to work with'. She didn't mention that now. She said she'd try to find Anna a psychiatrist and a drug and alcohol counsellor through Headspace, a government organisation that helped young people with their mental health. At twenty-five, Anna just qualified for this service by squeaking into the upper range of 'young'.

Six days after that visit to Dr Deb, perhaps inspired by Deb's pep talk, Anna announced that as of tomorrow, she was giving up alcohol and dope, both real and synthetic. This terrified me. Of course I hoped the plan could work, but I knew her pattern of expecting perfection and then, when she couldn't achieve it, falling into a suicidal heap.

It was a Tuesday when she told me of her cold-turkey plan. She made it through Wednesday and Thursday. On Friday she told us Billy, the plumber boyfriend who John and I both liked, had invited her out for Saturday night, to a party at a pub on Sydney Road in Brunswick. Sparklers of joy lit up her blue eyes. A party! With a good-looking guy!

'How are you going to handle that?' Icy fear was running through my veins.

'I don't need to drink to have a good time,' she answered blithely. 'I'll just have soda water. Or maybe a Red Bull.'

Billy picked her up after work on the Friday. It was the 23rd of May, a week before the official start of the Southern Hemisphere winter. And it heralded the most chilling season yet for our family.

Chapter 28

After Billy collected Anna on Friday night, she stayed at his place for the weekend, and on into the following week. She answered my daily texts inquiring whether she was okay, so I knew she was alive. I didn't ask whether she'd been able to get through the party without drinking or smoking dope.

Actually, I enjoyed those days she was away. John and Katie had gone camping, so it was the first time I had the house to myself in what seemed like ages. A couple of months earlier, another pretty stressful event had happened in our lives. John had retired. Border Force (still called the Australian Quarantine and Inspection Service in those days) had invited its officers to apply for redundancy packages. John had taken up the offer and been successful, so his working life, the salaried one, finished at the age of sixty-two. I was happy for him to be starting this new phase of his life when he was still healthy and vibrant, but I think the retirement of a spouse is a challenge for a lot of couples, and it certainly was for us.

John wanted to be spontaneous, to head off on trips to interesting pockets of the state while we planned longer journeys around Australia and perhaps across the world. But I hated car trips longer than an hour and a half, and besides, I needed to stay home during the week because I didn't want to give up any of my tutoring. This was the best holiday for me: to focus my mind on how to help a year 9 boy – whose

passions were fishing and umpiring junior footy – to internalise
the structure of a basic five-paragraph essay. This let my aching brain have a break from worrying about Anna in a way
that wandering through the Ballarat Art Gallery or hiking in
the Grampians never could.

On Monday, while Anna was at Billy's, I did my tutoring, then picked up my friend Mina and drove us to the Nova
to see the seven o'clock session of *The Babadook*. It was
a bit close to the bone, with a sinister spirit taking over a
home. 'It was scary,' I wrote in my journal. 'I didn't want to
leave Mina.'

On Tuesday I met up with my pal Margie for a coffee.
She was off work that year, devoting herself to finishing her
master's in psychology. Before I headed off for tutoring, I spent
some time on the back deck, fiddling with my succulents. This
was a sort of meditation for me: I'd planted miniature cactus
gardens in various containers I'd scouted out at op shops.
Some of my favourites were a sugar bowl with a spotted horse
on it, a one-person teapot in the shape of a fish, and a lopsided
mug made in a pottery class, hand-painted with golden wattle.
I had twenty-five or thirty such containers, carefully arranged
on the three shelves of a bamboo credenza. Each cream jug or
teapot held a variety of succulent sprigs, propped up and held
apart with the perfect, minute seashells I'd searched beaches
for, on holidays with John and the kids. To keep these bonsai
creations looking their best, I picked off any crunchy brown
leaves and snapped off straggling bits, making my girls all
neat and beautiful. I thought of them as girls who appreciated
me, who liked to surprise me with their little flowers, some
of them so tiny and unassuming you had to get right up close
to see them. From the window over the kitchen sink, I could

admire their many shapes and colours, as I washed dishes or peeled vegetables.

On Wednesday morning Billy, on his way to work, must have put Anna on a train, because as I sipped my morning coffee I saw her through the window, dragging herself up the driveway at eight o'clock. She went straight into the bunga- low. Before I left for tutoring I crept in there to check on her. She was heavily asleep, in jeans and a hoodie that smelled like she'd been wearing them for days, but she was definitely breathing. So off I went to do my tutoring and when I got home hours later, in the early evening, she was lying in the same position as when I left. 'She must have been bombed out on Seroquel,' I wrote in my journal. 'I enticed her into the lounge room, so I could keep an eye on her, and she lay on the couch. But she didn't really wake up.'

She finally did wake up – in the same spot on the couch, looking bleary and confused – at nine o'clock the next morn- ing. She'd slept for twenty-four hours. I got her some coffee and toast with Nutella, cut into triangles the way she liked when she was little. 'Look,' I pointed out, 'I found your Minnie Mouse plate.' This plastic kid's plate, brought home from Disneyland when she was five, was still her favour- ite, but it often went missing among the heap of rubbish in her room.

While she was at Billy's, I had embarked on one of my peri- odic fossicking excursions through her stuff, not because I wanted to snoop – in fact, I'd rather not know what she had in there – but because I'd learned from some disgusting experi- ences that it was better to find and clean out the food remains before they rotted or were discovered by a happy band of ants or mice.

I sat down in my rocking chair beside the couch. Anna managed to sit up, sip some coffee and scoff a couple of chocolate toast bits. She smiled at me and murmured, 'Thanks, Mummy.' We had a saying in our family, which we used when we were in a good mood. When someone accidentally broke something or guiltily ate the last Tim Tam, we'd jauntily remark, 'There's more at the store.' Now Anna said to me, 'There's no more of you at the store.'

I wanted to ask how the party went, wanted to know if she had managed not to drink, but I kept my wanting quiet. When she'd finished her toast and coffee, she didn't rush straight out to the backyard for a cigarette or a bong. She lay back and gazed out the french doors, through the last of the leaves on our liquidambar, to the sky. I took her hand, her beautiful slender hand, and held it flat in both of mine. I ran my fingertips over her long fingers, and I made myself not ask for anything else.

That afternoon she agreed to go for a walk with me. That's when she told me, unprompted, what happened at the party. Apparently, when she and Billy arrived at the pub, she decided to have just a couple of drinks, so she started a tab at the bar. Of course, the two drinks became four, and then six . . . who knew how many? Eventually the bartender said, 'I think you've had enough.'

I can remember exactly where we were when Anna was telling me this. We'd crossed Pacco Road and were heading north on Station Road, which runs parallel to the railway line. Anna said, 'I told the bartender he was doing exactly the right thing, not to let me have any more. Remember I did the same course he did, Responsible Service of Alcohol? I closed my tab and gave him a twenty-five dollar tip.' A sharp toothpick of pain shot into my heart as I imagined what that bartender must have thought of her, slurring and swaying, dishing out embarrassing compliments.

Anna told me her memory was a bit patchy after that. She did remember Billy and his friends leaving the pub with her, and when they were all out on the street, Anna suddenly realised she was ravenous. There was some dispute about what they should eat, or where, or when . . . Anna couldn't recall exactly what made her leave the group and stagger off into the night in a huff. She didn't use the verb 'stagger', but I figured that would have been her gait. Now, as we made our way up the street adjacent to what is now called the Craigieburn Line, I could hear the pain in Anna's voice. 'I thought Billy would come after me,' she said, 'but he didn't!'

It caused me intense pain to visualise her wandering alone on the post-midnight streets of Brunswick, drunk and hungry and with no sense of direction. There is a pedestrian tunnel that runs under the railway line about halfway between Oak Park and Glenroy. Anna and I were walking through that tunnel when she told me what happened next on that Brunswick night. She started talking to a guy – he walked beside her and held her hand. She couldn't remember if he'd approached her or if she'd spoken to him first. I recorded in my journal her description of what followed: 'He dragged me into an alley and got my pants off. I had enough survival instinct to get my pants back on and get away from him.'

So there it was: a part of the terrible thing I had felt approaching, a raw and jagged piece of the horrible fantasies I tried to block from my mind when I lay awake at 2 a.m. A man had grabbed her. I remember what I felt, in the instant that my daughter told me about that man. My soul didn't blaze with anger. I felt relief, almost gratitude. He didn't kill her. Apparently, he didn't rape her.

Anna couldn't remember how Billy found her, or she found him, but obviously they met up somehow, because the next day she woke in his bed.

I was so thankful that my girl had survived that scenario, so similar to the one that cost the life of beautiful, talented and much-loved Gillian Meagher, two years earlier in the same suburb. I didn't realise until much later how deeply the incident had affected Anna.

Eventually, I would come to understand how that encounter in a Brunswick alleyway had punctured another hole in Anna's faith in life. It made her afraid in ways she had never been before. On the day she told me about it, as we walked through the tunnel under the railway line, I didn't understand. It was just one more awful incident that I had to find the energy to help my girl deal with. Now, sitting quietly in my peaceful little study, in a new house where Anna has never been, I can see that at the time of the assault, Anna's poor brain was already trying to cope with paranoia and hallucinations. Afterwards, it had to find room for acute anxiety as well.

When we got home from that walk, Anna said she was exhausted. I reminded her I'd bought tickets for both of us to go to a film screening that evening at the Westgarth in Northcote. It was a fundraiser for a carer's organisation that my friend Marcelle was involved with. Anna said she was looking forward to it, but she needed a nap. I encouraged her to drink some water and eat some cantaloupe and I tucked her up in bed in the bungalow. I suggested that she view her drinking over the weekend as a slip up. 'Nobody expects you to be perfect,' I assured her, smoothing out the bumps in her doona.

'I know,' she mumbled, already half-asleep. 'I'm never drinking alcohol again.'

A couple of my students had cancelled, so I only had one to visit after school that day. He lived just ten minutes away, my year 9 fishing enthusiast with the blond curls and the sweet smile. I'd been tutoring him since the summer he finished grade 6.

As I drove back home after this session, I mentally prepared for the challenge of prying Anna out of the bungalow and getting her into the car, because we needed to leave more or less straight away. I'd agreed to meet Marcelle at Nando's, across from the cinema, for an early dinner before the film. To my surprise, Anna was up, waiting in the kitchen and ready to go. In fact, she was especially jaunty. So off we trundled through the peak-hour traffic, up the Tulla to Brunswick Road and then High Street. Anna was telling me about a doco she'd seen on the internet, which profiled a pair of conjoined twins, girls in their late teens. 'They're so in denial,' Anna reported. 'They go on and on about how they're two completely different people, but really they're one body with two heads.'

'What?' I queried. 'How can that be?'

'Look!' She googled a picture of them on her phone which, when we got to the next red light, I peered at. They did indeed appear to be one girl with two rather attractive heads.

'Imagine that,' Anna said, popping her phone onto the car charger and stowing it in the console. 'The twins would be going for a walk and one would be like, "I'm desperate for a poo. Let's stop at this servo." And the other would be like, "No way I'm going into that filthy hole!" Or, say they were having sex . . . with . . . um . . . their maths teacher!' Anna was really getting into the story now. 'One head would be all

groany and moany . . . "Oh, Mr Baker you're soooo good!"
And the other one would say, "Are you kidding? That purple
vibrator we got is like a hundred times more exciting than this
smelly old dude! Let's get him off us and go home and watch
Breaking Bad again. That episode where Grandpa explodes."'

Anna's voice slowed down as she thought about something. 'That's kind of how my mind works, and I've only got
one head, in theory . . .'

I looked at her. Was she beginning to slur? Oh God,
she was.

That's what she'd do in those days. She didn't sip her
drinks. In a murky corner of her bungalow, she'd glug
down an eye-watering amount of vodka in an unbelievably
short time. The alcohol wouldn't kick in straight away. So
she'd appear sober, but then, suddenly, she would be totally
sozzled, sometimes so drunk she could barely walk. That's
why I dropped her right outside Nando's and told her to go in
and chat to Marcelle while I parked. I didn't know how far I'd
have to go to find a parking spot. One thing I did know was
that Marcelle would already be in the restaurant – she hated
to be late for anything.

It did take me a while to find a park. As I was locking
up the car I realised Anna had left her phone in the console.
I grabbed it and headed for Nando's. Sure enough, Marcelle was
already seated at a table . . . alone. 'Where's Anna?' she asked
me brightly.

No. My heart felt like it couldn't take this. I rushed outside
and looked up and down High Street hoping to spy her smoking. But she was gone. She'd disappeared in a suburb she was
completely unfamiliar with. And the thing that provided me
the only hope of connecting with her was sitting in my pocket!

Right now she was probably latching onto some random guy, and this time it would be someone who would drag her into an alleyway and not let her go when she tried to get her pants back on. Where was she? How could that little bitch *do* this to me? I wanted to scream. I wanted to cry.

I think I was crying when my phone rang. No caller ID.

'Hello?' I answered. 'Mary speaking.'

'Oh . . . hello . . . my name's Rob. You don't know me, but I've just met your daughter. Anna's with me.'

'Where is she?' I gasped.

He named a pub which we worked out was a few doors down from Nando's.

This time the man she'd approached was in his mid-thirties, responsible and kind. He'd seen Anna not as an easy sexual conquest, but as a girl who needed help. She'd been able to recite my number when he asked, as she always could when she was conscious. And he had rung me to fetch her. Which I did, with alacrity, and thanked him profusely.

So we did make it to the movie. It was a good one – *Chef*. The audience was full of young people with physical or intellectual disabilities, and their carers. While we were in our seats waiting for the film to start, I glowered at Anna and informed her sternly that if she decided to go out for a smoke, I was coming with her. 'You'd better not try to get away from me again!' I was shaking, and could still taste the coppery taint of terror. She frowned and stared grimly ahead at the curtains that were yet to be opened to reveal the screen.

When I was pregnant with Katie, John and I went to antenatal classes for first-time parents. One evening the instructor asked us class members to say what we feared most about the birth process. Most of the fledgling mothers, and fathers, mentioned loss of control or coping with pain. While I wasn't looking forward to the sweaty screaming portrayed in movies, it looked to me like a temporary state I'd get through somehow. My real fear, which I voiced when my turn came, was of something much more permanent. 'What if my baby is disabled?'

During both my pregnancies, I undertook every test I could convince my obstetrician to order. John and I were willing to abort a fetus that had a detectable abnormality. Now I looked wistfully down the row, at a composed-looking young woman with Down syndrome, quietly engaged in nibbling at her choc-top. No, I would not have swapped Anna for that girl. But I also certainly didn't believe, as I once may have, that her mother had been dealt a worse hand than me.

Chapter 29

The morning after we'd been to the Westgarth, I woke at 6 a.m. John was still away, camping with Katie. At 6.30, Anna crept into bed with me. 'I didn't get any sleep at all,' she griped. There was accusation in her voice, due to me making her promise before she went to bed not to take Seroquel on top of all the alcohol she'd had. I wasn't feeling too pleased with her, either. 'That was really sneaky of you to run off to a pub.'

'*What?*' She couldn't remember that. 'I only came to half-way through the movie,' she claimed. I offered a brief recap of what happened and she told me she was sorry she'd scared me. So we lay there as the chilly pre-dawn light began to seep into the room. I held her close, with her back spooned against my chest.

That week, when Anna was assaulted, knocked the stuffing out of both of us. When John and Katie returned from their bushwalking, they wanted me to look at their photos, and though I held the phone in my hand, my brain could not connect with the scenery that scrolled across the screen. I wrote in my journal: 'I feel like I'm flailing in a river of grief.'

And yet, as always, good things happened, too. A letter from Centrelink arrived for Anna, giving an appointment time for her to meet with an officer to discuss a medical exemption. Anna was glad it was in the middle of the afternoon, but I figured it would mean we'd have to wait ages, and we were both dreading another encounter with a brusque official who barely looked at us and couldn't wait to shoo us out of there. Surprisingly, when we arrived on the appointed day and went up to the reception counter, instead of being directed to wait with the sixty or so people sitting there at that hour, we were ushered straight in, past the rows of workers at their computers, into one of the little private offices I hadn't known existed.

Behind the desk was a kindly looking guy in his mid-fifties, who stood up and shook our hands. 'I'm Terry,' he said.

'Terry was an angel,' I gushed in my journal. 'He treated Anna like a precious flower. She now has until mid-November to work on her mental health, then instead of having to find jobs by herself, she'll be in a disability support scheme to help her find part-time work. I couldn't wait to tell Katie!'

Terry gave me a form to fill out which, after I had lodged it and it was approved, made me Anna's official carer. I didn't qualify for any money or benefits, so the only thing my new title really changed was that I would now receive copies of any correspondence that Centrelink sent by post or emailed to Anna. This was actually very useful, as my daughter was preternaturally talented at making physical objects, such as letters, vanish. And I had never been privy to her emails. Now that I was being copied into the ones from Centrelink, I could keep track of important information for her, including dates for appointments.

Both Dr Deb and Terry had stressed that Anna should use this vacation from applying for jobs to work on her mental health. I took to this idea with grateful enthusiasm. First I went to Officeworks to buy two new ringbinders. All the most important aspects of my life – my manuscripts, my students' work, handmade cards from my girls, paintings by Charlotte, years and years of letters from my mother – have two holes punched on their left side so they can be neatly stored in a binder. For this new project, 'Saving Anna', I used one binder for official documentation from Centrelink, Merri Health and any other organisation I managed to connect with. The second binder was for brochures gathered from libraries and learning centres, plus printouts from the internet, all detailing activities that Anna might try: singing groups, walkers' mornings, volunteering at the Cat Protection Society. Free from the burden of applying for jobs, my daughter could build a life.

John and Katie pitched in with the newly revitalised Saving Anna project. While I was tutoring, John ferried Anna to the frequent medical appointments she insisted I arrange: for example, to the gastro clinic at the Royal Melbourne Hospital, to find out if she had stomach ulcers. It seems obvious now that she was scouring Google to try to find a cause for the unrelenting pain she felt. That's why she spent so much money on supplements, and had a $300 customised mouthguard made to try to ameliorate the jaw pain she had been complaining of for some time, which she self-diagnosed as temporomandibular joint dysfunction, or TMJ, a disorder that was exacerbated by grinding one's teeth at night. We were pretty sure her condition could not be treated by antibiotics or surgery, but for the sake of peace, if nothing else, we took her to her doctors' appointments. Katie went with her to various appointments at Headspace, including anti-anxiety classes.

Did Anna make an effort to get involved in all of this? Well, she did try. Sadly, she was not tempted by any of the enticing activities outlined in the brochures I had collected. But she did give up dope, including synthetic. This was great, except that it meant she stopped seeing Billy, and her old friend Dan, as it would have been too hard to not smoke with them. She no longer disappeared on secret train trips, and we were grateful for that, though I would come to realise this had nothing to do with a sudden upturn in her common sense. Rather, she was becoming increasingly afraid to leave the house on her own.

So, with no stoners to visit, or trains to catch, she was home all the time with us. And, in the absence of dope, she began to consume ever more ridiculous amounts of alcohol. This was on top of her prescription medication, which she never took as prescribed. With no routine of regular sleep or meals, she swallowed her pills randomly, when she remembered them or felt like she desperately needed them. I didn't keep a precise list of exactly what she was on. My journal is sprinkled with notes like, 'took A to Dr K to get script', 'drove A to chemist to pick up meds'. Apart from the many mentions of Seroquel, there are also references to Cipramil, Effexor, Temazepam and Nexium.

I can see now that even as John, Katie and I were toiling to help Anna create a functioning adult life, she was becoming more and more crippled by mental illness. At the same time, I felt crippled by annoyance. She had transferred her mess of blankets, along with her computer, bottles of Red Bull and packets of muesli bars to the lounge room, where she was forced to sleep on the couch because her own bedroom was again 'occupied by evil ghosts'. (Father Ron's holy water had dried up long ago.) Sometimes at night, even the lounge room became too frightening, and she'd climb into bed between John and me. This really annoyed me. I'd never liked the kids getting into bed with us, even when they were little. In my view, I'd contracted to give them the best possible care during waking hours, but the night hours were mine. Now I was being squashed to the far side of my bed by this tall, gangly person who hadn't had a shower or changed her clothes in days. She smelled of unwashed hair and stale cigarette smoke, with the reek of alcohol seeping through her skin.

She must have been so lonely. I knew this. I kept suggesting activities she could try so she could meet good people and be less alone. Although I can see now she was unable to act on my advice, at the time I found her inertia increasingly aggravating.

One evening during this time, a friend did come to visit her – Dan, the 'best mate' she'd stayed with after she left Andrew and while she was doing the hair and beauty course. I was so happy to see a friend of Anna's come by that I didn't even care if he had brought dope for them to smoke. I was just so glad she was out in the bungalow with him, giving me a chance to clean up the lounge room and have a peaceful glass of wine with my husband.

At about 2 a.m., John and I were jerked awake by an almighty crash. We both rushed out the back door to find that the bamboo credenza where I kept my miniature cactus gardens had tipped over. The deck was covered in broken crockery and bits of cactus and potting soil. Anna, too drunk and stoned to walk properly, had staggered outside for a smoke and fallen into the credenza.

John was checking to make sure that Anna and Dan were okay. They were. I was checking on the welfare of my two zygocactuses, which had sat in pride of place at the very top of the credenza. They were the thriving result of two tiny potted sprigs a friend had given me when we moved into this house. It had taken many years and multiple careful re-pottings for them to grow so large. They bloomed in July. Every autumn, as soon as the last of my petunias had died off, I would start to look forward to the delicate little scarlet lanterns that would dangle for weeks from the ungainly tendrils of my ziggy cactuses, as I called them. Now those tendrils with the plump red buds, that I had looked at with anticipation every day, lay strewn around the deck, severed from their source of nourishment.

As I gazed at the destruction, I told myself they were only plants. The little teapots with their spouts and handles broken off, the shattered sugar bowls and cups, which had given me squirts of happiness when I discovered them in op shops . . . they were only things.

But they were *my* plants, *my* things.

I turned on Anna. In front of her friend I screamed, 'You useless, selfish, drunk little *turd*!'

Chapter 30

The next day, after she sobered up, Anna was horrified by what she'd done to my cactuses. She knew how much time and care I had put into creating and maintaining each tiny garden. She had even given me some of the tiniest ones, bought when she was still with Andrew. There's a kiosk on Swanston Street where an old guy sells succulents so small that they live in terracotta pots the size of thimbles, or in ceramic dishes meant for dolls. Anna was delighted by these, and had brought several home for me.

She helped me clean up the deck without a single complaint. We sorted through the crockery shards and the potting soil and the tiny seashells, picking up the remains of cactuses. Even though they were broken, the pieces could be saved to be planted in new containers. They waited patiently among the debris for us to rescue them.

I wasn't feeling so patient with my daughter. 'I'm done with not nagging you about the amount you drink!' I informed her crossly.

'Fair enough,' she sighed. She sure was being Good Anna that day. I pounced on the chance and announced that I was going to take her to Alcoholics Anonymous (AA). 'Even if you don't stop drinking completely,' I reasoned, 'you can meet some people to be friends with who know how to have fun without alcohol or dope.'

'Okay,' she agreed.

And so began the AA face of the Anna saga. It was one of the ideas I'd clamped into the Saving Anna binder that dealt with activities. And the idea started out well. I located a meeting near us, at a church, and off we went the very next Friday evening. I couldn't believe how eagerly those people welcomed Anna. After the formal part of the meeting was over, they literally embraced her, pressing brochures and booklets into her hand. A lovely young lass from Ireland, Brenna, told Anna that she would be more than happy to pick her up once or twice a week and take her to other AA groups she belonged to. Carol, who was middle aged and looked like the quintessential Aussie matriarch from the bush, offered to take Anna to a regular table tennis night run by one of her groups. (I was surprised to find out that many AA members attended several meetings a week at different venues.)

Anna sailed through the next few days, or so it appeared to me. On Saturday I took her to an AA meeting in Fitzroy, which each week concentrated on a different one of the twelve steps to recovery. On Monday, when I was tutoring, Katie went with her to a beginners' AA group in Glenroy. On Wednesday, Carol from the first AA encounter picked Anna up and took her to one of her regular groups. Then, on Thursday, Anna had a meeting with a drug and alcohol counsellor at Headspace. I joined the initial part of the session. This situation provided just another example of how naive I was. Did I really believe that six days of AA could drag Anna out of her murky hole? Evidently, because there it is in my journal: 'I was disappointed and dismayed when Anna said AA was not really helping, and she hasn't had a week of not drinking as I had hoped.'

That evening I dropped Anna at home and went off to tutor; when I returned I found her 'well on the way to being drunk'. But this was the night Carol was going to pick her up for table tennis! 'I'm still going,' Anna assured me. 'I just needed something to take the edge off.' She wasn't quite slurring, but she'd blurred the edges pretty effectively.

I assumed you weren't supposed to attend an AA function sozzled. But I so wanted Anna to have friends, to get out and do things, I didn't discourage her from getting into Carol's car when she pulled up out the front. A few minutes later, when John and I were settling down in front of the TV, we heard a car stop in front of our house. *Please don't let that be Carol bringing her back*. It was. I don't blame Carol. She thought she was dealing with a young alcoholic who'd decided that she wanted to be sober. How could Carol have known I'd recruited her to help me save my sick and lonely girl, even if she was drunk? I understood Carol's rejection, but it was a big blow to me as well as Anna.

The next day, Anna had an appointment at our local clinic to find out the result of some test she'd insisted she needed. I coaxed her out of bed and drove her there at 11.15. In the waiting room, I realised she wasn't just sleepy, but very drunk. A dark muck of disappointment and disgust filled my head. How had she managed to get herself into this state? I hadn't taken her shopping lately, nor had I noticed her heading to the licensed grocer in our local shopping strip. Dr Khoo wasn't on duty that day, so we were scheduled to see someone we'd never met, but it didn't matter because we only needed the test result. When Anna's name was called I got up and marched down the corridor, leaving Anna to follow me. I was so pissed off, I didn't want to even look at her. Then I heard a muffled bang: she'd fallen onto the floor. I kept on walking away from her. I sat down in the doctor's consulting room, shaking. A nurse I recognised appeared at the doorway with her arm around Anna, helping her walk. As she eased Anna into the chair next to mine, I kept my eyes on the floor. I didn't want to see the disapproval on the nurse's face, wondering how I could have left my daughter lying in a heap. I didn't want to watch the bruise begin to form on the delicate skin my daughter had inherited from me. I didn't want to start bawling in that colourless, disinfected room. And it turned out we need not have bothered even going there, because the result of the test wasn't in yet.

I took her home and put her back to bed. That's when I saw, peeping out from under her bed at the edge of that particular mess, an empty bottle of our good Tahbilk Shiraz. And another, of Cab Sav, half gone. She'd raided our 'cellar', cartons of wine we'd stored away in the deep shelves of the closet in the spare room. Bottles which, unlike her, were guaranteed to improve with age.

She slept for the rest of that day, and on into the next. Halfway through the next morning I went in to check that she was still alive. I shook her arm and she mumbled, 'Everything is ending.'

'What do you mean by that?' I demanded, but she didn't answer. She turned over, away from me, the blank of her back making it clear she would not respond to my words. So I left her in the smelly murk of her room and went out for lunch with John in Moonee Ponds.

It's as if my mind, in those days, was fighting for its right to enjoy anything. Our favourite cafe in Moonee Ponds was a cramped little joint across from the bus exchange. It looked like a place where the coffee would be awful, and actually it wasn't great. But the food tasted like it came straight from a big, rustic kitchen in the south of France. And it was astronomically cheap. The owners, a skinny couple in their mid-thirties, kept the prices down by renting a small space around the corner from the main drag, Puckle Street, and by not hiring any staff. They ran themselves ragged doing the greeting, order taking, coffee-making and table-waiting themselves. The husband's mother did the cooking.

I loved walking in there and saying 'Hi, Sally!' to the wife, who always smiled, no matter how tired she looked. I admired the flourish with which her husband set down our glasses of water and menus, though I didn't really need the menu, having long ago memorised its simple offerings. On the day I left Anna sleeping with her dark thoughts and went out for lunch with John, I could taste the lemony tang of the hollandaise sauce atop my eggs, which were poached just right. Yet, even as I savoured the good food and the atmosphere, a dark shape hovered at the edge of my brain. *How dare you have fun,* it hissed, *when your daughter is in so much pain?* It kept reminding me of a line I'd heard years ago: 'A mother can only be as happy as her least happy child.'

If that was true, and I believed it was, then I'd have to be bloody miserable. But I didn't want to be! Sure, I'd had some pretty serious quibbles with this mortal coil, pain I'd squashed down with cookies and corn chips and Hershey's chocolate kisses. When I was ten years old, sitting on a dark wood pew of our little country church, our preacher bellowed at us that this life meant nothing, it was only a tedious blip to be endured on our way to eternal redemption. Though I would not have dared to put it into words even to myself, I didn't believe him. I knew this life – this life I had been given, this life I was living right now – was precious. To say it had no value, to cast it aside as just a bunch of temptations with which God tested us, that seemed to me, and still seems, to be a great sin.

The Tuesday after that Saturday brunch with John, I took Anna to Dr Deb. My journal doesn't record why we had that visit scheduled, or how I got Anna out of bed to get her there. What I detailed, and remember, is how I reacted when we got into Deb's office. I saw her beautiful, concerned face. I recalled the many hours she'd spent trying to nurture teenage Anna. The previous week at the local clinic when Anna fell down, I'd managed not to cry. Now, I couldn't keep the tears locked up. 'I don't know what to do any more,' I sobbed. 'I don't know how to keep her alive! She's been asleep or drunk since last Thursday.'

I felt pathetic, crying in front of Deb, but she was on my side. She handed me a tissue and gently suggested that I give her some time alone with Anna. I didn't want the people in the waiting room to see my face contorted with the effort to hold back more tears, so I went out to my car, which was parked in front of the clinic. Safe in the driver's seat, I gripped the steering wheel even though I wasn't going anywhere. And as I gazed through the windscreen at the grey drizzle, I gripped this thought: *Just let me get her through until we go on our holiday to the Gold Coast.*

The challenge of keeping her alive indefinitely seemed insurmountable, but was it possible we make it to Dreamworld? I couldn't bear the thought of disappointing Charlotte again, as I'd done the previous summer when I had to cancel dance camp. I was so looking forward to watching her little face as we hurled down the runway towards her very first take-off. It was seven weeks till that was scheduled to happen.

In my mind, the Gold Coast sparkled with sunshine and fun. I longed to be at Sea World, buying Charlotte and Anna sky-blue icy poles in the shape of dolphins, not finding money for a funeral. It seemed inevitable that John and I would have to do that. But maybe, please, not till after our holiday.

Whatever Deb said in her office that grey winter's day, it got to Anna. I'm a little sad that Anna never really thought of her in the same way after that. Before, Deb had been among a tiny group of people whom Anna idolised. Now, suddenly, she'd been catapulted into the 'hard-arse bitch' category. Anna didn't say anything on the drive home. Or when we got into the house and discovered that John had been to Bunnings and bought a steel box the size of a coffin. He'd fitted it into the closet of the spare room by tossing out everything that had been on the floor of the closet. He ushered Anna and me in to show us that he had deposited our crates of wine and his whiskey into the steel box. He clanged the lid shut and secured it with a sturdy padlock. Fixing Anna with his famous mega-glare, he warned her, 'You'd better not try to break in there.'

John marched off, leaving Anna and me among a bunch of plastic and calico bags that he had flung out from the far corners of the closet. From one bulging calico bag, a little giraffe's head and an elephant's trunk protruded. 'My Beanie Babies,' Anna sighed. There must have been forty small animals squashed up in that bag. She'd collected them for over a decade, from when she was about five. Some she chose for herself on trips to the States, while others had flown over the Pacific for her birthdays and Christmases, sent by Joan or Linda or Stormy. The wiener dog, the butterfly, the pterodactyl – I was grateful to them all, for each had provided her with moments of happiness.

Anna turned to me. Perhaps prompted by what Deb had said to her, or by my crying in Deb's office, or a combination of both, topped off by the steel box and the Beanie Babies, she said, 'I'm going back to AA. And this time I'm making a commitment not to drink at all.' She told me she needed help detoxing, so I took her to see Dr Khoo at our local clinic. This time he said she could have Valium, on the understanding that I hide it and dole out to her 5 milligrams a day.

The gang at AA welcomed her back with heart-warming enthusiasm. I now understood that alcoholics in the early stages of recovery needed to attend meetings most nights. Brenna came good with her promise to pick up Anna twice a week. Carol did her bit, too, and John, Katie and I provided transport when needed, to various meetings in Glenroy, Moonee Ponds or Essendon. Anna didn't drink for an entire week. This stretched to two weeks, and then three. Did I believe that these rectangles of time on a calendar were the building blocks to a life of purpose and sobriety? No. Because I could see that without the solace of dope or alcohol, Anna struggled more than ever. The demon that drove her to get into bed with me and John came back to roar in her head. One night, in the middle of her first non-drinking week, when John was out and Gill was visiting, Anna told us that the voices were telling her terrible things, putting pictures in her head so horrible she would never describe to anyone what they were. Gill and I made urgent suggestions: she should expel the voices and the pictures by putting other stuff in there. Read, pray, try out the drama group I'd found a brochure for, go to the gym!

Did she follow up on even one of my good ideas? No. She went to bed; using a combination of Valium, Seroquel and her various other meds, she worked on staying asleep for as many hours as possible out of every twenty-four. She did manage to get out of bed some days, especially when Charlotte came to stay during the July school holidays. And most evenings she would attend one of her AA meetings, trudging down to the end of the driveway to be collected by Brenna, or whoever it was that was taking her. I must say that on her return from those meetings she was often more alive than at any other stage of the week. Sometimes she'd tell us stories about people she'd met there.

But then came the Wednesday evening when Brenna walked Anna up to our front door instead of dropping her off as usual. 'She's upset,' Brenna said, stepping into the lounge room with her, as if handing back a little child. Anna reached out to me for a hug. She was shaking with distress. It turned out that when they'd been having a smoke outside the church before the meeting started, Anna had told a smutty joke and the leader called her out on it, saying it wasn't appropriate for a young woman to be talking like that in front of the men at AA. Most likely she'd been thinking of Anna's safety, cautioning her not to be provocative, but Anna had been devastated. Brenna stayed for a cup of tea, reassuring Anna that it was nothing, that by the next meeting it would be forgotten. I spent until after midnight placating her, as I had done so many nights before, telling her how beautiful and good she was. We sat on the couch, her head in my lap. I stroked her hair and said, 'That's the demon talking to you, don't listen.' Inside I was begging that same demon, *Please don't destroy us yet, with less than a month until our holiday.*

Finally, she took her Valium and went to bed. An hour later I was woken by a dull and rhythmic bang, bang, bang. I'm a lighter sleeper than John, and I figured this would more likely be Anna than an unwanted intruder, so I got up to investigate. There she was, in the laundry, banging her head against the wall over and over. I grabbed her. 'Stop that!' I beseeched. She said she wanted to die, that she was going to kill herself by drinking the metho we kept in the hall cupboard. I bought her off with a second Valium and stowed the metho in the steel box.

Anna managed not to touch alcohol for four weeks. Then she said to me, 'I did this for you. But I feel worse than ever.' What could I say? I already knew this was true.

Even though Anna wasn't cured during her time at AA, two important things did happen. Since I was now, according to the government, Anna's official carer, I contacted an organisation that offered support to carers. The action of picking up the phone and ringing the number of these kinds of services for the first time always felt good. It might just be a gateway that would lead to some sort of help.

The call to this particular organisation was pretty satisfying: rather than wading through a swamp of number-pressing, I was able to talk to a real person straight away. The woman I spoke to told me I was entitled to something like twenty-five hours of respite care. Not per week, or month, but as a one-off deal. She said I should think about how I'd like to use those twenty-five hours. A day or so later I got back to her. I'd talked it over with John and we'd decided we'd like to have someone pick up Anna a couple of nights a week to take her to her AA meetings and bring her home again. Brenna was already doing that when she could, but it would be nice for John and me to have a few extra drama-free dinners, so we could do what we'd never got tired of since we met at the age of twenty-nine: chat over a good meal and a bottle of wine. (To support Anna, we no longer drank alcohol when she was home.)

The woman who organised respite said this was an unusual request, but she thought she could arrange it. And so, one evening soon after that, a man called Jim appeared at our door, ready to be Anna's chauffeur. Slim, with a weathered but friendly face, he looked to be in his early fifties. I admired his nicely cut black leather jacket, and tried not to stare at his pointy-toed white shoes. John went out to inspect his car and decided it was safe enough for our daughter to ride in.

There should have been lights flashing on Jim's forehead, spelling out a message: *Watch this one. He's going to become quite an important character in the story of your life.* That night, though, he was simply a stranger we'd allowed through our front door. There could be no warning of the part he would play.

The second important development to occur during our AA days was that John decided we should get a cat. A few months previously, he had lost his temper over all the cardboard boxes and poo in the kitchen, so we'd taken the guinea pigs to a shelter to be rehomed. The rodent-loving woman there had assured us that our furry trio would be snapped up by the end of the day, as they were so healthy and used to being handled.

Now John thought it would help Anna's mental health to cuddle a mammal whose intelligence went beyond recognising the rustle of a bag of salad mix and responding with an excited squeal. 'She needs a pet who's glad to see her!'

I wasn't so sure. My old ginger pal Basil had died several years before, aged seventeen. I knew for certain that no other cat could match him. But research did say that patting a cat had health benefits, like lowering a person's blood pressure. So Anna and I began looking online.

When Charlotte was at our house during the school holidays, we found a cat online that we thought might suit us. So we put in a request for her, and on a crisp July afternoon, Charlotte, Anna and I drove up to meet her at a shelter in Woodend. She seemed nice enough, but while we were there, Charlotte and Anna spotted, in a corner cage, a tiny black scrap of a feline, a scrawny eight-week-old kitten. Anna took the kitten out, and she clung to the front of her hoodie, meowing piteously. She was so young she couldn't yet retract her claws. 'I want this one,' Anna pronounced, hugging her close to her chest.

'Can we get her?' Charlotte was jumping up and down. 'Can we, can we, can we?'

We got her. The tag on her cage read 'Dora', but we changed her name to Poppy. Anna, who hadn't bought dope or alcohol in many weeks, had accumulated enough money to pay for Poppy's purchase, and for her collar and expensive food.

So Anna had at last what she'd longed for since she was a toddler: her own kitten. Surely this would make her want to live, I hoped, at least till Poppy got old enough to maybe not want to sit on Anna's lap . . . and that would be *after* our Gold Coast holiday!

Chapter 31

The same week Anna threatened to kill herself by drinking metho, I went to my first Al-Anon meeting. This was another hope I had plucked from my binder of possibilities. Having studied the brochure and researched online, I already knew that Al-Anon was not an official organisation, but rather a worldwide 'fellowship of relatives and friends of alcoholics who share their experience, strength and hope'. There was also Nar-Anon, especially for the families and friends of drug addicts, but I couldn't find any meetings for this near us. And, since at the time Anna's main drug was alcohol, I figured Al-Anon was worth a try.

The meeting was held at a church in Moonee Ponds. It was scheduled for 10.30 on Thursday morning. I set out much earlier, catching the 9.05 train. I like taking the train when I don't need the car for shopping or for lugging around my tutoring supplies. Apart from allowing me to feel self-righteous for burning less fossil fuel, the train gets me out walking, and it reminds me of the months many years ago, when my babies were just shiny ideas, when my world was squashed into a backpack and I had a Eurail pass that took me over the Swiss Alps and up into Scandinavia.

This train took me to Moonee Ponds, eleven minutes up the line from Oak Park. But the world still looked shiny to me, on this bright winter morning. I went into a cafe across the street from the station, around the corner from the sex shop where Anna used to buy her synthetic. This cafe, due to its proximity to trains, was called Chew Chew. Not the greatest pun I've ever heard, but the coffee was a lot better than at the tiny family-run joint with the lovely food that was also nearby. It felt so nice to be in that clean, quiet place, a shaft of sunlight falling across the solid, dark wood table in front of me, and a mug of good cappuccino to warm my hands. I got a hit of dopamine by clicking onto Facebook on my phone and seeing words from people I loved, both in this country and the States. And yet, as always, in moments when my mind was clear and quiet, that voice would begin to mutter. *You shouldn't be feeling like this when your daughter is suffering.* I tried arguing with it: *She has her little kitten.* When I left home, Anna was sleeping on the couch with Poppy snoozing on her chest; they both looked really peaceful. It irritated me to recall the rumpled blankets on the couch and the mess around it, which Anna would just stroll away from, if and when she got up. But at least when I was pissed off with her, I could more successfully ignore the voice.

It was 10.15 by the time I headed down the street towards the Al-Anon meeting, walking past elegant old houses with their gardens of roses and lavender, trimmed back tidily for the winter. I wasn't nervous about going to a place I'd never been before and meeting new people. In my professional life I'd done that thousands of times. I still did it, going in to a school or a student's home for the first time. As I walked towards this new group, I harboured a little hope. Perhaps these people who lived with addicted loved ones could give me a clue or two about how to help my ailing girl.

The church was not hard to spot because there was a sandwich board out the front announcing, 'Al-Anon Here Today'.

Inside there were helpful hand-lettered signs that I followed through a cavernous vestibule, down a ramp, through a kitchenette and into a meeting room.

In my memory, as soon as I stepped into that room, a tall, middle-aged woman with big, capable hands and the kindest face you could imagine enfolded me in her warm arms and said, 'It's not your fault.' Of course, this must have happened after the formal part of the meeting, after I'd had my turn to tell my story (the short version of it), but in my mind, as soon as I'd found my way through the narrow kitchen with its counter of tea bags, Nescafé and heavy brown mugs, this tall woman drew me into her embrace. The next thing she said was, 'This group isn't about your daughter's recovery, it's about taking care of you.'

You don't need to believe in God to benefit from Al-Anon. What you need is to hear the words the kind, tall woman, whose name turned out to be Jo, said to me: It's not your fault. You need someone to ask you, as Jo did me, if you are sleeping well, and eating proper meals. You need to be assured of something that may not have occurred to you, and may take some time to believe: No matter what happens to your child, your life is valuable. You deserve to live!

Al-Anon turned out to be a great comfort to me. Katie came to quite a few meetings too, before she moved to the country. We went to the Moonee Ponds group on Thursdays and another in Brunswick on Sunday nights. I don't know about Katie, but I recall only scraps of the twelve steps we recited at the beginning of every meeting, and almost nothing of the official manual, which we took turns reading from at every meeting. What I remember is how warm the people were, despite their sometimes harrowing stories. I remember how a man my age kept on loving his wife through endless cycles of rehab and relapse. One Thursday morning, I sat there wiping tears away through most of the meeting because I was so tired; I'd been up for hours during the night, again, talking Anna out of killing herself. At the end of the meeting, after we'd stood in a circle, held hands and recited the Serenity Prayer, this man with the relentlessly alcoholic wife opened his arms to me and without saying anything, gave me the most generous, tightest hug.

But after each Al-Anon meeting, I had to go home. Though I might postpone this by checking out whatever weird specials Aldi had on offer, eventually I had to return to the mess and pain of Anna's life.

The week before we were scheduled to leave for our holiday was particularly hard. With Anna continuing to go to AA but drinking again, it felt like the terrible thing was galloping towards us from some distant and fetid corner of the universe. I was desperate to confuse it, cajole it, outmanoeuvre it so that before it could get to us, we could take off into the sky and land safely in a state of sparkles and sun.

Then, on Wednesday, five days before our departure date, Anna announced that she was going to lodge a form with Centrelink by herself, taking the train to Broady. I didn't like that idea. I said I'd drive her, as I usually did, but she insisted, reminding me that she was supposed to be working on her mental health. 'I have to start doing more stuff on my own,' she argued. Of course I wanted this to be true, to believe that she could begin to take baby steps towards control of her own affairs. I was beyond relieved when she returned sober, happy even, more confident than I had seen her in ages. Brenna picked her up for AA that night, and the next day Anna was awake before noon. She said she wanted to move her bedding back into the bungalow because she felt ready to sleep in there again. Could I help her with that? Could I ever! We made her bed, all fresh and clean. I even found her an electric blanket to make it cosy, and she gave me a big hug to thank me. Then she helped me tidy the lounge room. So off I went to tutor, feeling light with the freedom of having my space back.

When I got home, according to my journal, 'Found A asleep on her freshly made bed . . . in a pool of piss!' There was a bottle of vodka on the floor beside the bed, with maybe seven centimetres left in it. I was disgusted. I wanted to scream at her for being a filthy, sneaky drunk who caused me endless hours of drudgery. But then she began to stir. She mumbled to me, 'Go away. Leave me alone.' She was slurring, but I could make out the words I hated to hear most: 'Part of me just wants to die.' My anger was once again smothered by panic. I assured her that the wet bed was nothing. Sheets and clothes could be washed. An electric blanket could be replaced, whereas she could not. I helped her to the bathroom to wash and get into a clean nightie, then made her as comfortable as I could, back on the couch.

But now she couldn't sleep. Jarred out of her drunken stupor, she wanted to talk.

I sat beside the couch, in my little wooden rocker, for a large part of the night. She told me Brenna had said she could only pick her up for AA one more time, because she'd been promoted at work, and would be too tired from the additional hours for any extra driving. I said this sounded reasonable to me, while inside me, a less charitable voice was screeching at Brenna, *I know my daughter hasn't appreciated your efforts enough, but why did you have to do this NOW?* Because

I knew Anna would take it as one more rejection in a life too full of them.

We were so close to our departure date! Katie Rose had texted to tell us that Charlotte had already packed her new bathers in her backpack in preparation for Wet'n'Wild. What could I do, what could I say to get Anna through to the water-slides? I didn't know, I was out of ideas. I tried the advice they gave at Al-Anon: don't try to reason with your alcoholic. It's not your job to cure her. Just wrap her in a blanket of love.

My alcoholic. I sat beside her on the couch and attempted not to care that a mess had returned to the lounge room. In my mind, I wrapped my baby up in the softest, pinkest blanket ever made.

Chapter 32

We were on our way to the Gold Coast! There we were on a midday flight on Monday the 18th of August. I sat in an aisle seat and across from me, in the same row, were Anna in the aisle and Katie by the window, with Charlotte wriggling with excitement between them.

I'd had a dozen books published and achieved plenty of professional promotions in my life, but this felt like my single greatest accomplishment.

It had been rough, getting Anna through the previous weekend. The Friday evening before we left was Anna's last AA meeting that Brenna would be taking her to. Anna wanted to skip it, since in her view Brenna had dumped her, but I insisted she go. After the meeting, Anna was up much of that night, with me trying to comfort her, but she pulled herself out of bed the next morning to play with Charlotte, who we'd collected the night before. Anna had been pretty good since then. She'd been incredibly anxious about packing for the trip, so Katie came over early and did it for her.

Now that we were safely – miraculously, it seemed to me – ensconced on the plane, we had some fun choosing our lunches from the snack packs pictured on laminated menu folders. We decided to share a couple of chicken sandwiches, plus some cheese and biscuits, and little chocolate bars for dessert. Anna asked if we could have wine, but when Katie and I responded in unison with a heartfelt *no*, she seemed content enough with peach-flavoured iced tea. It was one of the best meals of my life: the chicken sandwiches were surprisingly delicious. And beside me were the three girls that I loved best in all the world, safely belted into place so they couldn't get away. Even though the trip Anna and I took when she was in year 9 taught me that I never again wanted to be apart from John for a long period, I relished this chance for a girls-only holiday. Plus, John didn't like theme parks much. We'd taken the girls to the Gold Coast when they were little, at which time John had pronounced Movie World to be 'Piss Weak World'.

Once we landed, I trusted Anna to be good for Charlotte, and she was. She made it out of bed every morning by nine o'clock, so we'd have plenty of time at each theme park. Charlotte couldn't swim confidently, so at Wet'n'Wild Anna watched her every minute, waiting at the bottom of the water-slides to scoop her up. Then they'd race off hand in hand to the next attraction Charlotte wanted to try. At one point Charlotte cried extravagantly because she was too short to qualify for one of the most fun-looking slides. So Anna carried Charlotte around in her arms to soothe her. Anna didn't drink during the day. She had wine with dinner, which was simple fare like fish and salad that we prepared in our cabin. Katie and I drank wine as well. Anna consumed more than we did, making sure she had a bottle to herself, but that was minimal by her standards.

Charlotte, who by this stage had three little brothers, rev-elled in her role as the only kid. She also appreciated being free of parental expectations for a whole week. Over dinner one night in our cabin, she listed some of the privileges she enjoyed with us: 'I get to suck my thumb, have chocolate sprinkles on my toast, chew with my mouth open and drink milk out of a wine glass. Cheers!' We clinked our stemware together for the third or fourth time that meal.

Charlotte loves Katie and me, and tells us so often, but Anna is the one who has always been the most special to her. In one of my favourite photos from that holiday, Charlotte and Anna are sitting side by side on the sky train at Sea World. They are wearing identical white sundresses bought from the children's section of Kmart. Anna's is a size 14 and Charlotte's is a size 6. If you look closely, you can spot the anxiety in Anna's eyes and the tension in her smile but, just as I'd hoped, she had more fun on that holiday than she'd had in years. She especially liked the thrill rides. I remember thinking that if only I could supply her with a continuous supply of taller and faster roller-coasters, she might settle on adrenaline as her drug of choice.

On the Monday after our trip, Charlotte was back at school and we were home. The holiday I'd tried so hard to keep Anna alive for had been a big success, but now it was over. What had I thought would happen after this feat had been accomplished? That I'd be ready to accept my daughter's death? That I could say goodbye to this beautiful girl, who had invited Charlotte into her bed when she woke up crying in the night because she was missing her mother?

Looking back, it seems like Anna used up the rest of that year's allotment of sanity on the Gold Coast, because when she got home, the demons came roaring in big time. Anna stopped going to AA, or doing anything much during the day apart from drinking, fiddling with her phone and sleeping. John said I'd been putting too much pressure on her, endlessly encouraging her to try different activities and dragging her along to various organisations I had unearthed and filed details of in my trusty folders. 'She needs to rest,' he told me firmly. 'That's how she'll get better, by having a safe place where people aren't nagging her all the time.'

I knew John cared about Anna just as much as I did. He was making the same point that was stressed over and over again in the Al-Anon literature: 'You didn't cause it, you can't cure it, and you can't control it.' *If the terrible thing is going to keep on marching toward her, there's absolutely nothing you can do about it. Let go and let God.*

I can't! I wanted to argue. *I have to keep on collecting ideas and snapping them into my binders.* My journal says that doing nothing for my daughter was the hardest job I had ever attempted. Letting go felt way too much like giving up.

In saying that, I don't mean to imply that John was giving up on her. He tried so, so hard. He'd wanted to travel when he retired, to go to Nepal and trek in the Himalayas like he did when he was young. But he stayed home to try to help our girl. Every night at dinner – well, the ones Anna managed to be conscious for – he would suggest what they might do the next day. Not stressful stuff like anger-management classes or self-improvement courses, which she'd have to face alone, but nice things they could do together, like run along the bike path, or go to a movie, or take the train into the city to catch an exhibition at the National Gallery. Anna would usually agree that these suggestions sounded great, and once in a while would actually get up and do them. But most often she'd be too tired, and John didn't try to convince and bribe her like I used to. He would let her rest.

But it seemed to me that the more rest she got, the less we did. More and more often we'd be woken in the night by

her banging or clanging or raving. Often John would get up
to her. I'd hear him soothing her, giving her pep talks, offering her glasses of water and cups of tea. Sometimes, because
she would have been asleep for so many hours during the day
and missed out on meals, he would heat up leftovers or baked
beans in the microwave for her and sit with her while she ate,
until she was relaxed enough to crawl back into her smelly
nest on the couch. When John came back to bed, he was able
to go to sleep almost immediately; he told me he'd taught himself this trick when he was doing shiftwork at the airport, but
I couldn't learn it. I'd lie awake listening for the next crisis.

Then there were nights when it was my turn to get up to
her. I had never been as patient as John with this, even when
the kids were tiny. She knew I hated losing sleep and tried to
take advantage of my desire to go back to bed. One particular night I was brutally tired, afraid I'd have to cancel tutoring
the next day as I wouldn't be safe to drive. She demanded that
I unlock the Bunnings box and give her access to the whiskey
or overproof rum that she knew was in there. By this time she
had become so crippled by anxiety that she was agoraphobic,
never leaving the property unless John, Katie or I, or someone else she trusted, like one of my girlfriends, took her out.
This was handy in a way, because we always knew where she
was. But it was horrible in another way, because she would
cry, yell and threaten to kill herself if we didn't supply her
with alcohol. I know what some people may think: we should
have called her bluff. But anyone who knows John would say
he is the least easily bluffed person they have ever met, and he
wasn't willing to take the risk.

Much later, he told me he used to imagine she would
'do it' by getting up the courage to walk to the train one last

time . . . and throw herself under it. So, rather than forbid alcohol altogether, John had come up with a compromise: no vodka, but we would go to Coles and buy slabs of Hammer 'n' Tongs, a mid-strength beer, and she could drink as much of that as she wanted. Plus, each evening with dinner, she could have a carafe of cask wine. This was not a small carafe, either. It held a litre.

She hated that beer. She complained that it tasted awful, made her put on weight and that she couldn't get a buzz from it. But she drank it anyway, can after can, for all the hours that she was awake. Once I counted the number of beers I witnessed her consuming in a 24-hour period. Including the carafe of wine we allotted her, I calculated she'd ingested thirty-four standard drinks.

But on this night, or rather very early morning – sometime during that depressing stretch between 2 and 4 a.m., when I stood exhausted with her in the mess that she'd made of our lounge room – the beer and the wine were not enough. 'I need to get a proper buzz on,' she pleaded. The demons must have been howling in her head, but I was thinking about my own brain, and how it wasn't going to work well enough to analyse year 12 texts tomorrow, if I did manage to drive to my scheduled schools.

'I'm not giving you your dad's expensive whiskey,' I told her. 'He'd have a fit.'

She grabbed the baseball bat that I'd given John years earlier, and which he kept propped beside the front door. 'Then I'll break my ribs!' she shouted, raising the bat above her head. Now it was me doing the pleading, begging her yet again not to hurt herself. That night I bought her off with extra Valium.

Sometimes, if she got up during the day, she could still be fun. One late afternoon in spring, I returned from tutoring to find her and John out in the backyard with our fast-growing kitten. Poppy was in the harness Brenna had given us. Anna, with a beer in one hand and the lead from the harness in the other, was laughing at Poppy pouncing upon dry leaves under the huge gum tree that was the centrepiece of our garden. 'I think you definitely killed that one,' Anna commented to the kitten. 'Try this one. It flies!' She tossed a leaf into the air, and for that tiny point in time, Anna, John and I were united in the joy of watching a young cat leap.

But a couple of nights later I got up to investigate a thumping sound and found Anna kneeling beside the cupboard where we kept the tinned food, hitting her forehead over and over again with a can of corn kernels. I can't remember how I dealt with that. But somehow, I did. And then came a day that stretched me to the limit of my ability to cope.

It was nine o'clock on a Friday morning. Anna was sitting at the kitchen table, sipping a beer and reading a book. Two of these facts were highly unusual: for Anna to be up in the morning, and to be reading an actual book instead of scrolling randomly on her phone. I remember what the book was – *One Child* by Torey Hayden, an old-fashioned paperback with tiny print that Anna had found on the shelves in the spare room. Hayden was a special education teacher, and her book was an extended case study of a deeply damaged little girl she'd taught. Anna was starting to really get into material about abused children.

When John came into the kitchen and saw Anna, something in him went dark. 'Have you been sitting there drinking all night?' he demanded. This was not the kind and patient voice he'd been using with her since we'd returned from the Gold Coast.

Anna ignored him.

'I asked you a question!'

I flinched at his tone.

Anna answered with a none-of-your-business shrug. She stank of beer. Not just her breath; a stale stench seemed to be seeping from the pores of her skin.

John jerked open the refrigerator door and pulled out the few remaining beers. 'You've had enough. I'm locking these up.'

That made her respond. She jumped out of her chair. 'You can't do that,' she screeched at him. 'The deal is I get to drink all the beer I want!'

He fixed her with his glare. 'The rules have changed.'

What happened next was so quick and shocking, it is not a logical sequence of events in my mind, but a series of jarring pictures: Anna is no longer sitting at the table, but standing at the bench beside the sink. And now the butcher's knife is in her hand, our good knife that John keeps sharpened with a whetstone. She is holding the knife aloft. She's plunging its glittery blade towards her chest . . .

I don't know how John did it, but somehow he managed to grab the knife and toss it aside, wrestling Anna, shrieking and thrashing, to the floor. The only physical damage done was a tear in the front of her puffy black jacket.

'Mum! Muuuuum!' Anna was yelling. 'Make him let me go!'

But he wouldn't let her go. He had her arms pinned to the floor and was holding her down with the weight of his body. Over the years since it happened, this scene has replayed itself to me several hundred times. It has become mixed up in my mind with the final moments of *The Exorcist*, when the priest wrestles grotesquely with Regan. That awful morning in the kitchen, I don't believe John was fighting to overpower his daughter. I think, like the handsome priest, he had become fed up with the demon inside the girl.

At the time, I was only aware of Anna screaming at me to make her father let go, and John refusing to do it.

'We need help!' John barked at me. 'Call somebody!'

'Who?'

'You figure it out!'

With Anna now screaming 'Help! Fire! Rape!' to try to rouse the neighbours, I called the CAT team. An automated voice informed me that I'd been placed in a queue. I slammed a metaphoric receiver down on my phone and punched in Dr Deb's number. I figured she was probably with a patient, but the receptionist must have heard the urgency in my voice because she put me straight through. 'Deb! She's tried to stab herself. Her dad's holding her down. What should I do? Can you hear her screaming?'

'You'll have to call the police.'

A scene flashed into my mind. The sight of police at the door would give Anna the strength to break free, grab the knife and head towards an officer. 'I can't call the police! They shoot mentally ill people!'

'Mary.' Deb's voice was firm. 'That hardly ever happens. You'll have to call them.'

Anna screamed obscenities at me as I punched in triple 0 and reported that we needed help with our out-of-control, suicidal daughter.

It was the sound of a wailing siren that finally made Anna stop wailing. It turned out the car wasn't coming to our place, but it served its purpose, because when two officers did appear at our door a few minutes later, Anna had calmed down enough for John to let her go; she had promised to lie quietly on the couch.

The officers, a man and a woman, clomped into the lounge room and over to Anna. 'I'm sorry,' Anna said to them. 'Mum shouldn't have called you. It's a waste of your time.'

'No,' the woman corrected her, 'your mother did exactly the right thing.'

I fell in love with that police officer. She told us we could call her by her first name, Georgia. She sat down in my rocker beside the couch and calmly asked Anna questions. Anna, despite the amount of alcohol bathing her brain, was able to answer with eloquence. This facility with language, and her obvious intelligence, was what made it so hard for most professionals to believe John, Katie and me when we said that Anna was sick and desperately needed help. But Georgia, who told us she had a background in psychology, was able to see through the screen of Anna's extensive vocabulary. And she listened to me when I described Anna's symptoms. Georgia asked the other officer to sit with Anna while she had a chat with John and me in the kitchen. The words Georgia said to us that morning felt like the first raindrops falling onto a drought-stricken land. 'I think Anna needs to be in a hospital,' Georgia said. 'She needs to be monitored and have regular blood tests so she can be medicated properly. With that, and decent nutrition and sleep, in the long term she can have good days. She can have lots of good days.' I don't know if Georgia patted my hand. In my memory, it feels like she did. She concluded, 'So what I think we'll do is call an ambulance to take her to the Northern Hospital.'

She didn't ask if this was okay with Anna or us. But it was more than okay with me. It sounded like a slice of heaven. *Properly medicated. Lots of good days.* Time off from having to deal with her!

It turned out all the ambulances were too busy with more urgent cases. So Georgia said they would drive Anna there in the cop car. Anna had a hissy fit at that. Georgia produced plan B: if Anna would promise to behave, John and I could drive her to the Northern Hospital while she and her partner would follow in the police car. 'When we get there,' Georgia said to me, 'if Matt and I escort her in, I'm pretty sure they'll admit her to the psych ward.'

Anna did not like the term 'admit'. She declared she didn't even want to go to a hospital to be examined, let alone stay there.

Georgia replied that she didn't have a choice. She looked into Anna's glowering face, then gave me her mobile number in case something went wrong on the way to the hospital. 'You ride in the back seat with her,' Georgia instructed me.

As we were cruising north on Pascoe Vale Road at 70 kilometres an hour, my mind was flying into the clouds with thoughts of Anna getting well. Georgia had told us in the kitchen that once Anna was admitted to a psych ward, she'd be in the adult mental health system and 'would get some real help'. Anna must have sensed my momentary lapse in concentration. Her hand drifted over to the door handle. I heard it begin to open. 'Stop that!' I screeched, grabbing her. She tried to struggle away but I held tight. Before I could even think of retrieving Georgia's number, we heard the commandingly loud 'Errr! Errr! Errr!' of the cop car behind us. We pulled over and in an instant Matt was at Anna's door.

'You need to ride with us now. Come on nicely or I'll have to cuff you.'

When we got to the hospital, Georgia said to me with just a teeny hint of smugness, 'I knew she'd do that. I was watching for it.' She and Matt handed Anna over to the emergency department staff and then said goodbye. 'Good luck!' Georgia said, shaking my hand. I didn't want to let her go. I wanted to draw her towards me and keep her, with her thick, serious-looking vest and her gun and capable compassion. Couldn't she stay with me, to protect me and my broken girl?

I let go of her hand and said, 'Thanks so much.'

Not too long afterwards we were permitted to see Anna in her emergency ward bed. They must have given her a Valium or two because she was drifting off to sleep. 'She'll probably sleep for a few hours,' the nurse told us. 'It'll take that long for her system to deal with the alcohol. When she's sober we'll do our assessment, then we'll call you.'

'What assessment?' I inquired.

'To see if she should be admitted to the psychiatric ward.'

But I had assumed that she *would* be admitted. Georgia had seemed so sure about that. 'Don't we get any input into that?' I asked.

'Oh . . . um . . . well, I can tell the mental health nurse that you want to speak to them.'

'Is that who'll make the decision?'

It was. I stewed about that for the many hours that it took for Anna's liver to metabolise the alcohol. John and I trudged around Northland, the mall near the hospital. We had a coffee; we ate some sushi. John appeared to be too stunned to say much. In my head I wrote, re-wrote and meticulously edited what I would say to this unknown mental health nurse.

If I could package our daughter concisely into a few well-rehearsed paragraphs, surely the nurse would see that she needed to be cared for.

We had no idea when the hospital might ring, so we thought we'd better stick around the area. We wandered through Bunnings, which usually cheered me up. People look so purposeful there, with their minds on their projects, perusing putty guns or swatches of paint colours. From the gardening section, happy couples sallied forth with their arms full of flowering plants.

The afternoon wore on, fading tiredly into evening. I worried that the mental health nurse's shift might be over, or that they had forgotten our request. Finally, the call came and we headed back to the hospital.

Thank God, they had not forgotten. In fact, it seemed the process was being taken quite seriously, because we were ushered into a little interview room to speak with the mental health nurse. She was obviously exhausted. I don't remember her bothering to tell us her name or shake our hands. As I began my perfectly worded presentation, she looked as if she deeply longed for me to shut up so she could go home. In fact, shortly after I started talking, she interrupted me. 'Your daughter doesn't fit the criteria to be admitted to the psychiatric ward.'

'What? Why not?'

'I've assessed her and in my opinion she appears to be rational.'

I couldn't take this in, couldn't believe this woman was saying what my ears heard. 'Why are you taking her word for it?' I asked. 'She might sound rational but she's barely functioning!'

'Mary . . .' It was John's warning voice, but for once I was beyond caring how much my public display of distress embarrassed him. That morning, Georgia the police officer had opened a gate through which I could see a land bathed in the sunlight of hope. *She can have good days. She can have lots of good days.* Now, this woman was clanging that gate shut.

So much for the polished speech I'd prepared. I begged her: 'Please . . . can't you admit her? She's so sick. She's suicidal! And I don't know how much longer we can cope.'

I was on the verge of crying. The gatekeeper looked disgusted, thoroughly sick of me and my girl and our whole sorry situation. 'What good would a few days in the psych ward do?' she snarled.

The woman rose from her chair and was already heading to the door when she pronounced, 'Your daughter has a plan to stop drinking. Take her home.'

I wanted to scream but all I could do was sob. 'Okay, then,' I managed to choke out, 'we'll take her home to *die*!'

Chapter 33

When John and I took Anna home that horrible night she was refused entry to the psych ward, the mental health people did not send us off completely without comfort. Anna would, they promised, be visited the next day by the CAT team. And so two young women, different CAT team members from those that had visited us before, arrived at 9.30 in the morning. As John tried to persuade Anna to wake up and drag herself off the couch, I talked to the CAT team in the kitchen. I repeated the words that Georgia had uttered at the same table the morning before, and which, having heard them, I knew to be true: 'This girl needs to be in a hospital.'

'Oh, no!' Team member one shook her head. 'These days we much prefer home-based care.'

I knew those women were only doing their jobs, but I wanted to scream at the officials who had sent them out to us, 'Who exactly do you expect to do this home-based care? Even if Anna isn't in a drunken stupor when the CAT team comes around, they'll only be here for a few minutes, an hour at the most. Who is supposed to look after her for the other twenty-three hours? And how long do you think we can keep it up?'

One afternoon, a couple of weeks after the morning of the knife, Anna arranged to go around to her old high school friend Scott's house, and we were thrilled. She was getting out of the house! Maybe she'd turned a corner. She said she'd be home around seven, but seven came and went, as did eight . . . finally, I rang Scott. 'Ummm, she's asleep,' he admitted. 'On the lounge-room floor. I can't really wake her up.'

'Is she breathing?' My heart was thumping like a mad thing.

'Oh, yeah. She's just . . . really tired.'

Poor, sweet Scott. He still lived with his parents, who happened to be out that night. He didn't want to tell me that Anna had drunk half the contents of his dad's liquor cabinet. John went to fetch her. He couldn't wake her up, so with Scott's help he carried her to the car. When he got home, John carried her to the bungalow and put her to bed. He did this again, when a slurring Anna insisted on going to an evening church service with Marcelle and me, and then passed out while we were there. This was at Marcelle's very evangelical church. The plump lady pastor and several young people gathered around Anna's comatose form, stretched out on a pew, and prayed over her fervently. They managed to carry her to Marcelle's car, but it was John who manhandled her to bed when we got home. Yes, Anna was skinny, but after her anorexia was resolved, she had grown three inches and was pretty damned heavy as a dead weight. John told me that lifting her was at the very limit of his strength. He was sixty-three years old by then. How much more of that kind of home-caring could he do?

How many times did the home-care proponents expect me to get up in the middle of the night to be with my whimpering daughter? 'Mum!' She'd cling to me. 'I'm so scared. I'm scared of almost everything now.' How many exhausted nights would I have to spend, trying to persuade my girl to choose life?

A few weeks after she tried to stab herself, the CAT team brought around a psychiatrist to talk to Anna. An actual psychiatrist! 'Can't you get her admitted to a hospital?' I pleaded. Surely he had power.

Maybe by this stage we would have paid to put her into a private psychiatric hospital. But there were no involuntary ones, and there was no way she would have signed herself into one. We couldn't make her do it. She was, technically, an adult. It had become my opinion, since Georgia the police officer had planted the idea, that Anna needed to be placed in a locked psych ward.

The psychiatrist and I were in the bungalow. I had ushered him in because, being daytime when the ghosts went into hiding, Anna was in there asleep. The psychiatrist glanced around Anna's chaotic abode, at the things she had in bed with her: a laptop, a sleeping kitten, four teddies and half a dozen empty beer cans. He saw the ragged holes in her walls that on more than one enraged occasion she had created by smashing through the plaster with her foot. 'I don't have the authority to have her admitted,' he said sadly. 'I'm afraid my hands are tied.'

And so, I planned my daughter's funeral. I didn't want to. I was disgusted with my mind and ordered it to stop. But when it wasn't actually engaged in a task, say preparing a lesson or arguing with John about how long to cook a leg of lamb for, it would imagine leafing through all the years of our family albums, choosing photos to project onto the big screen behind the priest officiating at her farewell. Which music would be best? How much should we spend on the coffin?

We hadn't had any contact with John's family in over a year. John and I used to, once in a while, invite them all over for a barbie or to a book launch. These were things of the past for us now. If the rest of the family was still having get-togethers, they didn't invite us. And I could understand why. Having Anna around, the way she was now, made parties too painful.

I liked John's family a lot. Plenty of our albums featured pictures of his beautiful nieces and their lovely, affectionate children. I couldn't stand the thought of breaking the silence with them by ringing to tell them that Anna had died. So I sent a text to John's sister and his two nieces. 'Anna is in a really bad place. We've been trying hard to keep her alive but I don't know if we can do it much longer.'

One of the nieces rang me straight away, asking if there was anything she could do. It was wonderful just to hear her voice, invoking the sun and sea and laughter of Christmases we used to spend together. John's sister rang a couple of days later, with suggestions for motivating projects Anna might do, such as raising a Guide Dog pup. The other niece never responded. This hurt at the time, but not any more. Maybe she didn't get the text. And even if she did, what could she have done? Maybe she just couldn't decide what to say. Or maybe she knew that there was nothing she could say that would make any difference.

Chapter 34

How to survive being raised by a narcissistic mother.

This was an example of the many links that Anna began to share on Facebook at this time. It was a theme that had been bubbling away all through the year, but it only came to prominence in the last two months of 2014. She began to rail about the night when, as a six-year-old, she ran away with Christian, and the police helicopter circled over our little suburb looking for them. 'Nobody hugged me!' She accused us over and over. 'Dad *beat* me!'

She wasn't mad at us all the time. There were moments when she could be apologetic, loving and clingy. But as I read through the pages in my journal describing the waning weeks of that year, I can see that she was definitely shifting John and me from the sparsely populated 'Good People' corral in her brain, to the overcrowded 'Bad People' paddock.

I have a theory about why this happened. She hated her birthday that year. She was white-hot angry at the idea of turning twenty-six and having no job, let alone a career. No car, no boyfriend, no prospects. She looked in the mirror (often) and saw an attractive young woman. How could she be so spectacularly unsuccessful?

Anna had studied psychology. She'd read dozens of books and who knows how many stories online about damaged children. She came to the logical conclusion that her problems must stem from her own terrible childhood. And there were people who encouraged her in this belief. Anna had online friends in various corners of the world who admired the fiction she used to write and publish on the internet. I know that at least one of them claimed to have an extremely troubled background. She and Anna used to spend hours chatting online and I now believe they exchanged quite a few 'war stories' about their upbringings. I don't resent that woman. She gave Anna a lot of support. She was a distant soul sister, but a soul sister nonetheless, when Anna had no girlfriends close by that she could confide in.

I no longer resent Jim either. Jim was the guy in his early fifties that the carers' organisation had sent to drive Anna to AA, so that John and I could have some respite from shuttling her to meetings. He did that two evenings a week for a month. During the last two weeks of that month, he would arrive earlier than necessary so he could have a cup of tea with us. John liked talking to him about cars and plastering. Jim was a bit of a jack-of-all-trades. As well as working as a carer, he did odd jobs like painting, plastering and car detailing.

Jim was sad when our respite money ran out and his official duties with Anna ended. He told us this was the best job he'd ever had, driving a beautiful girl to meetings and chatting with her in the car. 'You're like family to me now. Would it be okay if I still came around to visit sometimes?'

John and I are suckers for sentiment like that. We said of course, he was welcome any time. So Jim became a regular fixture, showing up once or twice a week. He'd stop in the kitchen to have a cup of tea with two sugars, and a Scotch Finger. Then he'd wander out to the backyard for a smoke, and if Anna was awake, she'd join him. Sometimes they'd chat for hours. Did I find this inappropriate? A little. But any qualms I felt were tiny compared to my relief that Anna had a friend who didn't drink alcohol and was disparaging about drugs.

Then came the day when Jim wandered outside, having had his cuppa and bickie and man-talk with John in the kitchen. Anna was asleep in the bungalow and I was under the gum tree, working on my cactuses at the green picnic table, creating my tiny gardens in new teacups, pots and sugar bowls that I'd collected to replace the ones Anna had broken. Jim sat on a lawn chair and lit up a smoke. He said to me, 'I really like Anna. How would you feel if I . . . um . . . asked her out?'

He was old enough to be her father. In fact, though he had never mentioned them to us, I knew he had an ex-wife and three kids in their early twenties. Marcelle, who seems to know approximately half the population of the northern suburbs, had divulged this information to me. Jim was once the drummer at her church. I didn't bring up any of this. What I said was, 'I think that would be a really bad idea. She's not ready for a relationship with anybody. She's very unwell.'

Jim looked decidedly unconvinced. He mumbled something about her needing just one good man in her life, 'a man who understands her'. And so I gathered, and found out for sure in the months to come, that Anna had been telling Jim how hard done by she was, being raised by parents as irresponsible and selfish as me and her dad.

There is someone I do resent, who, unlike Anna's cyber pal or her misguided chauffeur, was a professional and should have known better. After the morning Anna tried to stab herself, John relaxed his insistence that she needed to rest all the time, so I reinstated my campaign to get her help. One of the organisations I got in touch with arranged for her to see a drug and alcohol counsellor. I'll call him Charles, and I need to say upfront that I have absolutely no hard evidence to back up the accusations I'm about to make. I'm basing them on the three hours or so I spent with him, and on what Anna reported that he said to her. He and I had two sessions together when Anna wasn't present, and on another occasion I sat in on one of Anna's sessions. I got the impression that Charles, while well meaning, was inexperienced and not especially intuitive. He seemed to rely a lot on what he'd studied in textbooks. For example, in my first solo session, when I expressed exhausted exasperation at Anna's tendency to give up substances for a couple of days then hatch plans to run marathons, which only ended up being marathons of alcohol and sleep, Charles looked at me in a chilly manner and said, 'Addiction is a chronically relapsing condition.' Like I wouldn't have realised that if he hadn't quoted from the script in his head.

He naturally would have wondered, when pondering Anna's mental problems, whether she'd had a particularly difficult childhood. I don't know if he came right out and asked Anna if she'd experienced parental abuse, but I'm pretty sure from what Anna said to John, Katie and me that Charles encouraged Anna's ravings against us.

One night at dinner, I was trying to make conversation with Anna, but she looked at me with hate in her eyes. She was sitting in the place at the kitchen table that had been hers since she was able to sit up in a highchair. She turned to her dad and told him in an ugly voice that we had ruined her life. She brought up, yet again, the time John spanked her after she ran away. She said, 'You change the structure of a child's brain when you abuse them!'

John's face was grim. But when he spoke, it wasn't to berate her. Instead, he said, 'Do you want to beat me? Would that make you feel better? Go ahead, if you want to, because no physical pain could be as bad as the pain of seeing you the way you are.'

'All right,' she agreed.

I couldn't believe it. John stood up and pulled his pants down, and she whacked him, hard. Then she grabbed him around the throat. She was putting real pressure on his windpipe and he didn't raise a hand in defence. She choked him harder, with a look on her face that scared me.

'Stop it!' I screamed, pulling at her arms. She was a lot stronger than me, but finally she let go.

We all sat back down in our accustomed places. John rubbed his throat a little, then he said to Anna in a calm, cool voice, 'You know, when I used to ride my bike to work, I'd ride under a bridge where some homeless people had set up camp. That's your future.'

The next morning, she got into our bed for a cuddle. She said she was sorry. I know that what her dad said had an effect on her because I recorded the following unusual behaviour in my journal: 'She had a shower and washed her hair and did the dishes from last night.'

Should we, should someone, have realised that Anna was capable of extreme violence? With hindsight, the indications were there. When a seriously underweight teenager can kick in the plate glass of an estate agent's window, doesn't that show the strength of the rage that can erupt from inside her? But that was an isolated incident, and it would be years before we would see that particular demon bare its teeth again.

We had a glimpse of it the night she nearly choked her dad,
and later that year, when John and I left Marcelle in charge
for a couple of days so we could have a night away. When
we got back, Marcelle told us with bemusement, and perhaps
even a hint of amusement, of an incident that happened in our
absence. Jim had come over to see Anna, in a strictly 'good
friend' capacity, according to him. Marcelle was relaxing in
front of the TV when Jim burst in from the backyard and
accused her of being deaf. 'Didn't you hear me? I needed your
help! Anna was choking me!'

Apparently, Marcelle had doubted that slender Anna could
overpower a guy who counted security work among his several
occupations.

'Of course, I know how to defend myself,' Jim is reported
to have huffed, 'but I didn't want to hurt her.'

Then there was the day, in November, when it took nine
people – ambulance officers, security guards and various
medical staff – to wrestle Anna from an ambulance to a bed
in the emergency ward at the Northern Hospital. And she still
managed to bite a nurse. I didn't witness this scene, but a horrified John did, and he has described it to me several times.

It was, however, me who had called the ambulance. The
night before, Anna had told us that she was thinking of volunteering at Vinnie's again. It had been at least a year since
she'd managed to get there. John had jumped on this proposal
as a great idea. He said that tomorrow he'd take her out for
lunch at the Dairy Queen, then they'd go to Vinnie's and sign
her up. I'm sure the part of Anna that was still healthy wanted
to do that. But she had become so anxious about leaving the
house. As John prepared for their father–daughter date, I grew
nervous, because Anna had got up from her couch nest and

gone into the bungalow a couple of hours before, announcing that she was going to dress in something special. She hadn't emerged for a smoke. It was suspiciously quiet in there. Most likely she was asleep, but the rat of worry was gnawing away.

So, just as I'd done a hundred times before, I went in to make sure she was alive. And this time, she barely seemed to be. She was sitting on the floor, her back slumped against her bed, and she was surrounded by blister packs of medication. I grabbed her arm and shook it. She didn't respond. This in itself wasn't unusual, but her eyes were rolled back in her head and her lips were blue, so I called triple 0.

By the time the ambos arrived, a man and a woman, we'd put Anna in the recovery position as instructed, and she was conscious enough to mumble that she didn't want to go to hospital, she just wanted to die. But with that thought in her head and her heart rate high, the male paramedic explained to her that they were obliged to take her in. The female paramedic inspected the blister packs and found they were mainly aspirin, with only a few of the tablets missing. Anna couldn't or wouldn't say what else she'd ingested to cause unconsciousness.

The male officer asked me if I'd like to come with them in the ambulance.

'Uhhh . . .' I responded, 'not really.'

He seemed surprised and a little rebuffed that I'd declined his invitation to accompany my suicidal daughter. But some vital part of me had been squashed into unwilling submission on the day that I rang the police and Georgia had given me hope that Anna might be helped, only to be turned away hours later by a mental health nurse. Over and over, I replayed the question the gatekeeper had put to me in sour tones: 'What good would a few days in the psych ward do?' I longed to shoot a few questions back to her, although I knew my voice would not contain her authority. It would be a strangled cry: 'Don't you see how much it would mean to me to have a few days off? Do you have any idea how exhausting it is to try to keep a beloved child alive? Why can't you realise what an energising gift it would be, if you gave me some help and kept her safe for even half a week?'

That's why I said no to the kind-hearted ambulance officer. I couldn't bear the thought of spending another dreary day hanging around the hospital, only to be handed back a sobered-up Anna with promises of visits from the CAT team. With her whisked off in an ambulance, I could at least have a few hours to myself, knowing she was in the hands of people who would keep her from killing herself. I would sit under our gum tree, sip a coffee and look at the sky, maybe read a book. John went with Anna to the hospital. When they arrived she was fully awake, and fought like the devil not to be taken in. That evening, just as I'd anticipated, she was back with us.

Like the abused children Anna read about, who had so little control over their own lives, I was sad, resentful and angry. Thank goodness I had a psychologist I respected and trusted. Coming from my generation, with my Bible Belt background, it wasn't easy for me to reach out – and pay – for help with my mental health. But during the worst times with Anna, that support was vital. I'd forgotten, until reading my journal recently, how dark some of the thoughts were that I expressed to Margot. In one session, on a Tuesday, I told her how angry I was at Anna. Dan, who was still very fond of Anna and missed her visits, had driven over to our place to pick her up on the previous Saturday, because he knew she could no longer manage train travel. This had given John and me the heaven of an Anna-free weekend. But on the Monday morning, Dan rang me. In a disgusted voice he informed me, 'Your daughter is passed out on my kitchen floor. Could you come and get her?'

Oh, God. Another person she'd driven to the point where he probably wouldn't want her in his life. I couldn't stand to see her, and I had a good reason not to. I said I needed to honour my tutoring commitments. John didn't feel like driving across the city through peak hour traffic either. I recorded his response in my journal: 'I'll do a lot for her, but I'm not going to be her slave.'

Poor Dan didn't think he should leave Anna unconscious on his floor and go to work. So Katie, bless her heart again, managed to get to Dan's place in the early afternoon, and with his help, pry her sister off the floor and drag her into her car.

I told Margot that once John had carried Anna in and put her on the couch, she began to come to, and started whimpering and asking me to cuddle her. I couldn't do it. I was so sick of her destroying every opportunity that anyone presented to her. What I wanted to do was scream at her, 'Sometimes I wish you *would* commit suicide! It would make my life a lot easier, you messy, inconsiderate, selfish drunk!'

Margot listened to my imagined rant with her characteristic intelligent kindness. She said I shouldn't berate myself for thinking these horrendous thoughts. 'If you measure stress on a scale of one hundred, you, John and Katie would be in the upper nineties. You're operating with your lizard brains.' She also suggested it might help me to cope with Anna sleeping in the lounge room if I visualised her as a frightened young animal who needed to feel safe.

Now I gaze back at the picture that Margot put in my head and I feel so sorry for Anna, my frightened little animal, lying on the couch crying for her mother. But I also feel sorry for me, and for John and Katie, and for all the parents and sisters and brothers who are expected to provide 'home care' for their non-functioning adult offspring and siblings.

They tell you at Al-Anon, 'Hate the disease but love the person.' My online support group promotes the same message, and I totally agree with the sentiment. But as 2014 wore on, I was finding it harder and harder to see the girl I adored inside the often mean-mouthed addict. She informed me more than once what a terrible carer I was. 'Look up the definition of carer on the internet! You don't deserve to call yourself one!'

She complained that all I did was nag and criticise her. I protested that I only made suggestions and reminded her of her commitments because I loved her.

'Oh, yeah,' she mocked me, making me sound like a whining bitch, '*I only do it because I love you*. That's just a get-out-of-jail-free card!'

Another favourite line of hers was, 'All you think of is yourself – it's just *me, me, me*!'

Her accusations didn't corrode my self-confidence the way my mother's used to, but they sure did thoroughly annoy me. I was amazed at the depth of Anna's capacity for self-destruction, pushing away the person who had walked beside her for twenty-six years. I longed for her to be safe. I wished she could be happy. But I was sick of living with her.

When I was a senior in high school, girls across the nation had to sit the Betty Crocker Homemaker of Tomorrow exam. I won the award for our school. I'm sure it wasn't because I scored high on the multiple-choice section, as I hadn't taken home economics since year 8. I remember there was a question about cream of tartar and I had no idea what that was. It would have been the essay question that cinched the deal for me. It asked something like, 'What makes an ideal wife and mother?' This was 1969, when the women's movement in Iowa was a hesitant toddler wondering if it had the right to squall. The main message I got across in my essay was that a good mother needed to have a life of her own, separate from her children. Four and a half decades later, words that I'd written in that classroom at Baxter High School flailed around in my bruised lizard brain. The words made me feel guilty, but they spoke the truth. I wanted my daughter out of my house. I wanted my lounge room, and my life, back.

Chapter 35

Charles, the drug and alcohol counsellor I resented, did do something that seemed at the time like a fine thing, even a breakthrough. He convinced Anna that detox would be a good idea and he helped her arrange for an intake assessment at Curran Place, the residential facility that Dr Roberts had told us about on the day we spent so many hours at the Grantham Street clinic. Anna ended up going to Curran Place for two ten-day stays: one in late October and early November of 2014, and another in December. I remember her first stint as positive – she wasn't yet saying nasty things about me all the time. I was proud of her for packing up the terrible fear of strangers she'd developed and heading off to stay in a place she'd never been. In the reception area, when we dropped her off, she was shaking. She gave John a long goodbye hug and clung to him desperately until the nurse gently separated them, like a kindergarten teacher taking charge of a frightened four-year-old.

When John and I returned to the car park we danced a little jig – ten days of freedom! Despite this, one of us visited her every day she was there, either John or me, Katie or Marcelle. She was our scared little girl, trying hard. She told us, and the nurses confirmed, that she got up by breakfast time every morning, and went to group sessions, and did her chores. Taking care of the rabbits and chickens in the yard was her special joy. But one of the head nurses recognised the damaged young woman inside the compliant girl. She said to John and me, 'Anna needs at least two years of residential rehab.'

'Two years . . .' John breathed as we walked out to the car after that visit. He made the words sound sacred and I knew what he meant.

As we were to discover, there was a downside to detox. With the help of the Valium they gave her, Anna soon overcame her shyness around new people. After having been marooned for so long without friends, she loved being with the other young residents, hanging out with them in the smokers' courtyard, chatting for hours. But the ten days flashed by, and she had to return to her lonely life with her annoying parents. Within a couple of days, she was drinking again. She needed long-term rehab, as the nurse had said, or some kind of structured help to enable her to learn to be an adult, but no one told us where we might find it.

Anna had picked up a few tips at detox. It was after her first stay that I found her unconscious with blue lips in the bungalow and called an ambulance. At the hospital she'd confessed that what made her lapse into unconsciousness was what she'd swallowed on top of a litre of wine, endless beers, Seroquel and a few aspirin: mouthwash and hand sanitiser. Someone at detox had suggested she try those substances, which is why we started storing those items in the steel box.

The second time Anna was scheduled for detox, she wasn't nervous at all. In fact, she was looking forward to it as a fun holiday. This made me realise how long it had been since she'd looked forward to anything. Before the Gold Coast trip, I'd been counting off the days till departure, but Anna hadn't shown a lot of interest. She was much more excited about returning to Curran Place. She'd noticed that the more wasted people were when they got there, the more Valium they were allowed. So she demanded extra alcohol in the days leading up to her admission date, threatening not to go if we refused. She couldn't sneak off to the shops and buy her beloved vodka, because the first detox stint hadn't cured her anxiety. She was still afraid to leave the house without one of us. We humoured her with a few extra litres of wine, because we were as desperate for the holiday as she was.

Would we have withheld the alcohol and kept her home if we'd known what would result from those ten days in detox? Maybe. Because that's when she met Robert. The clients at Curran Place weren't supposed to exchange phone numbers. They weren't meant to meet up once they left detox. But of course they did, at least in Anna's case. Four days after she got home from detox, on Sunday the 14th of December at three in the afternoon, she left the house on her own for the first time in months. She said she was going to catch up with Robert in the city.

At the time, I was glad she'd at last found the motivation and courage to go out on a summer's day. It always opened up a little corner of sunshine in my heart when she found a way, even for a few hours, not to be lonely. John was really worried about her. Writing this now, I wonder if he feared that her sudden courage to face the outside world meant she'd decided to keep that appointment with the front of a speeding train. He kept asking me if I'd heard from her; she did text me a couple of times during the evening to say she was okay. I stopped hearing from her around nine, and when eleven o'clock rolled around and she wasn't home, I went to bed but didn't really sleep. John stayed up in the lounge room, waiting for her till she was dropped home by Robert at 1.30 in the morning. The next day I woke feeling as if I hadn't slept at all. I slumped into my rocker and switched on the TV to find live coverage of the horrible siege at the Lindt Cafe in Sydney.

Anna, on the other hand, was the opposite of tired. She'd decided she wasn't going to sleep in the lounge room any more. She was moving back into the bungalow, but first she was going to thoroughly clean it. This involved taking every piece of clothing out of her closet, from socks to frocks, and piling them on her bed. From the shelves along the wall and the large cupboard under her TV and from the storage boxes under her bed she pulled all her DVDs and books, plus years of high school and university notes. These became a jumbled hillock on the floor, topped with karate trophies. Sprinkled over and around all of this were tubes of lip gloss, tiny flat boxes of eye shadow plus bottles of hair products and jars of health supplies. Glittering among it all was her extensive collection of bling.

John had always been more appalled than me at the state of Anna's room. I hated her mess migrating into my space, but as long as there wasn't any rotting food in her room, I was resigned to shutting the door and ignoring it. But John was forever wanting her to clean up her room, bringing home bedside shelves he'd unearthed at an op shop or a filing cabinet he'd found on sale at Officeworks, attempting to inspire her to control the chaos. So he was pretty thrilled when she was up early, with plans to tidy. Ten or so hours later, he went out to the bungalow to see how she was going and tell her that dinner was ready.

He returned to the kitchen with anger in his eyes. 'She's been in there all fucking day and it looks exactly the same!'

I went in to see what was going on, expecting to find her asleep or re-watching some favourite DVD. Instead I found her in the most enthusiastic organisational mood I'd ever encountered. She was arranging her books into categories and then shelving them in alphabetical order by author name. 'After I get this done,' she chirped, 'I'm gonna sort all my university notes into chronological order. I've still got all my textbooks . . . I can do the whole course over again!'

She wouldn't come in to eat, and stayed up all that night working on her project. The next day, when I told Katie what Anna had been up to, she confided her suspicion about what Anna's motivation had been in meeting up with Robert. Oh God, I groaned. I had to admit Katie was probably right. All Anna's efforts to stop drugs, and now she was back on ice. Was she going to ruin another Christmas?

As the effects of Robert's magic potion wore off, Anna grew too weary to pursue her room-tidying project. Now she couldn't even sleep in there, because the bed was buried in stuff. John was disgusted and disappointed. She was back to drinking and snoozing less than a week after leaving detox. Although, this time, there was a plan for rehab: it wouldn't be residential, or long term, but it was definitely better than nothing. ReGen, the organisation that ran Curran Place, had scheduled her for a six-week rehabilitation course called Catalyst, designed for people addicted to alcohol. It was to begin at the end of January. She was to attend this program five days a week, from nine in the morning till four in the afternoon. According to Catalyst's website, 'The core components of the program utilise Cognitive Behavioural Therapy and relapse prevention strategies to help participants identify and change unhelpful thinking.' Sounded good to me. Apparently she would also learn to cook! But first we had to get her through one more month.

John was desperate for her to restore some order to the shambles of her room, but she didn't want him helping her.

'I don't want you taking over and doing it all your way!' she fumed. So John suggested an idea: 'How about you get Jim over and just tell him where to put stuff?'

This plan actually worked. Jim was delighted to be invited to spend time with Anna. Day after day, he worked for hours helping Anna with Operation Bungalow. They had plenty of breaks to sit under the pine tree, drink coffee (Red Bull for her) and smoke. But then they would go back to converting the chaos to meticulous order. John and I got into the spirit and bought Anna a deluxe model Dymo labeller. A year later, when the bungalow had been silent and clean for many months, her shelves and drawers still bore their neatly printed labels. Make-up. Jewellery. G-strings and Bras.

One evening, after Jim had completed a day of sorting and stowing with Anna and had gone home, Robert from detox turned up. Great, now another addict knew our address. He didn't seem crazy like Lance. Rather than talk our ears off, he hardly said anything. But who knew what he might do if he grew desperate for his drug of choice? Who knew what mates he might bring around?

We were polite to him. John gave him a cup of tea and a Scotch Finger. But when Anna casually mentioned that he was going to spend the night with her in the freshly organised bungalow, John said no, he didn't think that was a good idea.

'What?' Anna spluttered. 'Can't I even decide for myself if I want to have a friend stay over?'

This exchange was unfolding in front of Robert, but rather than get up and excuse himself with dignity, he just sat there, looking from John to Anna as if to see who would win.

'Robert,' I addressed him directly, but I hope not unkindly, 'you'd better leave now.'

So he did. Anna was furious with me. 'You've really crossed the line this time,' she screeched. 'I'd go home with Robert but his dad says I'm not allowed at their house!'

She stormed out to her room. For half an hour or so I was too angry to care what damage she might be doing to herself out there, but eventually, of course, that morphed into concern and I went to check on her. She was sitting cross-legged on her bed with her laptop open in front of her. She looked at me and what I saw in her eyes seemed to be real hate. She snarled, 'My friends say it is majorly weird how you control me!'

And who might those friends be? Faces on a computer screen. People typing messages from across an ocean, who had never had to talk her out of breaking her bones with a baseball bat at 2 a.m., or spend a hundred dollars at Coles to try to make her happy with hair products, energy drinks, magazines and cigarettes. People who had never had to wash her sheets after she had pissed in her bed.

It all boiled up in my brain: the countless nights when she was a kid and I would sit beside her until she could fall asleep, when I had to get up early the next day to act like a fully focused assistant principal. The trips I'd taken her on, the pets I'd looked after for her. The guinea pig shit that I'd scraped off the kitchen floor on a sweaty summer morning, when I was still grieving over her leaving Andrew. What did all that count for? Nothing, it appeared. Bloody *nothing*. She hated me.

When she was three months old, I would hold her in my arms as she drank from my breast and gaze at her in wonder. I couldn't believe I'd been given such a beautiful baby. Now I stood in the doorway of her room and screamed at her, 'If your so-called friends are so fucking wonderful, why don't you go live with *them*?'

Chapter 36

The next morning Anna came into our room and said she was sorry for how she had spoken to me. She crawled into our bed for a cuddle. But John and I were both fed up with her. I knew we were in serious danger of not just threatening to kick her out on the street, but actually doing it. So that evening, while she drank herself stupid in the kitchen, we sat on our bed, propped up against the pillows, and came up with a plan. If she actually completed the six weeks of Catalyst, the non-residential rehab program she was scheduled to begin at the end of January, then we would let her stay, and when she finished we would help her find and maintain a place of her own. But if she bombed out of the program, if she couldn't manage to sober up and get herself there every day, then she was going to have to leave. As John put it, 'If all she's going to do with her life is drink and do drugs, she is going to travel that road without us.'

I didn't want to tell Anna about this plan at home with just John and me, or even with Katie there. We were all so emotionally fragile by that stage. Our decision, I was certain, would cause Anna to hurl accusations at us, and I didn't think we had the self-control to keep from screeching back at her. I thought it would be best to outline our proposal in the office of a professional, whose presence would keep us all calm, at least outwardly. The obvious choice would be Dr Deb, but ever since the day Deb gave Anna an honest opinion of her behaviour, Anna had refused to see her.

So I rang Charles, the drug and alcohol counsellor, and ran the idea past him. This was before I began to suspect he had encouraged, if not suggested, the idea that John and I had abused Anna as a child. I figured Anna would probably agree to see him, because she liked him a lot. Charles said okay, he'd go along with my wishes. Anna and I visited him together on the 11th of December, and though my heart was thumping, I kept my voice steady as I explained why I didn't feel we could allow her to live with us indefinitely. I'd written down our plan, so emotion wouldn't get in the way of me presenting it as simply and logically as possible. She'd need to go back to detox before the Catalyst program began, and Charles said he could arrange that. Then I got to the conditions: if Anna couldn't manage the nine-to-four routine of the program, over the six weeks, she would not be welcome to drink and smoke and sleep away her days at our house.

Charles looked at me with something like disdain in his eyes. He didn't say, 'Yes, you and John have done all you can for her.' He didn't say to Anna, 'You do need to start living your own life . . . or not. Your parents' plan sounds entirely reasonable.' Instead, he turned to Anna and asked her in a voice you might use with a delicate and damaged little girl, 'How does that make you feel, to have your mother threaten to kick you out?'

'Terrified!'

Looking back now at our meeting in that office on a warm December day, I want to cry. I am so sorry my daughter was terrified. I see that she was indeed delicate and damaged. But so were John and I.

This was two weeks before Christmas.

During all the years when our girls were babies, then children and teenagers, and then willowy young adults, on the 1st of December, John had set up our tree in the corner of the lounge room. It was the same spruce, in a succession of larger and larger pots, which grew taller as our daughters did. That room used to spring to life with the scent of the living tree and the fairy lights and our growing array of beautiful ornaments. From the tree, among the dozens of baubles and handcrafted silver icicles hung a little glowing, golden church that I'd brought home from a trip to Iowa. Across the mantelpiece marched the collectible ornaments, angels and shepherds and cherubs, each engraved with the year that my sister Joan sent them across the sea, to the nieces she rarely saw but never forgot.

My favourite ornament was an angel Anna made in grade 4. Its body, created from a cardboard cone, listed to one side. Its gauze gown didn't fit properly and its wings were different sizes. But it had so much character it looked like it was about to speak. Every year when I unpacked it, I was amazed by the expression on its styrofoam face. How could Anna have conveyed that much personality with a few strokes of a permanent marker?

In former years, when the lounge room was set up, we'd celebrate nearly every Friday and Saturday of December, inviting friends and neighbours for drinks, barbies and present exchanges. Not any more. This was the third year of no parties. The ornaments that used to mean so much to us stayed packed in their cardboard boxes, on the high shelves of the spare room closet, above the steel box from Bunnings. The spruce was just another outdoor pot plant. Anna's disease had pulled the plug on any twinkling lights at our house.

The previous year, in the hours before Anna ran off to be with Lance, we'd at least had a low-key Christmas lunch with her, Katie and Tom. Now John said he couldn't face even that, and I agreed. We had reached compassion fatigue with Anna's brand of celebrating: first she'd be smoochy, then nasty, then comatose.

A couple of days before Christmas, listening to the local ABC radio station in the shower, I heard there would be a free brekkie at Fed Square for anyone who needed it. On the morning of the 25th, Katie was with Tom's family in the country and Anna was in a virtual coma, after being up for three days and nights in her mania of cleaning, arranging and organising. So, praying our girl would still be breathing when we returned, John and I headed off on the train to the city.

It was a perfect summer morning, the air just cool enough to make the sun a welcome gift. We held hands as we crossed Flinders Street to bells pealing from St Paul's Cathedral. I'd expected a crowd in Fed Square, a queue of homeless people eager for a free feed. But there were just a scattered few of us. Only one or two guys looked a little scruffy. Mainly there were couples and young families, well dressed, quietly speaking a variety of languages. Were they a little subdued and sad? Missing their families or places of origin? I thought so.

There were long tables set up, tended by smiling volunteers in Santa hats. We took an orange each, a bottle of water and a bacon and tomato roll. There were also croissants that looked fresh and delicious. 'Want to share one?' I asked John.

'You can have one each!' a young volunteer chirped. She was around Anna's age and was so pretty, so alive and healthy. She really wanted us to have our own croissant.

We sat on a sun-warmed step. My grief felt like a jagged, frozen object in my chest. Twenty-six Christmases earlier, I held a perfect blue-eyed baby in my arms, and loved her so much it was terrifying. I'm glad I couldn't know then what 2014 would bring to us. The nights of screaming and pleading, begging her to choose life. The locking up of knives. The frantic calls to police, the ambulance rides to psych wards.

I pulled my mind away from that and accepted a mince tart from a smiling older woman proffering a wicker basket. I watched a tiny Asian girl in a new dress twirl in the morning light. And I felt one of my own addictions clamouring: I needed caffeine.

'Excuse me?' The Asian man sitting to our left, most likely the father of the little girl, was speaking to me. He gestured towards the next level of the square. 'They're serving coffee upstairs.'

'You must have read my mind!' I responded.

'It was speaking very loudly,' he replied in a serious tone.

That made me smile.

Over the years since then, when we've had to make decisions I never could have imagined we would need to consider, I've often thought of that Christmas morning. It shines in my mind, a little warm splash of quiet goodness. It's made me love Melbourne, my adopted home, more than ever.

Christmases are still hard for us. For a different reason now: our quirky little girl who made the wonky angel can't celebrate with us. Lately, Katie and I have been wondering if we might start a different holiday tradition, and join the volunteers who dish out comfort not only to the homeless and the homesick, but also to the broken-hearted.

Chapter 37

It was the beginning of 2015. Anna was scheduled to go back to Curran Place on Monday the 19th of January for her third stint of detox. The plan was to spend a week there, then start the Catalyst program on Tuesday the 27th, just after Australia Day. As I read through my journal entries on those first two weeks of January, I see that I was still ringing Odyssey House. This had been a major project of mine, trying to get Anna into their eighteen-month residential rehab program, designed to help people addicted to drugs. I'd cajoled her over to the Odyssey House headquarters in Richmond on several occasions for information sessions and interviews. But in order for her to be accepted for the program, she had to prove that she herself wanted a substance-free life.

The residential program sounded so good to me that I could taste my longing for Anna to do it, after she completed the six weeks at Catalyst. Eighteen months of learning life skills would give her excellent preparation to leave home and get her own place. John and I wouldn't mind helping her with that. If only she would become sober, and employable, and nice to us. Now, I look back at the person I was just three years ago and shake my head. *Mary, you're dreaming. Your girl is far from being capable of any of that.* The staff at Odyssey House had already figured that out. After I'd rung them perhaps a dozen times to see if Anna had made the waiting list, they finally told me they'd decided her mental health problems were too tricky for them to handle.

But at the time I wanted to believe that, somehow, Anna might be helped down a path to normal adulthood. She was still able to behave well if she really wanted to: she was good in the days between Christmas and New Year when Charlotte was staying with us. I have some nice photos of the 'cubby-house' they built together, behind the silky oak in one of the secluded spots in our sprawling backyard, that nearly unmanageable piece of suburbia that was a kids' paradise.

But then, on the 2nd of January, John and I returned home from an afternoon stroll along Southbank, and found Robert in the bungalow with Anna. He left without any fuss around midnight. But something kept me from getting to sleep. I went to check in on her at 1 a.m. and found her lying on the floor of her room with her head wedged between the bed and the corner shelves. Thankfully I was able to wake her and help her into bed. A couple of days later, Dan arrived to take her to his place for the weekend. John and I thought this was a pretty bad idea, since last time she visited Dan she ended up in a coma on his kitchen floor, but I had it on good authority, Victoria Police to be specific, we could not lawfully keep our daughter at home by force.

This time, we didn't have to go to Dan's place and scrape her off the floor. Dan dropped her back home at ten o'clock on Monday night, and, according to my journal, 'She was a complete, crazy, nasty *mess*. John wouldn't leave Anna alone in case she did "something stupid", so she yelled at him and he called her a piece of shit, off and on until 3 a.m.' This was really unusual behaviour on John's part. He was often impatient with me, and less often with Katie, but all Anna's life he had treated her like a special gift, an especially breakable one, that he had to handle very carefully to protect. Now something in him had broken.

A heart can break in a single moment. My mother's did, in the second that it took my dad to tell her why the phone had rung at two in the morning: her beloved mama was dead. But hearts can also break a little bit at a time over months and years.

By January 15th that year, our hearts had just about had it. If only we could have made it through to the holiday of detox – the sweet respite of just a few days off – things might have turned out differently. But Robert came back for more visits, and we're pretty sure he brought the worst refreshment with him. Ice. What a lovely, silvery kind of name for a truly evil drug. Synthetic weed made Anna paranoid; her mishmash of prescription meds made her cranky and comatose, but ice made her mean.

On midnight between Thursday the 15th and Friday the 16th, three days before Anna was due to go to detox, my phone rang. It was Katie, crying. 'I'm sorry I woke you up,' she sobbed, 'but Anna just called me. I've never heard her sound so crazy! It's not fair she says those things about you! I told her I didn't want to listen to her bitch about you but she yelled at me in this really scary voice. She said, "Katie, listen to me! Mum's not who you think she is! She pretends to be this nice, sweet person but she's turned into someone *else*. And Dad has, too. You don't see the things they do to me!"'

At the time, I didn't take a lot of notice of what Anna had said about us. I was annoyed at getting jarred awake by what didn't seem like big news. After all, Anna had been railing against our 'life-destroying' parenting for months. Much later, I would listen to the voice recording Katie made soon after that call, in which she recalled as many details as she could about the conversation. Then I realised that the depth of Anna's delusions about John and me were truly chilling.

The day after the call, Anna's main accomplishment was to stock up on cigarettes for detox. Mind you, she didn't even do that on her own. I drove her to Glenroy and she spent $105 at the little shop where they sold cheap smokes in branded packets, even though the law requiring plain packaging had been around for some time. Yes, I guess I was still enabling her. I should have discouraged her from making friends at detox, instead of aiding and abetting her procurement of the legal drug she could distribute for momentary popularity. And since I'm confessing my sins here, I admit I also took her to Coles and bought several bags of mini KitKats and Snickers bars for her to share at her special summer camp. I just wanted her to get there, and if cigarettes and chocolate would help, then I would make sure she had them.

That evening, Friday the 16th, Robert was back at our place. Since the night that John and I had made it clear Robert wasn't welcome to spend the night at our house, he had always left by about midnight. But on this particular evening, around ten o'clock, Anna came into the house from the backyard and announced that Robert was staying over; even though she'd asked about this earlier, and John had said no. Now he said no again, louder and more firmly. 'Can't you get it through your head we don't want him here?' he asked her.

Anna marched out, then after a few minutes reappeared in the kitchen. 'I'm going on the train with him to make sure he gets home safe,' she announced. Then, because she was not allowed inside his parents' house, she would get the train back.

'I'm going to talk with him,' I said. What sort of man would allow a young woman to escort him home, then travel back alone on a train in the middle of the night? Before I could make it out the back door, she got there first and, facing me, blocked my way. 'Don't you go near my boyfriend!' she hissed.

'Bloody hell,' I responded. 'He's your boyfriend now, is he?'

I tried to push past her; she grabbed my arm, using the force she'd come by when she had choked her father. John was beside me now. 'Don't you touch your mother,' he commanded.

She dropped my arm, turned to him, and uttered four words. Later, John repeated those words to me many times, reliving the moment when he understood he should be afraid of his own daughter. In the voice that made her sound like Regan from *The Exorcist*, she growled, carefully emphasising each syllable, 'I'll. Fuck. You. Up.'

She bolted out the back door, and went off into the night with Robert. About an hour later she called me. She said they'd missed the train they'd been aiming to catch, and, somehow, the one after that as well. 'I'm going to sleep on the street with Robert.'

Good grief. I said to John, 'Can't they just spend this one night here?' I so wanted to get her through to Monday morning, when we could drive her down Banksia Street towards detox.

John wasn't happy about it, but he agreed.

The next day, around midday, Anna and Robert were in the backyard smoking. I went out to tell them John and I were heading off to the city for a walk in the Botanic Gardens. Robert said he would be leaving soon, as his dad was expecting him home for a family barbie.

When something bad happens, you look back and question every move. Would it have made a difference, if we hadn't left her that day? If we'd hung around in the murk of our home instead of indulging in a summer afternoon of peaceful green lawns graced with swans, and world-class scones beside the lake?

At about 3.30, Anna sent me a text: 'I'm out and about. Call me if you're worried.' Of course I was worried. What had given her the courage to be 'out and about'? I did call her, twice, and also texted her. No response. As always, I had taken the precaution of entering the number of her current so-called boyfriend into my contacts. I texted Robert, and later he called me. 'She walked me over to the bus stop near the golf course and I left her there,' he told me.

'When was that?'

'Around three o'clock.'

I tried to reach her a few more times, but her phone went straight to voicemail. Finally, at about eight o'clock that evening, when John and I had been back for a couple of hours, my phone rang and the name 'Anna' appeared on my screen. But it wasn't Anna's voice I heard. It was a very angry, unfamiliar woman. 'Do you realise,' she shouted, 'that your daughter is covered from head to foot in bruises?'

Well, I could have said, I think it's an exaggeration to say she's covered from head to foot, but I do know she has plenty of bruises from bumping into things and falling over drunk. Instead I asked, 'Who is this?'

She wouldn't say. 'I've never seen such bruises on a person's thighs!' she bellowed. 'And she has rope burns on her arms and legs from being tied up and tortured. I'm taking her to the police.'

I tried to keep my voice calm. 'Please do that,' I said. 'Take her to the police. She's mentally ill and delusional and she needs help.'

'That's what people always do. They always deny it!'

At that point, I put the phone on speaker, so John heard the worst of the accusations against me, and especially him. I don't want to commit these to writing. They were so vile, and utterly untrue, that I didn't even bother to try to refute them as the woman continued her diatribe. She screeched, 'You're an arse of a mother!' Then she hung up. John said, 'That's it. Anna's not coming back here.'

What did I feel then? That I should fight for my little girl's right to come back home? No. What I felt was incalculable relief. I don't think I could have kicked her out myself, not permanently. But I knew that when John used that tone of voice, with that look on his face, there was no one in the world who could make him change his mind. And I was grateful.

Not long before that night, Anna had told me that I'd crossed the line. Now she had done that. By denigrating and threatening us, by manipulating us into admitting a person into our home whom we didn't trust, by going out and finding people on the street who would call us and level unspeakable accusations at us, she had finally made herself unwelcome. We banned her from the place where she was conceived, where she'd squirmed and swam for the first oblivious nine months of her life, where she'd returned six days after she was born, to a mother, father and sister who could not have loved her more.

Chapter 38

I didn't try to get hold of Anna again that night. I rang the police to report the call from the unknown woman, and to say that we were feeling unsafe. At two in the morning John's phone rang. Since I was lying next to him, I could clearly hear Anna's voice. Usually she spoke irritatingly softly and slowly, but now she was fast and loud. 'Dad! I'm in an emergency situation!' She didn't sound scared. She sounded angry. 'Send $200 to my account, *now*!'

John hung up. He wouldn't speak to Anna again for over a year.

My phone rang. 'What's wrong?' I asked her. 'If you're in an emergency, ring triple 0.'

'I owe people money!' she yelled. 'If I don't pay them, they're gonna stab me or bash me!'

'Ring the police,' I said.

'Muuuuuum!'

I hung up, rang triple 0 and was put through to the local police station. A senior constable told me they couldn't trace Anna's call to find out where she was. When I said we were feeling unsafe since our daughter was associating with people who sounded like criminals, and no doubt knew our address, the constable informed me that there was nothing they could do unless someone actually showed up at our house.

Thankfully, no one did show up, including Anna. We didn't

hear from her until the following evening, Sunday, when my phone rang announcing 'Private Number'.

Anna's harried voice said, 'I only have 50 cents, but Mum, listen to me for *once*! You and Dad be on alert!' The line went dead. That freaked me out, but John and a prayer calmed me down.

I see now that in her addled way, with that little phone call she was trying to protect us. But I was too hurt to think that way then, and too disappointed. The next day, Monday the 19th, was when Anna was scheduled to go to detox. Instead of driving her to Curran Place to begin a more productive and independent phase of her life, I rang and told the intake nurse that it was highly unlikely Anna would be turning up there.

I was able to relate this information calmly. For the first time in Anna's life, I wasn't frantic with worry when she was missing. Something in me had changed. This hadn't happened instantly. It felt like a force had been welling up inside me since we returned from the Gold Coast. It felt like the small, fierce light burning in my heart as a child, which had made me feel guilty for not wanting to believe our preacher in that little country church beside the cornfield when he shouted at us that this life we were living now meant nothing. That force, that light, still dragged guilt along behind it. But it also brought joy, and the joy had become stronger than the guilt. It proclaimed, it shouted: I want to live! Maybe she doesn't want to, but I do! No matter what happens to her. I want to savour the coffee at Chew Chew, and squish a cumquat from our tree between my fingers because it smells like citrus from heaven, and walk beside the creek with John, looking forward to a glass of wine with him on our front deck afterwards. This voice of light reminded me how blessed I was, to have made it into my sixties with my health pretty much intact. So many good people I knew hadn't made it this far. There was our sweet and funny brother-in-law, Brian, who left our girls money for international travel. And his wife, Wilma, who was so in love with her man that she didn't see the point in living without him. There was my friend Roslyn, a quiet but fervent believer in God, who died of breast cancer when her boys and my girls were still in primary school. And especially there was Rhita, the beloved soulmate of my childhood years, my cousin who lived a mile up the gravel road from our farm, the one whose fragile blondeness I had envied. One summer night when she was in her early fifties, her partner stubbed a cigarette on the wooden deck at the front of their mobile home. But the butt was not squashed well enough, it kept on burning, right into the wood, which smouldered through the night. There must have been no functioning smoke alarm. My cousin and her man were finally woken up by the terrible heat of flames that had engulfed the front of the trailer. The back door was blocked off by furniture. They covered their heads with wet towels and tried to jerk aside the dresser or bookshelf or whatever it was, but they were too late.

The life-force voice demanded that I remember them: Brian and Wilma and Roslyn and Rhita. You've been granted these extra years, it said, let's bloody well appreciate them. And by the way, you know that aphorism you're so fond of toting around in your head, 'A mother can only be as happy as her least happy child'? Well, I have to tell you, I hate that saying. I have decided that particular piece of wisdom is total crap.

This doesn't mean I stopped loving Anna, or caring for her. I knew if something happened to her, I would grieve deeply.

But, somehow, I no longer felt that my life would have to end. So that's how, on the Monday afternoon when Anna was supposed to have gone to detox, I could go to the movies when I still didn't know where she was.

John was off at the Australian Open, watching what was happening at the outer courts on the first day of play. I went to the Nova with my pals, Margie and Marcelle. The film was *Birdman*. I switched my phone to silent, but left it on vibrate in my lap. Even though I no longer felt that Anna held my life hostage, I didn't want to make myself unavailable for communication. Halfway through the film, my phone shivered and lit up with an unfamiliar number. I ducked out to the corridor to answer: it was a nurse at the Sunshine Hospital. 'Your daughter is here,' she told me. 'She was brought in earlier today by the police. She's in the emergency department if you'd like to come in and see her.'

'Is she okay?' I asked.

'She seems to be fine physically,' the nurse demurred.

I texted Marcelle, who was still inside the cinema with her phone on her lap, to say I was heading to the hospital. I respected John's decision not to see or speak to the daughter he had adored since he first held his hand flat against my swelling belly and felt her move. But I still wanted to see her, to touch her, to do what I could for her, even though I was determined not to even consider trying to talk John into letting her come back home.

Marcelle and Margie both came out of the cinema and went with me to the hospital. Gestures like that – when my friends walked beside me without being asked, when they never judged my daughter but just kept on loving her – meant more to me than words could say.

At the entrance of the emergency department, the nurse looking after Anna came out and introduced himself to us. 'I'm Greg,' he said. 'I wanted to let you know Anna's pretty bad. She thinks I'm a plant.' Into my head popped an image of a large potted palm. Jeepers, she had really gone off the deep end this time.

Greg said it would be better if Marcelle and Margie waited near the entrance until after I'd seen Anna. He led me down a row of curtained cubicles to where Anna lay in a hospital gown, flat on her back on a bed, being held down by thick velcro straps around her wrists and ankles. She strained against them. 'Get these off me!' she demanded.

'Are you gonna be good now your mum's here?' Greg asked her. 'You won't try to jump off the bed?'

'Okay!' she said crossly.

'Promise?'

'Yes!'

Two nurses were summoned to stand on either side of the bed while Greg loosened Anna's restraints. When they were satisfied she wasn't going to bolt, they left us alone. But they'd said not to draw the curtain across, so the cubicle was open to the ward, and we could still see all the bustle of nurses and aids.

'Why are you in a hospital gown?' I asked her.

She didn't answer, or even seem to take in what I'd said. She was looking around, scared and anxious. 'There's one,' she told me in a hoarse, urgent whisper, pointing towards a maintenance guy fixing a light.

'One what?' I inquired.

'Shush! Don't let them hear you. They followed me in here!'

'Who?'

'The gang who are after me! They're pretending they work here.'

So that's what Greg meant when he said she thought he was a plant. That day, Anna was more psychotic than I'd ever seen her before. As far as I know she only smoked ice a few times, but later she admitted to me she'd binged on it that weekend. I didn't need to know that to see that something had tipped her over into la-la land.

She gestured around the bed, indicating the array of medical equipment that stood at the ready to monitor, measure and alert. 'They're watching me with all that,' she informed me in a tiny voice. She was a caricature of a crazy person, somebody you might guiltily chuckle at in, say, an episode of *Father Ted*.

I found this kind of fascinating. 'Is she one?' I asked of a nurse passing by.

'No, but she is.' She nodded towards a different nurse, dressed in the same hospital uniform.

I didn't find it entertaining, however, when she told me the people who demanded the $200, which we refused to hand over, had stolen her phone and wallet.

'At least you've got your glasses,' I said.

John and I had replaced these several times over the last couple of years, at $400 a pop. The last time was barely two months earlier, when Anna had promised she'd be good for Katie's birthday dinner at The Retreat Hotel in Brunswick. Actually, she didn't cause a scene as we had feared she might; she began the night sitting beside me on a bench seat, and before long put her head in my lap and quietly passed out. So I was able to converse with Katie's lovely friends while stroking Anna's hair. A couple of hours later, one of those friends helped me wrangle Anna to the car. She wasn't comatose, so we were able to persuade her to walk, with one of us on either side of her for support. Anna said she needed the toilet, but we didn't quite manage to get her onto the toilet seat in time. She pissed on the floor, then slipped in it and smashed her glasses. Like me, she was severely short-sighted, with astigmatism in one eye, so she relied on them to see clearly.

After a while, Greg said it would be okay for Margie and Marcelle to spend some time with Anna. He wanted to speak to me alone. So he and I went off to a far corner of the emergency department.

I was hoping that Anna's stolen phone and wallet were a part of her fantasy, that Greg would tell me they were safely tucked away under the counter in the nurses' station. But no, Greg said that when the police picked up Anna, at a service station in Footscray, she'd had nothing with her. She wasn't even wearing clothes.

'What?' I gasped. 'Why not?'

Apparently she'd been afraid to contact the police herself, because she believed that members of the gang who were out to get her would hurt her, or worse, if she tried doing that. If only someone would ring the police on her behalf . . . so she hatched a plan. She walked into a service station on a major road, fully clothed, and politely asked the young guy behind the counter if she could use the restroom. When she emerged, she was naked, and proceeded to stand by the entrance, where customers coming in would clearly see her.

I shook my head while my brain attempted to process this. In a nearby cubicle a woman screamed, savagely cursing the nurses who were trying to help her.

'Ice,' Greg sighed.

Then he said the magic words, 'We're going to admit Anna to the psychiatric ward, under the Mental Health Act.'

Thank God. It took her standing naked in a servo. It took her believing that maintenance men and nurses wanted to kill her, and evil gangs were spying on her through IV poles and heart monitors – but at last the system had agreed to keep her. I explained to Greg that once she was released she would still need help, because she could not come back to live with us. He said he understood.

When I returned to the cubicle to kiss Anna goodbye, she clung to me. 'Muuum!' she screamed as I extracted myself and walked away. 'Don't leave me here!' Of course it was hard to hear that, but I was so glad I could walk away and know that her gigantic, sticky needs would be met by someone else.

That night, I cancelled Anna's bank card and phone number and reported her learner's licence lost. There wasn't much I could do about the door key she'd had in her bag, except maybe get the locks changed. Meanwhile, John and I rejoiced, with Katie joining in by speaker phone . . . finally, *finally*, she was in a locked psych ward!

Anna was not nearly as thrilled as we were about this. She was desperate to get out of there. She soon stabilised in the psych ward, but she was still highly suspicious of the staff, and she couldn't smoke in there. I dreaded the moment when I'd have to tell her she wouldn't be coming home. But I knew I had to do it. I thought John was right when he said she would be much more likely to get help from the system if we stepped out of the picture. And this turned out to be true. A doctor spoke to me at the hospital and told me the mental health team had worked out a 'tiered approach' for Anna's care. Once she left the locked ward she'd be in the voluntary ward for a while, then she'd go to PARC, a short-term residential facility for the mentally ill. After that they would try to find her housing with 'a high degree of support'.

That sounded wonderful. With a plan in place, I just wanted to get the eviction notice over with and move on to a future that looked lit with clear colours instead of the sludge of grey we'd been plodding through. Anna didn't seem as surprised as I'd anticipated by my announcement. Maybe someone on the staff had warned her? Or perhaps some part of her knew that this 'abandonment' would come one day.

Not long after I'd spoken to the doctor about the 'tiered approach', Anna rang me. She'd been transferred to the voluntary inpatient part of the psych ward, and she wasn't staying. Jim was coming to get her and she was going to live with him.

'You're kidding!' I spluttered. Jim lived in Craigieburn, an outer northern suburb. I'd never been to his house, but I'd worked in Craigieburn for a term as the acting assistant principal of the secondary college. I remembered it as flat and dull, a suburb where young families could afford the relatively cheap houses but had to commute to somewhere else for work or fun. 'You need to stay where you are!' I said to Anna. 'They've got a plan worked out for you to get some life skills and a job. You can't just —'

'Mum!' she interrupted me forcefully, 'If you're kicking me out, you don't have any right to tell me what to do any more!'

I was numb with disappointment. How could she do that again and again – throw away her future as though it was as disposable as a used tissue?

I rang Jim and more or less begged him not to take her away from the psych ward. But he didn't care for my line of reasoning. 'She doesn't need to be there,' he informed me.

He then repeated something he'd said before: 'What she needs is a good man for once in her life, a man who understands her.'

'A good man for once'. So what did that make John, who'd fashioned flashcards for her when she was five years old and practised with her for hours when she was having trouble learning to read, who soothed her and cooked her eggs on toast after we arrived home on the night that she was refused entry to the psych ward at the Northern Hospital and I was too distraught to function? What did that make Andrew, who'd walked hand in hand with her around Loch Ness, sang 'My Lovely Horse' with her, and bought a little house for them to live in? And how about Billy the plumber, a hard worker who didn't complain about driving over from Point Cook to fetch Anna for the weekend? Was he not a good man?

'It's taken me a long time to get myself a nice house,' Jim said. 'There's plenty of room for Anna. I'm giving her a chance.'

With that he hung up, and for several days didn't answer my calls. He came by with Anna on the way back from the psych ward, to collect some of her stuff from the bungalow. John refused to speak to either of them and told me to warn them they'd better take all they needed that afternoon, because he didn't want them on the property again.

So off Anna went, with armloads of clothes and washing baskets full of make-up, DVDs and PlayStation games, to, as I put it in my journal, 'rot in Craigieburn instead of the bungalow'.

Katie was furious with Jim for removing Anna from a place we'd longed for her to be. And it took him a comically short amount of time to regret that he'd done it. Five days after picking up her stuff, he showed up at our place at six in the evening. Katie was there, but John was out. I reminded Jim that John didn't want him there, but he said he really needed to talk with us about Anna.

'You'd better make it quick,' I told him. We went to the backyard and sat under the young jacaranda that Poppy liked to climb. Katie glared at Jim as he lit up a smoke. His fingers shook as he told us, 'Anna was fine when I left for work in the morning. She called me about one o'clock and said, "Why didn't you tell me you have security cameras in the house?" And she's taken my steel baton. I don't know what she's done with it. I ordered that from America and I used it when I was a security guard. She could do some real damage with that!'

Katie let him have it then. 'You had no right to interfere with our family!' She continued, icily articulate, using the skills learned as a champion high school debater. I didn't record the exact content of her speech, but I remember how she ended it. 'You took her out of the psych ward against our wishes, so now *you deal with her*!'

Katie marched off into the house and Jim slunk out to his car. That night, around 7.30, Anna rang me on the phone Jim had given her. She sounded terrified. 'I don't know where I am!' I could hear a lot of voices in the background and announcements from a loudspeaker.

'It sounds like you're at a train station, a big one. Which one?'

'I don't know,' she answered miserably.

'Well, ask somebody!'

I could hear her do that. It was Flinders Street.

'I don't know how to get home.' Her voice was so small and scared. She was my little girl again. I needed to jump on the train and go to her, wrap her up in my arms and bring her back to safety. But I couldn't.

'Go to a PSO, one of those people in the fluoro vests. They'll help you.'

She promised she would look for one.

Later that evening Jim called me and said, 'Anna's back with me. It's all good. I forgot I put that baton in my boot.'

For the next few weeks, both he and Anna refused to have anything to do with me or Katie. I received a letter from Centrelink informing me that I would no longer be receiving copies of her correspondence. She'd sacked me as her carer. I called the number of the phone Jim had given her, but she never answered it or responded to my texts. But I knew she was okay, because of Caroline.

Back when I was working through the brochures in my Saving Anna binders, I'd contacted PHaMs – Personal Helpers and Mentors service. Their website stated that their purpose was to 'assist people aged sixteen years and over whose ability to manage their daily activities and to live independently in the community is impacted because of a severe mental illness'. I filled out an application for a helper, and Anna signed it. A couple of months later Anna was assessed and several months after that, just before we could no longer have her at home, thank goodness she was deemed mentally ill enough to qualify for a helper. This turned out to be Caro. 'Isn't she *cute*?' Anna had gushed on the way home from our first meeting with her. Caro was in her late twenties, a compact dynamo with hair that was dark brown and softly curled around her smart but infinitely caring face. She seemed to love Anna instantly, and worked so hard for her. I'm pretty sure she put in many more hours than she was paid for. When Anna and

Jim wouldn't communicate with me, Caro could at least let me know my daughter was alive, though confidentiality rules prevented her from saying too much.

A couple of weeks after Katie fired those home truths at Jim, Robert rang me. I hadn't expected to hear from him again. He was the guy from detox who we suspected gave Anna ice and who she insisted we permit to stay over on what turned out to be her last night at home. He sounded sober. 'I thought you'd want to know that I've spoken to Anna. She's in the Broadmeadows psych ward. She didn't want you to know, but I thought you'd be worried.'

Broady had a psych ward? I thanked him for telling me. A quick Google search showed me that the Broadmeadows psychiatric facility was at the back of what was now called the Dianella health centre, where I had taken Anna to see Dr Deb so many times for her anorexia. I rang the facility but, of course, without Anna's permission, they weren't allowed to tell me anything.

The next day Katie got a call from the psych facility: they'd allowed Anna to call her. 'Can you come and pick me up?' Anna asked. Apparently she wasn't keen on living with Jim any more, and Katie had told her she was always welcome to stay with her. But Katie and Tom were now living on a property his mother owned, a picturesque little spot on a billabong near Wangaratta. They were beginning their experiment with ethical farming, a project they were both passionate about, while Katie launched her career as a freelance journalist.

'You can come up here and stay,' Katie told Anna, 'as long as you fit in with our rules. But you'll have to get yourself up here. I can pick you up from the station in Wang.'

Anna seemed surprised and miffed that Katie didn't want to make the six-hour round trip to scoop her up from the psych ward. She handed the phone to a nurse who spoke to Katie for a while. Something the nurse asked Katie upset her a lot. Katie would repeat the nurse's question to me many times over the coming years. For her it encapsulated how so many professionals, though well meaning, seemed unable to comprehend the seriousness of our situation. 'Why can't Anna go home with your parents?' the nurse asked Katie. 'She's such a lovely girl.'

Even now, when Katie recalls this nurse's response, you can hear the hurt in her voice and her need to protect John and me. 'I said to that nurse, "With all due respect, do you think my parents would have kicked my sister out if they hadn't done *every single thing* they could think of to help her?"'

My journal says that the question, which Katie related to me straight after she had spoken to the nurse, 'threw me into a bit of a state. I calmed myself down with this thought: she's either going to die or begin to live. Out in the bungalow in a coma, the second choice was never going to happen. The nurse Katie spoke to said they'd keep her one more night, then arrange emergency accommodation.'

The morning after Anna was supposed to be in emergency accommodation, I wrote: 'Had almond meal porridge and read the second chapter of *Sapiens: A Brief History of Humankind* by Yuval Noah Harari. Made me feel smart! Don't know where Anna slept last night . . . she doesn't answer the phone when I ring.'

The next day I was pleased when she deigned to answer a phone call from Marcelle. 'Marcelle was here and we had coffee on the deck. She called Anna and Anna answered!

Apparently she sounded alert, at 11.30 a.m. Wouldn't say where she was.'

On Saturday night my phone rang. Another unfamiliar number. 'Mum, please visit me!' It was Anna, sounding extremely distressed. A nurse came on the line. Anna was at the Northern Hospital emergency department. The nurse was not allowed to say why, but she did tell me they were transferring Anna by ambulance to the Broadmeadows psychiatric facility. She had lasted in emergency accommodation, which I later learned meant a boarding house, for three nights.

Charlotte was with us that weekend, so she and I went to see Anna the next day in the psych ward. My journal states: 'I had thought Anna missed me. Turns out she wanted a cigarette-and-cash dispenser . . . oh, and "two large, cold Red Bulls". Charlotte and Anna played "Guess Who?" while I dutifully took myself over to the Broadmeadows shopping centre and fetched the required items.'

John was away camping that week. On Tuesday evening, after several hours of tutoring, I drove my usual route down Johnstone Street, which meant I went right past the psych ward. I thought I'd stop to see Anna, have a peaceful chat, maybe play a round of 'Guess Who?'.

When I got there, a nurse heading out the door at the end of her shift stopped to talk to me. She told me that she'd got to know Anna after caring for her during this and her previous admission period. In her opinion, Anna needed to remain in the facility for several weeks. 'She needs time to stabilise, and I intend to do all I can to make sure that happens.' My soul lit up with hope. Then I was buzzed into the ward and found Anna in despair. To my surprise, she agreed with the nurse I'd just spoken to: she wanted to stay where she was.

But apparently the guy in charge of making this decision was not of the same opinion. 'He yelled at me when I said I needed to be here longer. He said, "You're not staying here just because you want to! Either you go to Jim's place or we're sending you back to the boarding house."'

Jim. When she uttered his name, Anna must have gestured towards the courtyard, because I looked in that direction and there he was, sitting on a bench, smoking. He saw me, stubbed out his cigarette and wandered in. I can't remember much of what we said to each other, but I do recall him announcing that he would be taking Anna home because he was a man who didn't shirk his responsibilities. 'She's my partner and I'm standing by her.'

Her partner?

I approached the nurse in charge of the night shift and told her I agreed with the nurse who'd said Anna should be there for several weeks. I outlined a few of the more compelling reasons.

This nurse looked at me in a manner to which I had become familiar: she was tired, irritated, wishing I would shut up and get out of her sight. 'If you're so concerned about your daughter,' she inquired, 'why don't you take her home with you?'

I couldn't sleep that night. The events of the evening had brought to life other evenings and they clanged around in my head, voices like jagged pieces of metal biting into my brain.

She belongs in the psych ward.

No, she has to go!

She's my partner and I, for one, won't give up on her.

Why won't you take her home?

Why can't you care for her, you selfish arse of a mother?

Towards dawn I managed to drift off. Later, as I woke up, other voices crept into my head. One was my psychologist, repeating what she'd told me at our last session: 'You've done everything humanly possible for that girl . . . and then some.' Another voice was John's, from a dinner conversation we'd had before he went camping: 'You have to stop trying to fix her. The more you try, the worse she gets. You'll just end up killing yourself.'

That morning, I realised that my psychologist and John and my lovely pals at Al-Anon and the mothers in my online support group were right. I'd already decided I wanted to live. Now I had to stop attempting to micromanage my daughter's future. I had to find a way, as they say in Al-Anon, to detach with love.

Chapter 39

Down in the back corner of the Baptist church in Moonee Ponds, in the meeting room where I used to attend Al-Anon, there is a plaque that appears handmade. It's the centrepiece of the table in the middle of the room, where the brochures are displayed during Al-Anon gatherings. It's a ceramic rectangle and someone has glued multicoloured sequins on to it, to spell out 'HOPE'. This word is also emphasised in my online group. Never give up hope, the women say to support other mothers whose precious children have been lost for years to some drug, usually an opiate.

I mean absolutely no disrespect to these fine and harried mums when I say that I have come to deeply dislike hope, at least for a specific outcome. The day after my visit to the Broadmeadows psych facility, which began with me wanting to hang out with Anna and ended with my head in a mess, Caro rang. Our angel from PHaMs. She told me that she and a doctor at Broadie had come up with a plan: Anna would go home with Jim that night, but by the end of the next week they thought they could get her into PARC, the residential mental health facility. This was the place we'd been so happy to hear about, when the doctor at Sunshine Hospital had told us she'd be going there. A second chance! Hope bounded around in my chest like an excited toddler.

PARC did indeed approve her stay, and Caro dropped her

off there the following Friday morning. At last Anna would get some help with her poor, battered mind, for more than just a few days. Later that same day, in the afternoon, Caro rang me. She sounded sad. 'They didn't let her stay,' she told me.

'Why?'

'Because they said she was hoarding drugs.'

'What drugs?'

Caro couldn't tell me much. 'It wasn't anything illegal. It was medication she'd been prescribed. But she should have handed it in to them.'

'So what happens now? Will they give her another chance?'

'It doesn't sound like it. Jim came and picked her up. She's back at his place.'

Blood pounded in my temples, like it was trying to push my eyes out of their sockets. I wanted to scream, 'What kind of health system is this? They won't take her at Odyssey House because she's too crazy, and now they've kicked her out of a mental health unit because she's a drug addict!'

Months later, I asked Anna what happened on that day. 'Did they really kick you out for hoarding drugs you'd been prescribed?'

'Yes.'

'Did they search your backpack?' I'd visualised a mish-mash of pills stuffed into a plastic bag, as I knew that to be one of Anna's usual ways of organising her things. But no, she'd employed a different method.

'I didn't really think it through,' she told me. 'I just suddenly thought when I was waiting to go in that they probably wouldn't let me have all the Seroquel and Valium I needed, so I shoved what I had into my underpants. When the nurse came out and walked me to my room, the pills started falling out on the floor.'

That image makes me chuckle now, but the laugh is wrapped around a hard little ball of sadness and regret. If PARC or some other refuge had been able to see that a girl who sequestered antipsychotics in her underwear still deserved help, Johnnie could be alive today, listening to the SBS news blaring on TV while shouting at his friends to have another glass of Fruity Lexia.

On the day it happened, I only knew that another lovely dream I'd harboured for her was gone. I believe that build-up of hope, followed again and again by disappointment, corrodes the soul. The only way I got through that day was by repeating the first phrase of the Serenity Prayer over and over: 'Grant me the serenity to accept the things I cannot change.'

That day, I decided to jettison hope. I don't mean I gave up on my daughter. But I couldn't retain my sanity if I kept hoping for a particular prize only to have it snatched away. All I could really do, I decided, is love her. Even if she was never fixed, even if she remained messy and addled by substances forever, and didn't get a job and never left Craigieburn, I could still love her. I still longed for her to remain alive. Beyond that, I would hope for nothing.

This decision wasn't easy to implement. Going cold turkey with hope was hard. It took practice. Three days after Jim picked up Anna from PARC, she texted me. 'Mum, guess what?'

Hope is such a naughty toddler. It kept leaping up and running around after I'd ordered it not to. As I texted back the question 'What?', I couldn't help wondering if PARC had relented and she'd be going there after all. She'd be moving away from Craigieburn and on with her life.

My phone pinged with her answer. 'We went to Lort Smith and got a big ginger sweetie like Basil.'

A cat! Another bloody pet. I'd insisted Anna not take Poppy away from the home she'd known since she was eight weeks old. That scrawny scrap had grown into a beauty, with big amber eyes and silky black fur specked with gold. Technically she was Anna's cat, but I'd promised her that if she didn't take Poppy away from me, I'd finance another cat for her, once she got settled. I figured that would be months, if not years, in the future. Before I gave up on hope, I'd visualised a little flat where Anna would return after her day's work as a librarian or a school counsellor. It would be then that she'd sit on her Ikea couch and hold a well-behaved little moggy in her arms while she sipped a cup of lemongrass and ginger tea.

It was hard, to have that fantasy smacked out of my head. She didn't have the job, or the flat, or the herbal tea. She only had the cat.

Still, after Jim and Anna acquired their ginger boy, life did settle down for a while . . . or, at least, life for John, Katie and me became much more manageable. To his credit, Jim took Katie's words to heart about having snatched Anna from the psych ward. He did the best he could with her. He let her stay in his house for the next four and a half months, during which time he appeared to age by about ten years. At first, he was cold and distant with me, but as the weeks passed and he realised how hard it was to live with Anna, he came to appreciate what we'd done for her, and what we were still willing to do. He became more and more friendly, until he and I got to a hugging hello and goodbye status.

It was after we'd established a certain closeness that he told me what it had been like during the first weeks Anna was living with him. He had forbidden her to take illicit drugs in his house, and he didn't understand (nor did we) that her drug-induced psychosis wouldn't magically disappear when the ice left her system. He told me he took her out for pizza and she confronted a group of young Lebanese men on the street. 'I know what you're planning to do!' she reportedly said to them. 'I know you've been monitoring my movements, and you're going to regret it.' Jim said they just stared at her and walked away.

Katie told me that when she visited them one oppressively hot day, Anna was manic, drenching herself with water from a spray bottle and yakking at a frightening speed. 'You know the gangs were recording me that day. They have loads of my info on file now!'

'What day?' Katie asked, confused and worried.

'The day I got naked so the cops would pick me up! In the back of the police van, I could see a recording device. It had a little flashing light.' Anna lowered her voice and whispered, 'They recorded me today when I was at the shops, too.'

'Who recorded you?' Katie knew well enough by this stage not to question Anna's delusions. That only made her angry.

'The Lebanese gangs, Katie! They follow me everywhere. Actually, that reminds me . . . when you leave, make sure you let me check the street first. They patrol up and down looking for me and if they see you they might try to snatch you.' She shivered. 'I'll protect you while you walk to your car.'

Caro tried to address the problem of Anna's paranoia. After realising the disarray her medication was in, Caro arranged for the prescribed drugs and the supplements Anna insisted she needed to be dispensed weekly in a seven-day pack. This was prepared at a pharmacy in Glenroy: every

Sunday either Jim or I would pick it up. Each day was divided into four bubbles with multicoloured pills inside, each bubble clearly marked: breakfast, lunch, dinner, bedtime. It calmed my heart just to look at such a well-medicated and organised week. But the problem with this carefully arranged assortment of pharmaceuticals was that Anna didn't actually eat break-fast, lunch and dinner, nor did she have a regular bedtime. It would have been at least two years since she'd embraced the idea of putting on pyjamas, brushing her teeth, and slipping between clean sheets to drift off to dreamland. She stayed awake for however long it took for drugs, alcohol or fatigue to knock her out, then she stayed asleep for as long as pos-sible, wearing whatever she happened to be in when she conked out. She'd wear the same clothes for days on end; just before we kicked her out she was especially fond of a onesie with bunny ears on its hood that Katie and I had given her for her birthday.

As for meals, even while awake she would go for long stretches without eating, maybe ten or twelve hours, till she suddenly realised she was ravenous and then, grumpy as all get-out, she'd be desperate for a particular food immediately, usually KFC. When she was living with us, John and I used to try to head off her gastronomical crises by offering her nutri-tious food at regular intervals, regardless of the time. John's specialty was eggs. Mine was fruit. If I was feeling generous, I'd cut up her favourites – watermelon, kiwi and orange – and arrange the pieces attractively on a plate, maybe adding some sultanas and cheese, and deliver them to her in the bungalow or under the pine tree. Even if she'd just shared a link about the effect of parental neglect on a developing brain, she would always smile and thank me.

Jim, however, was exceptionally bad at feeding himself, let alone another person. His three main food groups were heavily sugared coffee, sweet biscuits and cigarettes. So after Anna moved in with him, even if she had been driven by hunger and good intentions to cut up her own fruit, there was none at hand. And supposing she hadn't been afraid to leave the house by herself, there were no shops within walking distance. Jim told me that when she first moved in, he took her to the local Woolies, with strict instructions not to spend a lot, as the money he earned from his hodgepodge of jobs paid for his mortgage, bills and car but not much else. I don't know what Anna did with her Centrelink money during this time, or even if she was receiving any.

After her eviction from PARC nearly made my eyes fly out of my head with frustrated rage, I had promised us both that I would never again nag her to do any programs, nor would I inquire about whether she was keeping up with the requirements to qualify for the dole. I removed all those carefully gathered brochures and printouts from their plastic sleeves and put them in the recycling bin. On the 16th of March I texted her, 'My only job now is to love you.'

Jim later reported to me that on that first trip to Woolies, he bought Anna a cask of cheap red. Although he consistently struck to his stance of no illegal drugs in the house, he did allow a limited amount of wine if either of them had the money to buy it. He also let her choose two kilos of beef mince, some tinned tomatoes, tomato paste and a family-sized packet of spaghetti. Apparently, when they got home from shopping at about midday, she drank a few glasses of wine and went to sleep. He told me, 'At two in the morning I heard all this clanging coming from the kitchen . . . I went out there . . . you wouldn't believe the number of pots she had on the go, or the mess she'd made.'

'Oh, yes I would,' I sighed. Soon after she had returned to our place after her break-up with Andrew, I'd insisted she make a contribution to the household by cooking dinner one night. On that occasion, too, it had been spag bol. Not only did it take her hours to prepare, she somehow also managed to smear every surface in the kitchen with red grease *and* gouge two sizeable chips out of the enamel on our new stovetop. I don't remember how the eventual meal tasted, but I do know I never asked her to make dinner again.

I felt a little sorry for Jim. He'd thought he was bringing home an attractive young woman who, with the kindness of his good manliness, would become his beloved partner. Instead, he got a grouchy, drunk, never-satisfied girl who complained a lot, imagined that ghosts and gangs wanted to kill her, and made messes everywhere in his formerly immaculate house. At least he liked the cat. And he did have one strategy up his sleeve: 'When she gets too stroppy, I shove that pack at her and say, "Take your medication!"'

What exactly did that involve? Popping several days' supply of Seroquel out of their bubbles, I imagined. Perhaps liberating a couple of cranberry pills and a capsule or two of acidophilus.

Somehow, Jim, Anna and Beuler, their big ginger cat, limped on together until the middle of the year.

Chapter 40

Tough love. It's a concept that is discussed a lot in the addiction community. In its purest form, the idea is that you kick your adult child out and give them zero help until they've reached their 'rock bottom' and begin to climb back up, clean and sober, to begin a 'normal' life. Many parents in my online group struggle with this, just as I did. They ask permission from the other members to break the rules, even just a little. A mother might post something like, 'It's so bitter cold out. Do you all think it's okay to buy my son a good warm coat, even though he's stole about everything I got?' A hundred other mothers ask a version of this: 'Should I pay for my daughter's phone? I know she'll use it to contact her dealer. But it's so darned hard not to have any way to keep in touch with her.'

I think the best and kindest answer to these questions goes like this: 'Do what your heart tells you. Do what you can live with.'

After we could no longer have Anna at home, John, Katie and I had to decide how to follow up that first dollop of tough love. John took the hard-line approach of not even speaking to her. Katie said that Anna was always welcome to stay with her and Tom, but there would be conditions: no drinking or illicit drugs. She would be expected to sleep and be awake at reasonable hours, to participate in daily life and make a contribution to the running of the household. Anna did try going up to stay

on the billabong while she was living with Jim. Katie picked
her up one Sunday afternoon after she'd been in Melbourne
for the weekend. They'd only been home for a couple of hours
before I started to get frustrated texts from Katie: 'She's moved
the furniture around in the room where she's sleeping and
spread wires all over the place. All she wants to do is sit in
front of her PlayStation!'

Tom and Katie were living in a converted dairy. They had
very little money at that stage, so they were grateful to Tom's
mother for their rent-free accommodation, but it was pretty
cramped. Anna was sleeping in the tiny lounge room, which
didn't have a door to close it off from the galley kitchen and
miniature dining area it adjoined. Katie was born a neat freak.
Like me, untidy living spaces caused her almost physical pain.

On the Monday morning after Anna arrived, Katie got tired
of watching her sleep so insisted she get out of bed around
eleven o'clock. Rather than leave Anna to her own (electronic)
devices, Katie took Anna with her to the Wangaratta library,
where she wrote for a few hours every day. She later told me,
'I said she should go for a walk, or to visit the art gallery or
something. She read for a while, but then she started whining
that she was bored.' Unless fuelled by ice, Anna was afraid to
do anything on her own.

Katie did say that Anna was fun company over dinner and
afterwards she volunteered to do the dishes. Katie had explained
in great detail how septic systems worked, and impressed upon
Anna not to put anything down the toilet apart from toilet
paper, and *especially* not to ever remove the strainer from the
sink, as even small chunks of anything could block the system.

The morning after Anna had helpfully washed the dishes,
Katie and Tom awoke to find both the toilet and the kitchen

sink blocked and overflowing. 'What did you put down the sink?' Katie screeched at the sleeping lump in the little lounge room. Anna woke up and mumbled, 'I did the dishes really well. I even heated up all the fat in the roasting pan to make it liquid and poured it down the sink.'

Katie rushed to the sink. She could see the lumps of solidified lamb fat floating in the water. 'You idiot!' she declared. For good reason. They were forced to fork out nearly $2000 to get the whole septic system dug up and restored.

After only a few days at Katie's, Anna decided to return to Jim's. She'd now awarded him the title of Melbourne's most boring man, but at least he let her sleep, drink, play her electronic games and watch her DVDs whenever she wanted to. Plus, she missed Bueler.

Katie never wavered in her promise to provide Anna with a home whenever she needed one, but she did stress that she would continue to expect Anna to cooperate with her rules. As for me, I learned as I went along how to inject 'tough' into loving my girl. It was a huge step when I stopped trying to fix her, but I couldn't stand the thought of her, or her cat, going without good food and medicine. So I visited her once a fortnight, on a Sunday afternoon, stopping on the way to pick up her medications pack from the young Glenroy pharmacist, who had such a kind and gentle face.

I'd also take a care package, which I'd assemble in the days leading up to each visit: quality cat food from the pet shop, plus worm pills or flea drops if needed. For Anna, I'd include some glittery earrings or a bracelet from the shopping mall, and cheap cigarettes from the little shop where the proprietor and I were now chatty pals. I'd hand her these items in a jolly gift bag and be rewarded with a big smile and a warm hug.

Now that she wasn't living with me, she appreciated me a lot more. I also paid for credit on her phone, and when she texted asking for money, John and I would usually transfer $20 or $30 into her account, or sometimes $50, but never more than that.

During my visits to Craigieburn, especially as the months wore on, Jim would usually be asleep. He'd told me before that he had a history of depression, and when it hit, it was very hard for him to get out of bed. Anna put it like this: 'All he does is sleep and cough.' I didn't ask if he managed to get up during the week to do his jobs. Instead, I'd take Anna to Woolies and let her buy whatever food she wanted, plus a limited number of products from the cosmetic aisle. But no alcohol. One Sunday I was in a different aisle from her, picking out a few things to take home for John and me. When I located her, she was in the section filled with baking ingredients. As I lowered my Bürgen bread and bananas into the trolley, I noticed there were about twenty-five bottles of vanilla extract nestled among the items she'd chosen. She'd cleaned out their entire supply. I picked up one of the little bottles from the trolley and peered at the ingredients: 35 per cent alcohol.

'I'm gonna do some baking!' she protested.

I looked at her sceptically.

'Can't you just ignore them?' she pleaded.

'Oh, for heaven's sake. If you're that desperate, I'll buy you a bottle of wine, but just one!'

Yes, I sometimes wavered. But other times I did manage to put 'tough love' into practice. One night my phone rang at 10.30, after I'd got into my pyjamas and done my yoga stretches. I was relaxing, watching a recorded episode of *Australian Story* with Poppy on my lap. It was Anna on the phone, sounding distraught. She missed her daddy. Couldn't

I persuade him to talk to her? When I heard that little girl voice, I always longed to do whatever she asked. But this time I couldn't. Her request that night jostled my soul so much that I lay awake for hours.

The next day I called to tell her and texted my friends to let them know that I had decided I'd be turning my phone off at 8.30 every night. Not just switched to silent, but turned off fully till the next morning. I'd reminded Anna what I'd advised her several times before: 'If you're in trouble, ring triple 0.'

This was my version of tough love, but I couldn't have done it if I'd hadn't had the granite cliff of John's resolve at my back. I know I would have caved whenever she whimpered that she was lonely and that she needed me. I'd have extracted a promise that she'd definitely be good this time, and I'd have let her back in the bungalow. I think that's partly why John took such a hard line with her: he had to say no for both of us. The few times I questioned our decision not to let her return home, John firmly stated, 'If she comes back, I'm leaving.' In my heart of hearts, that's what I wanted to hear. *You haven't got a choice. You can't let her come back.*

I got better at quarantining my anxieties about her. If a worry popped up, I would politely ask it to step aside and wait till three in the afternoon, the hour I'd allocated to consider it. Meanwhile, during the other hours of the day, I was still doing my tutoring. I didn't feel up to embarking on the writing of another book, but I started blogging and sending out articles to magazines.

And John and I got on with our marriage . . . finding things other than Anna to argue about and discuss. We managed to sprinkle in some fun as well. We went on a holiday to Mackay in Queensland. Most importantly, we embarked on a life-changing project: we decided to sell our home among the trees. I knew it was time to move to a place with a smaller garden that I could manage by myself when John went off on the adventures he planned for his retirement, like trekking in Nepal . . . or, at least, camping in the Grampians. But it was so hard to think of leaving. I experienced anticipatory grief for the skink who lived in a crack in the bricks of our wood-fired barbecue, and the shiny black spiders who guarded their silken egg sacs inside any empty terracotta pots I left upturned for later use.

Still, there was an upside to the downsizing. I was able to fill the plastic sleeves of a brand new binder, labelled 'Buying House'. Because we felt (well, mainly I felt) that we should first find a new home we really liked before parting with our current one.

It was hard work, especially emotionally, searching for the right house. But I was glad John and I could do it while we were still strong in body and mind, and had the time to make a rational decision together. And it was an excellent technique for taking our minds off what Anna might be doing, or more likely not doing, in Craigieburn.

While John and I were trudging up and down the stairs of various townhouses, Anna did begin to work more actively towards her sobriety. Or so it seemed. It also could have been that Caro, who regularly took Anna out for coffee, had begun arranging things for her.

On the last Tuesday in April, Anna rang to tell me she was going back to Curran Place for another round of detox on Friday. 'I know it would be a lot of driving for you,' she said, 'but could you pick me up and take me there?'

Perhaps the toughest of the tough love proponents would have told her she should get herself to detox. But I'd stated in that list of boundaries I'd drawn up for the CAT team that I'd always assist if she reached out for help with her addiction, and I still felt that way. I said I'd love to take her to detox.

Because she'd have to leave her beloved cat for a week, I foraged in my keepsakes box and unearthed a toy cat John's sister gave Anna for her second Christmas, when she was fifteen months old. That cat, too, was ginger, and Anna, my chubby toddler with white-blonde hair, had carried it with her everywhere, its long tail skimming the ground.

On Friday the 1st of May my journal states: 'Up at six o'clock. Waited with guys in hi-vis vests at the Dairy Queen for excellent cappuccino. Got to A's 7.25. She loved having her toy cat back. Good run to Curran Place. Got there 8.30 and checked her in. Out of four scheduled admissions, this is the best ever!'

Anna was out and back at Jim's in time for Mother's Day, on Sunday the 10th. The four of us couldn't celebrate together as John wasn't speaking to Anna. Katie promised to make me a special dinner next time she was down from the farm. Anna, still afraid of leaving the house on her own, couldn't meet me in the city like she used to do a few years earlier when she was living with Andrew. Instead, I drove to Craigieburn and picked her up so we could go out for lunch. I'd googled cafes in the area that served all-day breakfast but were not licensed to serve alcohol. As we munched our eggs Florentine, I looked across the table at my daughter and, despite everything, I was grateful to have her with me. Only a day out of detox, she was clear-eyed and sober. I could hear the pleasure in her voice as she described the board games she'd played, the meals she'd helped create, and the jokes she'd shared with her friends at Curran Place – repeat residents like her.

Concern nibbled at the edges of my resolve not to nag her. Shouldn't she be telling me about what she'd learned at the therapy sessions? Did she take away any strategies for staying sober? Hadn't they helped her make some plans for moving towards a future that contained more than a depressed older man and a ginger cat? I shoved a forkful of spinach in my mouth to keep the thoughts from coming out.

'Sorry I don't have a present for you,' Anna said. 'I'm broke.'

'That's okay,' I shrugged.

'But I do have this!' She reached down the front of her shirt, pulled out an envelope and handed it to me. On it she had printed, 'Mummy'. Inside was a Mother's Day card, the glittery kind you see in spinning racks at the front of two-dollar shops. I wondered how she'd managed to get it: she must have asked Caro or Jim to drive her to the shops. I opened the card and there, along with the printed line 'Happy Mother's Day', was Anna's own message, written in purple ink:

To my beautiful mum,
You are the best person I have ever known,
Forgiving, kind, generous, creative, constantly learning
and evolving,
The type of person who LIVES, not just exists.
Words cannot express how much I appreciate you.
You are insecure sometimes but you should never be.
You are everything a good woman should be, and like a
good coffee, you are sweet and strong.
I love you forever, Mummy. Anna

She knew how deeply I believed in the power of words. She'd laid on the adjectives a bit thick, but that was fine by me. Never again, to my knowledge, did she post anything on Facebook about being raised by abusive, narcissistic parents.

Chapter 41

On Sunday the 21st of June, I rang Anna early in the afternoon to confirm I'd be visiting her with her fortnightly supplies. She didn't answer. So I rang Jim. In a grim and shaky voice he told me, 'I kicked her out last night.'

'What? Why?'

'She got physical with me. She was mad at me and started kickboxing me, hard. I said that's it, you're out.'

'Where is she?'

'She went off somewhere in a taxi.'

The hard hand of panic didn't close around my heart as firmly as it would have in the past. She could afford a taxi because our writing money for that year had come through. And I was pretty sure where she would have gone . . . or to be more precise, who she had run to.

For the last three weeks she'd been attending Catalyst, the non-residential rehab program we had been hoping she would begin before we kicked her out. Although Anna didn't tell me so, I'm pretty sure Caro must have helped her arrange this. I was very impressed when Anna rang me one evening, her voice bright and eager, to let me know she had completed three days of the course and got there on time each morning. Jim later told me he'd dragged her out of bed and deposited her at Craigieburn station to achieve this. Still, getting herself the rest of the way to Coburg was a major step.

The following Monday, Anna rang me again, sounding even more chuffed. 'I've made a good friend at Catalyst. He's picking me up every morning and driving me back home.'

Ding, dong! The alarm bells clanged.

This guy was younger than Jim, she gushed a few days later, and a lot more fun. Plus, he had great hair. It turned out my guess was correct: she'd taken the taxi to his place. But his housemate didn't want Anna living there. Her writing money covered a few nights' stay at a hotel for her and the guy with the great hair. Then he introduced her to another guy, Harry, whom he'd met at one of his own rounds of detox at Curran Place. It was Harry who told Anna about an older Macedonian guy who sublet the bedrooms of his rented house in Lalor. He didn't require references or a bond. That's how Anna met Johnnie, and subsequently moved into his home in July of 2015.

I pulled up in front of this house for the first time on Thursday afternoon, the 9th of July. It was the school holidays so I had Charlotte with me.

Once we emerged from the car, we only had time to glance around the scruffy grass of the treeless front yard before Anna came rushing out to greet us. She scooped up Charlotte and spun her around, then gave me a long hug. She was thoroughly, exuberantly drunk. 'There's three cats here!' was her first exciting bit of news about this new home. 'The two kittens are kind of feral, but the mother is adorable. She lets me cuddle her for ages.' She shepherded us across a little verandah towards the front door. 'Come on in and meet Johnnie.'

We stepped into the lounge room, which was crammed with piles of stuff I didn't have time to identify, because it was so dim in there, my eyes couldn't adjust before Anna urged us through to the pokey kitchen. There it was much brighter, with the window uncurtained. The light allowed us to see a tall, overweight guy who looked to be in his late sixties, perched on a kitchen chair, with walking sticks leaning against him on either side. Two other men, a bit younger, sat facing the TV that blared from the laminex table shoved against the wall.

'Mum, Charlotte, this is Johnnie.' As she said this, Anna was standing beside him, resting her hand on his shoulder, as if he were a favourite uncle she'd known forever.

'Anna mumma!' Johnnie boomed. 'You sit!'

Since there were no spare chairs in the room, Johnnie picked up the walking stick on his left and waved it towards one of the other guys. That guy jumped up and stood in the corner. 'Sit, Anna mumma!' Johnnie commanded.

I sat, and Charlotte scrambled onto my lap, folding in her arms and legs to make her already small self as little as possible. She pushed her face into my chest. I was feeling a little unsure myself, so I was glad to hold her tight.

'Baby!' Johnnie roared. 'Say hello, Baby!'

Charlotte attempted to bury her face in the front of my jumper. 'She's shy,' I explained apologetically to Johnnie, hoping Anna wouldn't point out that Charlotte had never been shy before.

Johnnie poked Charlotte in the side with his walking stick, but very gently. 'Johnnie don't eat babies!' he declared. I was to discover he always spoke at top volume, and punctuated each sentence with an exclamation mark.

Giving up on Charlotte, Johnnie looked back to me. 'Anna mumma! You want drink? Have drink!' He pointed the stick towards a cask of Fruity Lexia beside the TV.

'Oh, no thanks,' I demurred.

'Mummy never drinks wine in the afternoon,' Anna told Johnnie. 'She waits till six o'clock and then has two standard drinks. She's got a glass with a line on it so she can measure it out, *exactly*.'

Johnnie squinted at Anna with interest but didn't seem to comprehend what she was saying. The guy in the corner informed me, 'He's deaf.' I was to learn that Johnnie was not really deaf, just hard of hearing. And he certainly seemed capable of carrying on conversations in several languages with the assortment of friends I saw sitting around his table in the months to come.

With Anna living in this new place, I kept on with my brand of tough love, turning off my phone at night and confining my visits to once a fortnight on a Sunday afternoon. Jim was no longer seeing her, so our nice Glenroy pharmacist agreed to let me pick up two medication packs to deliver to her when I saw her. Anna had agreed that I could give her one piece of advice each time I visited or talked to her on the phone. Sometimes I used this allocation to remind her she ought to take her medication regularly, instead of just plucking out Seroquel when she was suddenly seized with the need to be comatose. 'Okay, Mum, I'll do that,' she would cheerfully or churlishly agree, depending on her mood.

In general, though, her mood was a lot sunnier than when she was at Jim's. Most days when I spoke to her, she seemed to be having heaps of fun. At any one time there were three or four men renting sleeping space from Johnnie in that house, plus the ones who dropped by for the day and likely as not would crash for the night. And those guys, unlike Jim, loved to party. At first I had trouble keeping track of who was who, but Anna claimed to know and love them all: she created an instant family. This one was her brother, that one her cousin, another one an uncle. And Johnnie was Daddy. For a while there she took to speaking loudly in pidgin English like him. 'Mummy and me go shop now!' she would announce when I arrived to take her to Coles.

However, there was, as always, a dark side to Anna's elation. Sometimes she would decide that Johnnie's house needed a thorough scrub and tidy. Then she would demand, suddenly, that any men who happened to be in the place should put down their drinks, jump up from the soccer game they were watching, cease with their spirited conversations, and help her whip that house into shape. She had purchased a wide selection of cleaning products during our shopping excursions and now – *right now, this very minute* – she would insist they get put to use. She would assign the jobs. She would order one guy to disinfect the toilet and another to de-flea the animals. A third man should tackle the accumulated grease on the stovetop and still another begin to create order from the clutter in the lounge room.

On Monday the 20th of July my journal reads:

Turned on my phone at 9.30 . . . there was a message from the emergency department of the Northern Hospital from 10.45 last night . . . 'Your daughter has been admitted under the Mental Health Act.' I told myself not to chuck away another day being the actress in a supporting role in one of her dramas. When I called her, she said she'd 'got violent' with the men in the house the night before, because they wouldn't do the cleaning jobs she assigned. She told me she was being transferred to the psych ward and asked when could I visit. I said maybe tomorrow.

The pattern of escalating violence seems clear now. The previous year she'd nearly choked her dad, and Jim. More recently Jim had kicked her out for getting physical with him again, and now the guys at Johnnie's house had called the police because she was attacking them. But it didn't enter my head that she would really hurt someone. To be honest, my actual concern was that she would get hurt, that one day she would have a go at those guys and they'd be too fed up with her to call the police and instead retaliate themselves. I asked that worry to go away, or at least wait until three in the afternoon.

Meanwhile, I practised detaching with love. Later on that same day, Anna called me. She hadn't been admitted to the psych ward after all. She was back at Johnnie's house. 'YAY!' I wrote in big letters in my journal. 'I don't have to drive to the hospital tomorrow!' I had developed PTSD about visiting her in emergency departments and psych wards.

Gill came over for dinner that night and I decided not to tell her about Anna landing in the emergency department again. I didn't think it was healthy for Anna and her problems to be the focal point of our lives. Yes, Gill was Anna's devoted godmother, but she was also my professional colleague, as passionate about teaching as I was. So I sought out her ideas on how to reach the most challenging student I was tutoring, a girl who wanted to do well in year 12 but had no clue on how to analyse a novel.

Also, during this time, John and I were getting serious about finding a new house to buy, so that process was taking up more and more brain space. Just as we'd done when looking for our first home thirty-three years earlier, we drew up a list of features we were looking for, and printed out multiple copies. As we inspected each property, we'd go through our list and tick off the criteria which that house fulfilled. We had thirty-six criteria ranging from 'three bedrooms', 'plenty of natural light', through to 'small backyard', and 'view of garden from kitchen sink', and 'solar hot water'.

On the 20th of August, Anna rang me to say she'd been in the Northern Hospital for a couple of days with joint pain. This could have been real, as she'd suffered from some temporary arthritis-like symptoms when she was in VCE. I wondered how she'd got to the hospital and back, but I didn't ask. Perhaps one of her housemates actually had a car and a valid licence. Also, I wouldn't have been surprised if she'd called an ambulance. However she got there, this hospital visit marked an enormous turning point in all of our lives, in a way we'd never imagined.

Chapter 42

'Mum? I don't know how to tell you this —'

It was Anna, speaking to me on Monday the 24th of August.

'What?' My heart constricted.

'You know I was in the hospital last week?'

'Yeah.'

'Well, they made me do a pee test, and . . . I'm up the duff.'

Whoa! This was something I'd never worried about. Come to think of it, why hadn't I?

'I'm gonna keep him,' she told me. 'I'm gonna live with Katie and have a healthy baby.'

'Uh . . . does she know?'

'Not yet.'

My soul was singing. A baby! Something joyous for my little girl to look forward to. Something even better than a kitten.

Katie, when she found out a couple of days later, pointed out that I was absolutely, certifiably nuts. 'Mum! She can't even look after herself, let alone a kid!'

Of course, Katie was right. The next morning I wrote in my journal:

Had a bad night, more full of worry than any time since Anna left home. Realised since I heard A's news, I've indulged in magical thinking . . . a baby! This could be a new beginning! But A couldn't get herself to her appointment with Dr Khoo yesterday, instead she texted, 'I got really drunk'. At 3.30 a.m. I lay awake imagining the fetus's point of view, attempting to assemble its little organs in a bath of alcohol and prescription drugs and nicotine.

The next day I googled fetal alcohol syndrome, and what I read there was nauseating. Yet I couldn't do what Katie urged me to do – try to convince Anna to terminate. More googling told me that the embryo was still being nourished by its egg sack. If Anna would stop drinking now, maybe he would be okay. (Anna never doubted she was having a boy.)

When Anna told me she was pregnant, she was adamant that she'd made her boy all by herself; which was her way of saying she didn't know for sure, or didn't want to know, or wasn't prepared to tell me, who the father was. I didn't press her to find out. Apart from the men who came and went from Johnnie's house, who knows how many guys she met at detox and Catalyst who visited her? I don't think any of those men were ready or able to be a responsible parent.

Less than a week after Anna told me she was pregnant and wanted to go live with Katie so she could have a healthy baby, several people had started work on making that happen. Caro from PHaMs was arranging for another stint at Curran Place for detox, and this time Anna promised she would carry through with no drinking afterwards. Meanwhile, assuming Anna wouldn't be living with Katie forever, Caro said she'd look into public housing for her after the birth. 'Our goal is to keep Anna and her baby safe,' Caro assured me. By 'our' she meant her and a new care worker: they both wanted to meet with Anna at one o'clock that Friday at the Northern Hospital.

I was desperate for Anna to get to that appointment. Tom and Katie had been staying with John and me for a couple of days and were planning to head back to the farm Friday afternoon. They took Anna to the appointment, then on to their home with them.

Another person trying to help make Anna and her infant safe was our kindly Glenroy pharmacist. He had helped Katie to locate a pharmacist in Wangaratta who would make up medication and supplement packs for Anna, and with the cooperation of Dr Khoo, was sending Anna's scripts to this new chemist. Katie was anxious about all this: she wanted to make sure Anna had a new pack waiting when the current one ran out. So our hard-working Glenroy pharmacist promised he would post *and* fax the scripts to Wangaratta.

On Saturday, the first day of Anna's long-term residence on the farm, I texted Katie to see how things were going, crossing my fingers that no drains had been blocked or toilets clogged yet. 'We're good,' Katie texted back. 'Going out to look at the baby goats.' Phew!

That evening I turned off my phone as usual. The next morning when I turned it on, two texts sent during the night pinged to life. Both from Anna. The first one read, 'Tom is a pissy tight-arse. Don't tell Katie.' And the second: 'Katie loves Belle heaps more than she loves me!' Belle was Tom and Katie's darling, a staffy cross. That evening Anna rang me, her voice hoarse with emotion. She had a cold, and Katie and Tom's rules, according to her, were impossibly harsh. 'They don't understand! They expect me to be perfect when I'm in withdrawal.'

I encouraged her to get through the next week, because Caro had managed to get her into Curran Place the following week. So they – Katie and Tom and Anna with her minuscule passenger on board and the baby goats and Belle and other assorted mammals – did make it through that week.

Apart from liaising with the Glenroy pharmacist and attempting to address the glitches in Anna's medicinal requirements, Katie took Anna to a doctor in Wangaratta on two separate days. 'I appreciate what you and Dad did more than ever,' Katie texted. 'Looking after Anna eats up a lot of time.'

This doctor, apparently, advised Anna to have an abortion after he heard how much she'd been drinking. Katie reported to me that he said to Anna, 'You're young. Why don't you get yourself sorted out and then try again.' Katie thought his advice was spot on, but Anna was horrified. 'I hate that doctor!' she told me. But she did consent to the ultrasound he suggested, which showed she was approximately seven weeks pregnant.

Anna had to be at Curran Place early Monday morning to secure her right to ten days of detox. So Katie put her on the train in Wangaratta on the Sunday afternoon and I picked her up from Broady station. I couldn't take her home to John, so we drove out to Gill's to spend the night. We had a lovely evening in front of her open fire, just like we used to when Anna was a sweet-smelling baby fresh from Gill's bath, or a child tired from an afternoon's horseride, or a teenager making us laugh with her friend Ellie. Anna could be such fun company when she was in a good mood, and gracious, too. 'You and Gill go ahead and have a glass of wine, it won't bother me,' she assured us. But we both said we were happy not to. Ever since the day she got drunk instead of keeping her appointment with Dr Khoo, she'd been making a real effort not to drink.

The next morning, the 7th of September, my journal said: 'Shower 6.45. Crumpets and coffee in lounge room with G. Not too hard to pry A from bed. On the drive in, actually enjoyed convo with A. Delivered her to detox . . . totally sober! To Nova to meet Marcelle for eleven o'clock session of *Holding the Man*.'

The week flashed by with tutoring and house inspecting; it was the spring selling season, so auction boards had sprouted up all over the suburb. I felt calm, knowing Anna was safe and sober in a place she enjoyed.

On Friday I rang Curran Place to chat with her. A nurse answered and told me casually, 'Oh, she discharged herself yesterday.'

What? After four days? Where was she?

I called her and she actually answered. 'I missed my family,' she said. Meaning the guys at Johnnie's house. She was back there after all her ravings about the dirt and the fleas and how it would be so much better at Katie's; after everything that Katie and the Glenroy pharmacist had done to help get her medication packs organised in Wang, after all the persuading Caro must have employed to get Anna into detox in record time because she was pregnant . . .

I didn't make a big deal about it over the phone or in my journal. I didn't even ask who picked her up from detox. I just repeated the Serenity Prayer a lot and got on with my life. What else could I do? As I had learned so many times, in increasingly painful ways, I could not force her into a future of my choosing.

When I think about it now, I actually get some comfort from the fact that she left Curran Place early and fled back to Johnnie's house. Because I do sometimes feel guilty that we didn't pay for private rehab, but if she couldn't stick it out at a detox she liked, if she couldn't even live with the rules her own sister insisted on, why would anyone think she wouldn't have walked out on rehab we paid for? And I'm fairly sure they don't refund your $30 000 if your kid skips out after a few days.

With Anna back at Johnnie's house, I kept on as before, visiting her once a fortnight to take her shopping and bring her a care package. I didn't try to get the medication pack redirected. Maybe I was remiss there. Was this the point at which I could have derailed the tragedy train, if I'd made sure she had the proper meds? Katie and I, as well as the two pharmacists and Dr Khoo, had gone to such a lot of trouble to get the scripts to Wang. It was completely discouraging to think of starting the whole process over again. Plus, who knew? She might decide she was going back to Katie's anyway. At Johnnie's house, even if she did have the meds and supplements, I thought she'd probably just pluck out the Seroquel when she was desperate for sleep, and that couldn't be good for the baby, could it?

When I visited Anna, Johnnie was always so happy to see me, no matter how many friends he had with him in the kitchen, watching footy or chatting. 'Anna mumma! You sit!' he would shout as I plonked onto the table a bag of Anna's favourite treats from the local bakery. 'Here,' I'd say to Johnnie, 'have a croissant.' Johnnie would usually accept one to have with his glass of Lexia. 'You good mumma,' he would tell me fondly as he munched.

Johnnie . . . there was something about him that was so likeable. He was almost always surrounded by friends. I couldn't understand most of what they said, as they usually forgot to speak English in front of me and reverted to conversing in a variety of Slavic languages, but it was obvious that Johnnie was at the centre of their passionate discussions. And he was funny: the guys were always guffawing at some remark he made. Johnnie was delighted by life, and Anna was one of his delights.

A few weeks after Anna returned to his house, I think it must have been early October, Johnnie had to move. Anna said it was because his rented house had been condemned, but I suspect it was simply because the landlord had decided to sell. For whatever reason, Johnnie and his shifting population of tenants had to vacate. One of Johnnie's many Macedonian pals found a place for him in Thomastown, not far from his old place, but this was a two-bedroom unit so Johnnie decided he could only sublet to two people, with him sleeping in a king bed in the lounge room. The people he chose to take with him were Anna and another tenant, Grant.

I couldn't imagine how Johnnie was going to move all the stuff he had crammed into his house, and I'm still not sure exactly how it was done, but I assume his friends and family came forward to help. So Anna ended up living in a sixties-style unit on a quiet street. Her bedroom overlooked a little patch of lawn that nobody had loved in quite a while. As for her clothes and other belongings, they had been moved over in large garbage bags and were now piled up against the wall at the foot of her bed. The first time I visited her after the move, Anna said she would sort these out later. The most important aspect for her was that the movers had managed to catch one of the semi-feral cats and bring him along, as well as Anna's beloved Chi Chi with her five little kittens. Anna had made a home for them in a cardboard box at the bottom of her wardrobe.

So Anna and Johnnie, along with Grant and the feline family, settled into life at the unit. Grant is the man who was described as Anna's partner in the news items following Black Sunday. In my opinion, giving him that title was a bit of a stretch. She only had to know a guy for five minutes to start calling him her boyfriend. She also claimed to have an uncle and a dad and several brothers among Johnnie's friends.

I don't have anything against Grant. He was always warm and polite to me, even affectionate, telling me I reminded him of his late mother. He was forty-seven, and he told me his height and physique had helped him excel at sport when he was a teenager. By the time Anna met him, ice and alcohol had robbed him of his strength. All I ever saw him do was sit at the kitchen table with Johnnie, smoking and drinking. I did appreciate the fact that he almost always answered his phone when I was trying to make sure Anna was still alive. But I also rang Johnnie on a few occasions for that reason, as well as Walt, an older man I became quite friendly with when he had lived at Johnnie's house and later visited the unit. I think for Anna, the main attraction to Grant was that he had access to weed. It helped a lot with the nausea that came with her pregnancy. It was the only thing that allowed her to keep even a little food down. I thought it was also likely that without alcohol, she needed something to keep the voices quiet. I didn't try to dissuade her: what good would it have done? And I figured weed was actually less harmful to the baby than alcohol.

On the 22nd of October, I spent most of the day at the unit, helping Anna to tackle the mountain of garbage bags in her bedroom. She seemed incapable of making a start on unpacking. This was partly because, at fourteen weeks, even when she was smoking weed, she still had days when she was throwing up almost every time she tried to get out of bed. She complained bitterly about it, 'This baby is trying to kill me!' But I think it helped her honour her resolution not to drink. She couldn't smoke as many cigarettes as she used to either.

The unpacking process was astounding: I'd open a bulging bag and find clothes wadded up with unwashed dishes and open boxes of cornflakes and half used packets of flour and bottles of shampoo and DVDs. Anna was feeling pretty good that day, so I'd direct her where to take each item. I tried to get Grant to help too, but he found walking around painful due to a bad case of gout. Happily, scattered among the contents of the bags, I found some very useful things: Anna's disposable contact lenses. She had procured a prescription for the lenses and bought a box of them a year or so earlier, when she had some money. It was like a treasure hunt, finding those contact lenses, loose from their original box but still safe, in their tiny, sealed plastic disks. Anna squealed with happiness whenever I found a pair.

A few weeks earlier, when Chi Chi's babies were first born, I'd taken Charlotte to meet them. Charlotte had never seen newborn kittens, with their eyes sealed shut and their earflaps stuck to their heads. 'Are they really *cats*?' she'd marvelled.

Charlotte had loved holding those tiny, squirming new lives, but later that night during our cubbyhouse time she started to cry. 'I want the old Anna back!' You never have to ask Charlotte to elaborate on what she's feeling. 'Anna smells awful now and her skin's all spotty and she can't see properly!'

Of course. It hadn't sunk in at the time, but now that Charlotte had mentioned it . . . out on the verandah as we held the new kittens, Anna had been squinting, her usually bespectacled face bare. She'd lost her glasses again. Or broken them.

I told Charlotte that I wasn't going to get her another pair. It was no use buying her glasses because she couldn't keep them safe. That made Charlotte cry even harder. I told her to get out of bed and have a cuddle. She sat on my lap, sobbing for the big sister she'd loved ever since she could remember. 'I want Anna to be able to see!'

I held Charlotte close and said, 'So do I, honey. So do I.'

Chapter 43

In the months after we found out Anna was pregnant, I visited her more often. Now that she wasn't drinking, she was better company. Some days she was too racked by nausea to leave the house, but if she was having a good day, I could take her out. It was such a relief that I could now trust her not to run off and wipe herself out with vodka. One Thursday we met Marcelle and one of her thousands of friends at Northland for lunch, then went to a matinee showing of *The Dressmaker*. Marcelle's friend, who claimed to be psychic, rested her hand lightly on Anna's belly and predicted there was a boy inside. 'And you'll be a great mum,' she said. Anna beamed behind her sunglasses (she had come across an old pair of prescription ones, thank goodness).

On Sunday the 15th of November, when Anna was seventeen weeks along, I picked her up and, for a special treat, drove her to the Nova, as it was the only cinema north of the Yarra showing *Freeheld*, and we both loved Ellen Page. I remember Anna looking around in a kind of wonder as we meandered up Lygon Street, licking our gelati from Brunetti's. She said, 'I feel like someone's gonna grab me and say, "Hey, you're not allowed to be out here!"' I thought that was a strange thing to say.

The Friday after we watched *Freeheld*, I arrived at the unit early in the morning, to take Anna to her antenatal appointment at the Northern Hospital. She was out of bed when I got there, but she looked terrible, with her hair matted, her eyes dull and her lips pale and cracked. She hadn't been able to keep anything down for days, not even water. Much later I would learn that she and Grant had run out of weed earlier in the week. She didn't tell me that at the time. I only knew she was in desperate need of hydration, so after her appointment with the midwife, I took her down to the emergency department. They admitted her and put her on a drip.

I returned to the unit, to pick up Johnnie for the errands he wanted to do. As we drove from the post office to Centrelink, he told me how he was trying to persuade Anna to eat better. 'I tell her, "Shouldn't eat only sugar things. Shouldn't smoke neither. You got baby now! I cook you good fish!"' Johnnie had a mate who was a keen fisherman and another mate who shopped for him at Preston Market. Cooking was something Johnnie could still do. Anna had told me how he began every one of his dishes by 'cutting up, like, eight onions and frying them in a ton of oil'.

I also took Grant on an errand that day to the Epping police station. He'd missed a court date for drink-driving because the summons had been sent to their old place after he left. Katie and I had begged Anna never to get into a car with Grant behind the wheel, as this was not his first drink-driving charge. She'd promised she wouldn't, especially because a few weeks earlier his dad had bought him a car that Grant had crashed two days later. With a new court date in hand, I dropped Grant back home midafternoon. Anna was still at the hospital and I'm not sure how she got back to the unit, nor do I recall how I said goodbye to Johnnie and Grant. Most likely I waved fondly to Johnnie as I headed out the door, and a bit less fondly to Grant. It was the last time I would ever see either of them.

The next morning, Saturday, John and I walked one of our favourite kilometres – the street that runs up over the ridge bedside the railway line and ends at Ferrovia, an excellent little cafe across the road from Pascoe Vale station. We had coffee in the courtyard: flat white for John and long black for me. We shared a raspberry slice. Although it's not recorded in my journal, I'm sure we held hands across the little weather-beaten table, because that's one of the things we've never tired of. I know as we were leaving the cafe, the middle-aged owner, Danny, who sports a ponytail and a lovely smile, would have waved at us from behind the espresso machine and called out, 'Nice to see you guys again!' John and I walked back over the ridge towards home, admiring the view across the valley to Essendon airport, without a clue that in approximately twenty-four hours, we would crash into a land we had never imagined.

And so The Call came, early in the afternoon of the day we would come to know as Black Sunday. The initial information was horrible enough, when the police officer told me there'd been an assault involving Anna, and Johnnie had passed away. But then I learned it wasn't an accident, that our daughter had stabbed to death the man who had provided her with a home. At that point, my mind seemed to break off from its moorings and clang around in my head. *What am I supposed to do with this?* my consciousness screamed. *I can't feel this! I don't know how to!*

John held me tight. He said, 'We have to stick together if we're going to get through this.' I think he would have liked to hold me in our bed all afternoon, quietly united against the horror. But I needed to talk. That's how I understand things.

And the harder a thing is to understand, the more I need to talk. Katie was still on the train heading to our place from the farm. I texted my psychologist: 'Something terrible has happened. Can I see you soon?' I needed her, a wise and cool professional, to tell me what to do with the shards of information crashing against each other in my brain. Margot texted back saying yes, she could fit me in the next day. But I needed someone now, another woman to talk to . . . immediately! So I went next door to Sandy. Thank God she was home, my close friend who always welcomed me in.

There I was, at Sandy's kitchen table where I'd sat so many times over three decades, telling her what my daughter had done. I can't remember the words I used to articulate the unspeakable. But I have no trouble recalling the feeling. She greeted the news with her particular brand of gritty compassion. She didn't hug me. She listened to my shocked and confused account of Anna's life at Johnnie's house. She offered her own stories of her many interactions with my girl. I felt no judgement or pity from her. I felt only sad understanding.

The entire time I was with Sandy, I was waiting for a call from the Magistrate's Court. The lawyer had said that someone would be in touch after the police had finished questioning Anna. Finally, as evening was closing in, my phone rang. I walked out into Sandy's back garden as I answered, 'Mary speaking.' It was Anna. 'Mum!' she said. 'They're taking me to prison! They've charged me with murder!'

Somehow, I knew the words to say. Talking things over with Sandy for two hours had allowed me to find, among the dismayed storm of thoughts thrashing around in my head, a truth. I said to my daughter, 'I still love you, and you can have a future.'

Chapter 44

On the night of Black Sunday, Gina the pro bono lawyer called me one last time to say that Anna had been transported to a place called the Dame Phyllis Frost Centre. Gina said that she was only Anna's lawyer for that one day. Because Anna had no money, she would be allocated an ongoing lawyer through legal aid. This lawyer would get in touch with us, hopefully within the next few days. By the time I took Gina's call, I'd returned home from Sandy's and Katie had arrived. I wanted to call the prison and talk to Anna. I wanted to make sure the officers guarding her knew she was pregnant, and that she needed to be on suicide watch. So I googled the Dame Phyllis Frost Centre and learned that it was Victoria's maximum-security prison for women. I called the number given on the website and was relieved to hear an actual human voice answer. The person at the end of the line explained that no one was allowed to call inmates. And the prison, because of privacy laws, could not divulge any information about our daughter. We could write to Anna, but that letter would take many days to find its way through the system. Like all prisoners, I was told, Anna had a monetary account, into which we were allowed to deposit up to $140 a month. She would be able to draw on this money to call us. She could also have visits, but first she must provide a list of the names of potential visitors, giving their dates of birth and addresses, so the names could be submitted for police checks. Once they were approved, that didn't mean that Anna's family and friends could just show up at the prison, or even book themselves in for a visit. Anna had to arrange that from her end. How would she manage all those practical steps? I didn't think she could. I only hoped she wasn't too distraught to keep herself and her baby alive.

Katie and I decided we would compile a list of people who would like to visit Anna, along with the required details, and send it to her. Meanwhile, all we could do was wait. I don't think Katie, John or I really slept that night. I was afraid to let my mind drift off in case it floated into the image of Johnnie dying at the hand of a girl he'd trusted.

When morning finally came, John, Katie and I gathered in the kitchen over coffee. We desperately wanted to tell those who loved Johnnie how sorry we were. But how could we send our condolences to his family when we had never met any of them and had no idea how to get in touch? At that stage we didn't even know Johnnie's real name.

Then I remembered Walt, who had lived at the house with Johnnie and his crew. I really liked Walt. He was in his mid-fifties and was often in bed sick from too many years of alcohol abuse and depression. But when he was up and about, especially early in the day before he'd drunk much, he was smart and funny. He'd made me laugh a lot during one particular visit, by creating a comedy sketch of the day his wife kicked him out because she discovered he was conducting an internet romance from the computer in his garage.

Walt used to visit Johnnie, even after the move to the new unit, and sometimes stayed overnight, though he had been allocated his own housing commission unit in a nearby suburb. So I called Walt. I told him how sorry we were that his good friend, this good man, was dead. He answered, 'It's not your fault.' He sighed. 'I feel so sorry for Johnnie, but I feel sorry for Anna, too.'

Then I heard someone in the background, a female voice demanding, 'Who's that?' Walt told her it was Anna's mother. 'Don't you talk to her!' The woman sounded so angry, and anguished. 'They kicked their daughter out on the streets so she could . . . do *that*! You hang up now!'

Walt said to me, 'I'm sorry. I'll call you back later.'

I had no idea who that woman was. Walt might have been with one of Johnnie's family. I felt no desire to try to justify myself to her, even in my head.

Even though I didn't resent the woman who made Walt hang up, I did feel shaken by her. I was glad Margot, my psychologist, had said she was able to see me. I didn't think I was capable of driving so Katie drove me to Margot's office, which was deep inside a lovely old house in North Fitzroy. I asked Margot how I was supposed to fit into my brain these two gigantic but irreconcilable facts: a young woman had killed a virtually defenseless man. That killer was my beloved daughter.

Margot reminded me of a technique we had talked about before, in which you visualise your mind as a house with many rooms. In some of those rooms you keep your treasures. People you've loved but who are long gone can invite you into a spotless kitchen or a lounge where every chair is comfortable. You might make one room into a glorious aviary, where all the budgies you ever owned fly happily about and chatter to you. In other rooms you store your embarrassment, your regrets, the deepest of your hurts. You can choose not to go into those rooms. It doesn't mean you have to stay away forever. But you can decide to gently close a door, explaining to whoever or whatever you're leaving in there that you can't engage with them right now. *Maybe later*, you might whisper just before the latch clicks.

Into one of those rooms I ushered the terror of Johnnie's death. Sometimes, in that strange, unguarded space between consciousness and sleep, Johnnie would creep out of his room and stand beside my bed. The look of disbelief and betrayal on his face was the saddest sight I'd ever seen. 'Anna's a good girl,' he would tell me. He no longer had to shout. 'I call her Daughtie. She calls me Daddy.' No words could take away the pain he must have suffered in his final moments on this earth. But I would say this anyway: 'Johnnie, I'm so, so sorry.'

So the nights were sometimes hard. But Katie stayed for a week, and with her and John by my side, we got through the days that followed Black Sunday. On Wednesday, John and I drove out to the prison for the first time, twenty-five minutes down the Ring Road to the flat, industrial suburb of Ravenhall. No one had yet been approved to visit Anna, but we wanted to put money into her account so she could call us, and we'd been informed that this had to be in cash. The side road leading to the prison took us through a bleak landscape of scrubby open fields, and the car park was dusty. But the officers in the gatehouse were friendly, nothing like the wardens I'd seen portrayed on TV. The woman who wrote the receipt for our $100 told us that when Anna called me, the screen on my phone would say 'Private Number'. As soon as we drove out of the car park, I started hoping to hear my ringtone and see those words, even though I knew the money would not appear in her account immediately.

It wasn't easy getting through those initial shocking days, but I also know I'm incredibly lucky and privileged compared to many mothers in my online group who have had to face the horrifying debris of their addicted children's lives with little or sometimes no support. Apart from the incalculable comfort of having my husband and firstborn daughter by my side, I had my girlfriends. My six closest friends surrounded me and held me in a tight circle of love. They did this by going for walks with me and taking me out for coffee, and treating me exactly as they always had. Most importantly, they kept on loving Anna. All but Marcelle had known her since she was tiny. They all said in their own ways, 'It wasn't our Anna who did that.' Marcelle, my Christian pal, texted me this on the morning after Black Sunday: 'Mary, God loves you and He loves your daughter.'

I also had professional help, apart from that provided by my psychologist. On the Thursday of that first week I went to see Dr Deb. I had made this appointment at least a month before, as I needed to see her to activate the remaining subsidised sessions with Margot, provided through my mental health plan. When I walked into Deb's office that day she already knew what Anna had done, because I'd asked Margot to tell her so I wouldn't have to say the words. Deb said, 'After twenty years of practice, not much surprises me. But this has blindsided me.' We talked for over an hour. Deb instructed me firmly, 'Don't you ever feel guilty for kicking her out. I saw the way she was. No one could have handled her.' At the same time, she was doing her own soul-searching, wondering if there was something more she could have done for the patient she'd treated for a decade and a half. She shook her head, expressing the incomprehension I felt. 'I can tell you now, Mary, I thought she might well be dead by now. But I never thought she'd kill someone else.'

Later, Caro, Anna's devoted helper from PHaMs, got in touch with me. I'd called her earlier in the week to tell her the awful news, and she wanted to keep helping Anna, to see her in prison, but she found out that was not in her brief. But she was able to offer me, through her organisation, a social worker who I could see for counselling once a week. And so I met lovely young Chanel, who I saw weekly for quite a while and still visit regularly. Her sessions are completely covered by my mental health plan. So, if you are sober and well enough to get yourself to appointments, if you have the energy and literacy to fill out forms, if you have the confidence to ask for help, the mental health system of Victoria is a wonderful blessing.

Chapter 45

'We've made it through the first week of After.' That's what I said to Katie and John on the morning of Sunday the 29th of November 2015, as we once again sat drinking coffee at our kitchen table.

Katie and John agreed it felt like a milestone, to have survived for seven days. I thought Anna's phone money must have been processed by now, but we still hadn't heard from her. Every time my phone rang, I hoped to see 'Private Number' appear on my screen and then hear Anna's voice. But the hours kept going by with no such call. We did know she had arrived safely at the prison and been assigned to a cell, because an officer had rung me shortly after Anna's admission to tell us that much. But by the Monday of Anna's second week in prison, my worry rat was wondering if she was still alive. I thought she must have been avoiding talking to me because she felt so guilty about what she'd done. What if she was so despondent that even her baby wouldn't be enough to keep her interested in life? I called the prison, but the officer I talked to couldn't give me any information about Anna. She did assure me I would get a call from the prison 'if anything happens'.

On the Monday evening of that second week, Anna's lawyer rang me to introduce himself. He sounded smart, competent and kind. He had spoken to Anna, which was a relief, and he said he would pass on to her my eagerness to hear from her.

He also explained that because the charge against her was so serious, it would likely be a long time before any legal conclusion was reached.

On Thursday evening, eleven days after Black Sunday, Katie was back at the farm with Tom and their animals. John and I were sitting out on the back deck having an after-work glass of wine. I'd finished with my students for the day, and John had put away his chainsaw and extension ladder, after spending another few hours trying to tame our garden into a neat enough state to be attractive to buyers. As I crunched a plain corn chip (John calls them martyr chips) my phone rang and, finally, there was the longed-for 'Private Number'. For the first time I heard the recording of a woman's voice informing me in a serious tone, 'This call has originated from an inmate at the Dame Phyllis Frost Centre —'. When the woman had finished her spiel about not recording the call or letting it be part of a conference call, I heard at last my daughter's voice. She told me she was okay and that the prison had its own midwife who thought the baby was doing well. Then she asked, 'Mum, can you come visit me?'

I certainly could. On Black Sunday, Gina the pro bono lawyer had supplied the prison with my name and details, so I'd been fast-tracked on to Anna's visitors list. Anna said, 'I'll book you in for Saturday morning then.' She sounded as if she could handle that.

I was so happy when I hung up. Of course, this happiness bumped up against guilt. Another family had been robbed of a kind and funny man they loved. Yet how could I not also rejoice? We had known for years that a terrible thing was coming. Now it was here, and it was a terror more horrible than we ever imagined. But Anna was alive, and her baby was alive, and she was in a safe place where I could visit her in two days time.

John was happy, too, that I had heard from her. But, looking back, I think the whole situation was harder on him than it was on Katie and me. He didn't have the support systems we did, of friendships cherished and nurtured over many years. Katie, like me, had sought professional help for her mental health, something John would never consider. He loved Anna so much, the little girl for whom he took years off from paid work to raise, the young woman he tried so hard to help. And now he was estranged from her. I knew from experience it was no use for me to make suggestions on how to patch up their relationship. If he was ever going to forgive her for betraying him with false accusations, it would be in a way that he'd decide.

And so, on that Saturday morning, I went to the prison to see our daughter on my own. I had booked the first time-slot available, beginning at 8.30. This was not a popular time to visit, so there was no one else in the waiting room. As soon as I arrived, a woman's voice on the public address system commanded, 'Next visitor!' The door to the reception area clicked, and with some effort I pulled the heavy door open and went in. An amiable guy behind a high counter checked my driver's licence. I signed a book and was given a plastic pass to wear around my neck, just like at the schools where I tutored. I had to leave my phone and handbag in a locker, and was not allowed to take anything with me apart from money for snacks. Once I had passed through a metal detector and stood on a platform so an officer could check for weapons by scanning with a wand, I had to wait for the click of more heavy doors unlocking, before I could push them open. Then I was strolling, unaccompanied, down a path lined with rose bushes to the visitors' centre. I had expected this to be a clinical place, but it turned out to be a large cafe with about thirty tables. The room was full of natural light from two walls of glass. There were shelves with toys and children's picture books, and beyond the glass I could see a large courtyard with monkey bars, slides and a basketball ring.

At reception I'd been given a slip of paper with details for the visit. I now handed this to an officer at a desk just inside the visitors' centre. She smiled and cheerfully told me I could have table 22. There was a large sign proclaiming 'River's End Cafe' above a serving area, but the grille was pulled down, and a smaller sign informed me it wouldn't open until ten o'clock. So I just sat at table 22, watching a few other visitors drift in, feeling a bit exposed without my phone to fiddle with.

And then, out of a door beside the officer's desk, Anna appeared. She was dressed in a forest-green jumpsuit and she looked around, squinting, because she didn't have her glasses. I got up and went to her, taking her in my arms. She clung to me, and started to cry. She sobbed, 'Mum, I'm sorry!' I held her tight, realising it had been a long time since I heard her cry.

What did we talk about, at table 22, on that first prison visit? I can't remember many specifics. But I do know I asked her if she wanted to talk about Johnnie's death. She said no. That was a great relief to me. I wasn't ready to even peek through the door of the room in my mind where Johnnie waited. It would be well over a year before I heard the details of what happened on that horrible night.

I vividly recall one other thing about that first visit: Anna's voice. I hadn't realised, because it happened so gradually, that during the years of drug taking and desperation, her normal speaking voice had become a colourless monotone. Now, tones and shades that I didn't know I'd missed were back. As she told me little stories about the girls in her unit, and gave synopses of a half-dozen books she'd already read from the prison library, I detected notes of humour and hope.

Anna was allowed to have two visits every week, one on a weekday and another on weekends. As soon as other people had been approved for her visitors list, I drew up a roster so that Anna would never miss out on her two permitted weekly visits. Gill, taking her godmotherly duties as seriously as ever, was Anna's most frequent visitor next to me. Of course, Katie often came down from the farm to see her sister, and Margie and Marcelle were regular visitors as well. Jim, who now felt guilty about kicking Anna out of his place, asked if he could be on the roster, and Anna agreed.

Over the weeks, as the bump under Anna's jumpsuit grew, we all marvelled as the girl we thought we'd lost reappeared. With good nutrition and regular sleep, with medication monitored and handed out to her three times a day, her irrational fears and ravings disappeared. With no bed bugs or fleas biting her, her skin returned to its unblemished complexion. An optometrist came to the prison and tested her eyes. I was allowed to put extra money into Anna's account that month, to pay for glasses. At last, she could see clearly again. Best of all, Anna was making progress in her relationships. She still made mistakes. Especially during her first weeks in prison, she sometimes trusted people too easily and then became enraged when they betrayed her. But, unlike ever before in the friendship department, she began to learn from her mistakes. She no longer had to worry about adult responsibilities like keeping up her Centrelink requirements, getting a driver's licence or making sure her prescriptions were filled. She could concentrate on honing skills that most of us pick up by osmosis as children.

Anna got a paid job in the kitchen, which she enjoyed a lot. But what gave her even more satisfaction was looking after what she called her 'crack babies', prisoners as young as eighteen, newly admitted and suffering from the sudden withdrawal of drugs. Anna made them sandwiches while she offered them sympathy and jokes.

During those first months in prison, there was an important person missing from Anna's roster of visitors: her father. With her mind clearer than it had been in years, she really missed him. Katie, Gill and I urged her to write to John and tell him this herself. She hesitated, not knowing what to say, and perhaps afraid that he couldn't forgive her. But we kept telling her we knew how much he missed her, too.

Finally, on the 5th of February 2016, John got a card in the mail. On the front were two pink hearts and the words 'With Love'. Inside it read, 'Dear Dad, I am SO SORRY for everything I put you through. I can never make it up to you.' She went on to say that the accusations she had made against him were 'just ice-induced, psychotic, babbling blasphemy'. She ended her message with one more affirmation, 'If my son grows up to be like you I would be content. Also, his farts would smell like roses.' The last sentence was a reference to a claim that John was fond of making, which always brought a disgusted groan from his daughters.

Just as Gill, Katie and I had predicted, John was more than ready to forgive Anna. So, the Friday after John received that card, we four had a happy reunion over cappuccino and excellent jelly slices at the prison cafe. John has visited Anna once a week ever since.

Chapter 46

In prison, Anna was given very good care during her pregnancy. Apart from the warm and competent midwife who often saw her, she was taken regularly to the Sunshine Hospital for ultrasounds and other antenatal care.

There is a mother and baby unit at the prison. Anna's lawyer had told us that children could stay there with their mothers up to the age of four, and this is what we hoped would happen with Anna's baby. At the beginning of 2016, when Anna was five and a half months pregnant, I started investigating who would make the decision about whether Anna could keep her baby with her. This was not an easy task. After many phone calls to various people at the prison and several outside organisations, and even a phone consultation with a leading lawyer in the field, I figured out that the final decision would be made by the Department of Human Services. It took even more detective work to track down someone who would talk to me from that organisation. When I finally did speak with a person there, I was told, to my dismay, that the answer would most likely be no, it would not be in the best interest of the child to remain in prison with his birth mother.

No one seemed willing to give a definite answer, especially to Anna. I suspect this was because they feared she would self-harm if she was told she would be separated from her newborn soon after birth. But I thought it would be too cruel to spring this information on her at the last minute, with no chance to prepare psychologically. She and her friends at the prison were looking forward to the day when Anna would return from hospital with her little boy in her arms, whom she had already named Oliver.

So a few weeks before Anna's due date, when we were sitting out in the visitors' centre courtyard on a bench, I brought up as gently as I could the sad news that she might not be able to keep her baby. She started to cry, and so did I. In the past I would have tried to find the right words to soften her hurt, but I had learned at last that sometimes you just have to feel the pain. All I could do was hold her. And then, suddenly, we were aware of a couple of people kneeling in front of us. One of them was wearing a green jumpsuit. It was Gracie, one of the young girls Anna tried to help. With her was her mother, Amanda, whom I knew because I now visited at more popular times and I'd chatted to her in the waiting room. By this stage we had exchanged emails and long texts about our difficult daughters.

Gracie and Amanda had seen us through the glass wall of the café and come out to offer whatever comfort they could. It was a gesture of courage and compassion, such as I had seldom experienced. Gracie took Anna's hands in hers and said, 'After your mum leaves, I'll come and see you in your room.'

It was a great comfort to me to know that Anna was surrounded by young women who cared about her. But as her pregnancy progressed, I was jolted awake at 2 a.m. more than once, grappling with a huge question: if Anna couldn't take her baby, who would?

Katie had been horrified when she learned Anna was pregnant, and disgusted at me for not trying to talk Anna into getting an abortion. Before Anna went to prison, as the early weeks of gestation ticked by, the need to terminate grew ever more urgent for Katie. 'You're not thinking of the baby!' she angrily pointed out to me more than once. 'It's like when you used to buy her more budgies or hermit crabs . . . you just want her to stay pregnant because it makes her happy!'

Katie was right. I couldn't bear to encourage Anna to part with the lovely dream she held inside her. But Katie didn't believe the baby had a chance of being born healthy. During one of Anna's brief stays at the farm, Katie told me that she said to Anna, 'Have you ever thought about how this kid is likely to turn out after all the shit you've done to your body? I can't make you get an abortion, but don't expect me to look after him when you get sick of him!'

Even after Anna was incarcerated and receiving proper antenatal care, even after we knew it was unlikely that Anna would be able to keep her baby with her, Katie remained adamant that she would not be putting up her hand for the job. And I didn't try to persuade her. Katie wasn't sure she would be remaining with Tom long term, but for now he was definitely in the picture, so his views had to be taken into account. Katie and Tom, and to be honest John and I as well, feared that Ollie's health would be compromised to some degree. It appeared from the ultrasounds and other tests that he was fine physically, but no one could tell what damage Anna's consumption of alcohol early in the pregnancy had done to his brain, not to mention the nicotine and weed, as well as the stress hormones that must have been rampaging through his tiny developing self on the night of Johnnie's death.

John said, 'If no one else takes the poor little bugger then we'll have to.' But I couldn't imagine dealing with a newborn at our age . . . actually, I could imagine it too well. I really didn't think we were up to the broken nights and the toilet-training and the kinder run, let alone helping a boy through his teenage years when we were pushing eighty. I tried to dream up scenarios that might work. Maybe we could find a lovely couple who would agree to an open adoption?

Katie knew from first-hand experience what it was like to care for a profoundly brain-injured child. From the time Katie was four years old until her late teens, John and I were volunteers in the Interchange program, which provides respite for the parents of disabled children. We learned how to love the beautiful little girl we took into our home for one weekend a month, but she also showed us how much hard and endless work her parents put in to caring for someone who would never walk or play or speak.

If Katie had reached the third trimester pregnant with her own baby, I'm sure she would have cherished it, knowing she would adore it no matter how it turned out. But this was a child inside her troubled sister, a baby Katie had worried should never be born. That's why it was such huge news when, shortly before Ollie was scheduled to make his appearance, Katie rang me and said, 'Tom and I've decided that if the baby isn't totally disabled, we'll take him. We figure if he's just a bit slow, we can still love him.'

Katie still laughs when she remembers my reaction to that. 'You were so happy. I never heard you screech that loud before!'

By this time it was March 2016. John and I had bought a townhouse built in 2013, and we were settling in there. It was in our same little suburb, just a few blocks away across the railway line from our house with the big garden. We had sold that to a developer, but they couldn't settle till August. For several reasons Katie and Tom had needed to leave the little farm where they'd been living, so they were staying in our old house.

John and I had decided to go into the ethical farming business with Tom and Katie, and we were looking around Victoria for a suitable property. Most likely we wouldn't find this before August so, after settlement, Katie and Tom were planning to move into the third bedroom of our townhouse until we could locate our dream farm. All this meant that Katie and Tom could be the baby's primary caregivers, with John and me at hand to give lots of support.

Just a week before her due date, we were told that Anna and her baby would definitely not be going to the mother and baby unit at the prison. Out of respect for Anna, we hadn't wanted to prepare to bring him home until we found out for sure that she couldn't keep him with her. This left us with only a few days to assemble all the equipment necessary for a bottle-fed newborn. Fortunately, Margie had persuaded me to join the congregation of a wonderful little church she had discovered, and the people there were amazing. With the help of a mothers' group that one of the women belonged to, they made sure we had a cot, car capsule and a pram, plus plenty of bottles and a microwave steriliser. Katie Rose, Charlotte's mother, passed on armloads of clothes and toys from her three little boys. We greatly appreciated all these gifts. But far more important was what they represented: an outpouring of love to welcome Ollie.

I was allowed to be with Anna as she laboured and gave birth to her boy at the Sunshine Hospital. When I look back at that night, it's hard to comprehend how much joy and grief could be bundled up in one evening. When Ollie emerged, he was just as beautiful as my own babies had been. I looked into his luminous eyes, wide open and amazingly alert, and I knew that he was a smart and happy little soul. But then there was his mother, who so desperately wanted him, who had fought addiction to help him be well, who had angrily defied calls to have him aborted. She was awarded the privilege of his first cuddle, but she would be taken back to prison the very next morning.

I remain in awe at the strength Anna has shown in the face of this loss. She wanted to be brave for her boy, and never complained that for all practical purposes, Katie would be his mother. I think it helped tremendously that the staff and the girls at the prison showed her so much compassion. On her first afternoon back, two of the girls risked a $50 fine to pick a single yellow rose from the garden in the compound. They gave this flower to Anna, along with their hugs. They also reminded her that while many of the women at the prison had been forced to relinquish their children into state care, her baby was safe in the arms of her own family.

John and I took Ollie to visit Anna for the first time when he was five days old, and we've continued to do that at least once a week. When Ollie was tiny, Anna told us that a highlight of her week was holding her baby in her arms and feeding him his bottle, then patting his back so she could see his 'burp face'. Ollie also spends every Sunday afternoon with Anna, when prison staff, along with a dedicated group of volunteers, run a program called Fun with Mum. Katie drops him off early in the afternoon and picks him up a couple of hours later.

Ollie calls Katie Mummy, while Anna is Mumma. One Sunday, when he was about a year old, they pulled into the prison car park and Katie asked him, 'Are you looking forward to seeing Mumma?'

From his perch in the back seat he replied enthusiastically, 'Coke!' That's how Katie found out that Anna was not obeying her strict instructions to only give Ollie the nutritious baby snacks she provided.

Chapter 47

Anna's lawyer had predicted that her criminal case would take a long time to resolve, and he was right. He kept me informed of all the legal proceedings and the adjournments that occurred over more than a year, while we were concentrating on the progress of our daughter and grandson. There was never any doubt that Anna killed Johnnie. Grant had been an eyewitness, plus Anna herself had admitted she did it. She could have pleaded not guilty on the grounds of mental impairment, which would have meant a trial. If the jury had decided she was so mentally compromised that she should not be held responsible for murder, she would have gone to Thomas Embling Hospital, Victoria's secure forensic mental health facility.

Anna's lawyer did explore this option. He arranged for two experienced psychiatrists to interview Anna, separately and several months apart. They did not agree on what caused Anna's many problems. One of them concluded she had a schizoid-type illness, while the other diagnosed a personality disorder. Neither one of them believed she had been psychotic enough to justify pleading not guilty.

Over the course of Anna's first year in prison, she did mention the stabbing to me a few times, just snippets I never encouraged her to elaborate on. Once she said, 'I felt like I was possessed.' Another time, she told me she laid a towel over

Johnnie after she'd done it, to try to stop the bleeding and give him some comfort. Maybe two months later, she mentioned that after she was arrested, she'd lied to the police.

That's basically all I knew about Anna's crime before the 10th of February 2017. That was the day of her sentencing hearing at the Victorian Supreme Court. Because she had pleaded guilty to murder some months before, there would be no trial. The sentencing hearing was like a mini-trial, compressed into two and a half hours. The object was not to find out whether Anna had done it, but to present evidence, which the judge would consider in deciding what sentence she should receive.

So, on that summer's day fourteen months after Black Sunday, Anna's supporters sat in two rows on the main floor of the courtroom. As well as Katie and John and me, there were Gill and Marcelle and Margie. Someone needed to stay home with Ollie, so Tom had volunteered, though he would have liked to have been able to show his support. Jim was there – we had all forgiven him and we appreciated that he visited Anna regularly in prison. There was also Dr Julie Morsillo, representing our church community with its commitment to help Anna and her son. Our two rows were directly in front of the dock, where Anna sat quietly with her hands folded in her lap, dressed in the black slacks and white top I'd been allowed to buy for her. Her shiny hair was tied back as neatly as a private school prefect's. She looked so young and alone. When she first came in I had turned to mouth 'I love you', and now I prayed she could make it through this without losing control. Then, suddenly, everyone stood up as Justice Jane Dixon entered the courtroom. I could see why Anna's lawyer had called me, sounding very pleased, when he found out the judge would be Justice Dixon. With her wig atop her shoulder-length blonde hair, intelligence and compassion seemed to surround her with a white, pure light.

When Justice Dixon asked Anna to confirm the plea she had already entered, she answered in a clear and polite voice, 'Guilty, Your Honour.' At that, I heard rustling and a kind of dismayed murmur from our left. That's where Johnnie's family sat, off to the side of that ornate room, in a section of tiered seats. Anna's lawyer had advised us not to interact with them. I figured that the sight of anything or anyone to do with Anna would cause them pain, so I tried not to even look in their direction, though part of me longed to let them know how much I had liked and appreciated Johnnie.

The sentencing hearing began. Anna's barrister would be presenting evidence in her favour, while a barrister from the Office of Public Prosecutions argued the case for the Crown. Before the arguments began, however, we would hear what happened on the night of 21st November 2015. This was the moment I'd dreaded. I didn't want to know the details of what my daughter had done: I wanted to get up and rush out of the stately room so I wouldn't have to live with the pictures of that night in my mind. But I clamped a hand onto Katie's on one side and John's on the other, and I sat there, because I knew it would upset Anna if I left, and we wanted her to remain calm in the dock.

As for what those details turned out to be, I will quote from the judgement statement, which Justice Dixon later prepared. The statement is much longer than this, and covers many facets, but the words below are taken directly from that statement. Passages left out, which I didn't think necessary here, are indicated by ellipses. The man referred to as 'Mr Brennan' is Grant.

On Saturday 21 November 2015 you spent the day at home. Mr Brennan had been drinking wine with the deceased throughout the morning and early afternoon.

The deceased left and went to a bank to withdraw some money at around 3.45 pm. He was then collected from home and taken to a family barbecue in the late afternoon. He continued drinking at the barbecue and was in good spirits. He was dropped home at 8.30 pm.

Upon being delivered home the deceased was helped out of the car and assisted to the door by family members. He used walking sticks to ambulate and was a large man who moved slowly. He was handed over to you at the door of the unit along with an unfinished bottle of beer.

The deceased then sat at the kitchen table with Mr Brennan and dozed off for a period of time. When he awoke he continued drinking beer whilst Mr Brennan drank wine. Both men watched television and conversed from time to time whilst drinking alcohol . . .

At around 10.00 pm you became frustrated and your frustration erupted into violence. You were craving cigarettes and began to ask the deceased for money to help you out. He told you to wait until the next day. You argued with him for ten minutes or so complaining that he had promised to look after the pair of you, and that he was holding out on you. When you challenged him to show whether he had any cash, he produced a fifty dollar bill and a twenty dollar bill from his pocket. You snatched the money from his hands and headed quickly into the kitchen. You were followed by the deceased who asked you to return the money . . .

. . . you became suddenly enraged and punched him so that he fell against the plaster wall and then face down onto the carpet. The head of the deceased perforated the plaster wall when he fell. At some stage during this incident you obtained a knife from the kitchen, and after the deceased fell down you knelt beside him and repeatedly stabbed him to the upper back, shoulder and neck whilst he lay prone on the floor. The knife used in the attack was a large boning knife which belonged to the deceased.

Grant Brennan . . . yelled at you several times to stop and when you finally desisted he began to call emergency services with his mobile phone . . .

You then took over the telephone call from Mr Brennan . . .

You lied to the emergency services operator saying that someone had broken in and stabbed your 'daddy'.

When police and ambulance officers entered the unit shortly afterwards you were holding the head of the deceased . . . You were sent to a bedroom by them and seen to be extremely agitated and visibly shaking.

Nevertheless when spoken to by police both you and Mr Brennan maintained the fiction that an intruder had broken in and stabbed the deceased. You maintained this version in a false statement prepared at the Mill Park Police Station later that same night.

The statement you made included some plainly implausible details. There was also an obvious lack of con-sistency between your description of the intruder and that of Mr Brennan . . .

Naturally police became suspicious and when Homicide members then arrested Mr Brennan and interviewed him, he admitted telling lies and gave a true account of what had taken place. He was released without charge. He later admitted plac-ing the deceased's money in his own wallet after it was given to

him by you following the attack. You were charged with murder
on 22 November 2015 and remanded in custody.

John, Katie, Gill and I, along with the friends who flanked
us, first heard this horrible night described at the same time
that the media did. It was hard to hear it, and afterwards, hard
to read the headline that appeared in newsfeeds across the
country and still remains like an avenging ghost on the internet: Pregnant Woman Killed Man for Cigarettes.

But in one way, knowing the details brought comfort to
me, because I learned that Johnnie was almost certainly unconscious when Anna stabbed him. He never had to see, as I had
imagined, the girl he had trusted and tried to help lunging at
him with wild anger in her eyes and a knife in her hand.

So after the sentencing hearing, we knew what happened.
But we still couldn't understand why. This was a girl who
wouldn't read a novel before the age of twelve, because in
novels there has to be conflict, and things go wrong for people
and animals . . . and Anna couldn't bear the thought of anyone, ever, feeling bad or being treated unfairly. How could that
child grow up to be a murderer?

I don't think we'll ever know the answer for sure. But
through the writing of this book, I have formed a theory.
A number of factors coalesced on the night of the 21st of
November: firstly, she'd run out of Seroquel. I'd pointed out to
her that she now lived within easy walking distance of doctors
and pharmacies, but even when she wasn't nauseated she
couldn't bring herself to leave the house, so she didn't procure
new scripts. She refused to drink because of the baby. Grant
hadn't been able to get any weed for her, and then Johnnie had
denied her even nicotine.

Without any of her drugs, half-starved from relentless morning sickness and with pregnancy hormones racing around in her brain, I believe her mind imploded. It let in the demon. The one that thrived in my grandfather and was passed down to my mother, that made them lash out to smash and hurt. Grandpa did this with his fists and curses. Mother used words. Anna grabbed a boning knife from the kitchen bench and stabbed the man she called Daddy twenty-two times.

Chapter 48

On the 16th of March 2017, John, Katie and I, as well as our little band of loyal supporters, gathered at our house and trooped down to the train to make the journey to the Supreme Court. This was the day of Anna's sentencing, when we would hear the decision that Justice Jane Dixon had made. Anna's lawyer had warned us that it could take over an hour for her to read through her judgement, and we would have to wait till the end to hear the number we were waiting for: the years that our daughter would be incarcerated.

As we walked through the autumn morning from Flagstaff station down William Street, people with important purpose on their faces floated past us in their legal robes. I thought of the time nearly three decades before when I was an editor working in the city. Anna had come to work with me for eight months, tucked safely inside my belly. I remembered walking up Collins Street towards the Rialto, where my office was. I'd just missed the green man at King Street so I had to stop and wait. As the traffic, which had been halted in King Street, roared into life, my baby jumped inside me. 'Oh good,' I thought, 'she can hear.'

What would I have said, if someone had asked me then where I thought that baby would be today, two days after my birthday in 2017? Certainly not in the dock of Courtroom Two in the Victorian Supreme Court.

This time, Johnnie's family sat on the main floor of the courtroom and we were in the tiered seats on the left. We all stood up as Justice Jane Dixon entered, surrounded by her cloud of intelligence and wisdom. She read her judgement. It was indeed lengthy, but I was immensely grateful that someone so respected had minutely analysed Anna's actions and motives. Justice Dixon had assembled a picture of Anna more accurate than anyone, including me, had been able to piece together till then. She had access to all of Anna's medical records; she'd read notes on conversations with doctors, psychologists and counsellors, which had occurred at times when I had not been present. She'd studied the opinions of the psychiatrists who had interviewed Anna in prison. Justice Dixon was able to analyse these pieces of my daughter's life and fit them together with a mind unclouded by guilt and the terrible burden of love.

As for why Anna had stabbed a defenceless man, Justice Dixon's conclusions were basically the same as mine; in fact, some of my ideas come from her, though of course she stated the reasons in different terms.

I agreed with Justice Dixon that even though Anna's mental state at the time of the murder was compromised, she was not so out of it that she was unaware her crime was the worst thing you could do to another person. Justice Dixon cited the reports of the two psychiatrists who interviewed Anna in prison. They had advised that Anna was not psychotic enough to consider pleading not guilty on the grounds of mental impairment. However, Justice Dixon did believe there were mitigating factors she should take into consideration when sentencing Anna. Some of these were listed in the judgement statement:

Your plea of guilty, and obvious remorse;

Absence of prior offending;

The spontaneous nature of your offending and the lack of premeditation;

Your physiological condition at the time of the offence . . .

Your . . . lifelong psychological vulnerabilities and further deterioration following a sexual assault in 2014 . . .

Your prospects for rehabilitation being enhanced by your behaviour in prison and your willingness to seek and accept help;

The persistence of family and friends in their attempts to support you in ways that should assist your rehabilitation into the future;

Your good prospects for rehabilitation, founded in part on your acknowledged intellectual capabilities and past success in pursuing tertiary education.

Justice Dixon did not seem to view Anna's lying to the police as a huge issue. Although it was an aggravating factor and it did show that by concocting a story Anna knew what she'd done was wrong, Justice Dixon pointed out that Anna soon reverted to the truth, and had entered a relatively early plea of guilty. At last, after references to many past cases and their relevance to Anna's sentencing, Justice Dixon read out the following:

I am bound to impose a sentence which reflects general deterrence, just punishment and denunciation, having regard to the seriousness of the crime of murder and the objective gravity of the offending . . .

In light of all the factors I have already referred to I sentence you as follows:

On the crime of murder you are sentenced to 17 years
imprisonment with a minimum non-parole period of 13 years.

John, Katie and I, and our supporters, thought this sentence was the fairest we could have wished for. However, as
instructed by Anna's lawyer, we tried to show no response. At
our next visit with Anna, she too expressed relief at the length
of her sentence.

After the sentencing, I dreaded that there might be TV
crews outside the Supreme Court who would follow us, Anna's
family and supporters, on a walk of shame down the steps.
But by the time we left, having stayed behind in the courtroom
because Anna's lawyer wanted to speak to us, the steps and
the street beyond were blessedly empty. Later I would learn
there had been a TV crew outside the court. They'd spoken to
Johnnie's family, who said they didn't know if thirteen years
was enough to pay for taking the life of their loved one. And
I feel that this sentiment, too, is fair.

It hurts to think of Johnnie so close beside me, in the front
seat of my blue Jazz, on the last full day of his life. If I'd known
what awaited him, I'd have kept on driving. I would have
driven on for hours and delivered him to a safe place far, far
away from my daughter. But none of us knows what black
horror might be waiting for us in that rectangle of time we
call tomorrow. Just as Anna is more than the crazed, cartoon
monster portrayed in the paragraphs of clickbait that appeared
minutes after her sentencing, just as John, Katie and I are more
than the people who harboured and unleashed this caricature,
Johnnie was many things apart from Anna's victim.

Johnnie was a man with dreams for his future. And he
was taking steps to make them happen. At the Centrelink

appointment I took him to on the day before he was killed, he successfully applied for a loan to get Grant's car fixed. He had a plan: he and all the other men who hung out at his place had lost their driver's licences, but Anna, who was no longer drinking, would finally obtain hers. He must have imagined Anna driving them all around, with a child seat strapped into the back. Anna had said more than once, 'Johnnie's really looking forward to the baby.'

Johnnie was a guy who spoke several languages. He was also a man who pointed his stick at a peach-coloured kitten just learning to walk and said to me, 'He's a good one. Gonna keep him. His name's Daddy Man!'

Walt told me that at Johnnie's funeral, the church was packed. I hope and believe this shows how much he was loved by his family, and respected by the Macedonian community. I saw with my own eyes and heard with my own ears, how much he was loved by his friends.

Epilogue

When Ollie was a few months old, we found our dream property near Ballarat, within easy driving distance of the prison. The place included a good modern house, and that's where Katie, Tom and Ollie live.

The business is beginning slowly, with a small flock of sheep, one calf and lots of vegetables. Every Friday night, while Tom looks after the farm, Katie drives to the city to stay in the townhouse with John and me. John takes Ollie to visit Anna on Saturdays. Katie and I alternate weeks, going with John to help out. I also visit every Friday, which I look forward to all week. After two years and four months in prison, Anna is doing better than at any other time since before she started school. She has worked at various jobs, including kitchen hand and library assistant. She's even passed a driver's test! Well, it is to drive a motorised food delivery cart around the prison, but it's a start. Even more importantly, prison has brought an end to one of the most painful parts of Anna's life. As she expressed to me in one of her letters, 'It feels so good not to be lonely.'

Anna also attends a drama class at the prison. It's run by a wonderful theatre group called Somebody's Daughter. Early last year they began workshopping a full-scale production to be staged in September. The young professionals from the company listened to the prisoners' stories, then helped weave these into song, dance and drama. Anna was very excited about this, especially in the weeks leading up to the performance, which would run in the prison's leisure centre over three nights and two matinees. The other prisoners would get to see it, as well as people on the performers' visitors list, the prison officers and the many volunteers who work with 'the girls' in various capacities.

John, Katie, Gill and I went to the production on its final night. We weren't prepared for how beautiful and professional it would be: all those vibrant young women, and some crusty and funny older ones as well. When it was Anna's turn to tell her story, she paced up and down in a very small, imaginary cell. This was the one underneath the Magistrate's Court, where they took her on the night of her crime. She couldn't comprehend what she had done. 'I've never been arrested for anything before,' she said as she paced. She held her hands flat over her belly, as if to hold and shield the tiny life inside her. Then she stepped out of the cell and faced the audience, back now in the present. She looked adorable, like she was about eighteen years old. One of the other girls had done her hair in perfect French braids and she was wearing a little black tunic. She told us in a clear, strong voice, 'I'm here instead of a mental hospital. Basically the system failed me, turned its back on me and I wasn't diagnosed until it was too late . . . My parents tried their hardest to help. It was a full-time job just to keep me alive. But they didn't have the knowledge. I needed professional help.'

We already knew that Anna now understood we'd done the best we could, but it was fantastic to hear it publicly acknowledged.

On my Friday visits, I sometimes take a friend with me, or Charlotte, if it's school holidays or she has a curriculum day.

Charlotte, who started year 7 this year, has visited Anna many times. A few weeks ago I said to her, 'I'm really glad your parents have been so good about you going into a maximum-security prison.' Charlotte gave me her Miss Bossy Boots, big-sister-to-three-brothers look and said, 'Mary, not visiting Anna was never an option.'

It's nice to see Anna relating so easily to other people, but I also savour the times when I visit and it's just the two of us. We have a simple meal together, usually a ham and cheese toastie and a fruit salad, then we walk laps around the court-yard. Two hours are never enough to share all the stories we've saved up for each other.

Of course, I tell her lots about Ollie. At nearly two, thanks to the world-class care Tom and Katie are giving him, he is thriving. He's crazy about cars and trains, but like the rest of us, he's pretty fond of words as well.

And he knows how to manipulate me with words. Last weekend I wanted him to go upstairs with me so I could change his clothes, but he decided we should sit down on the bottom step instead. He sat, and then he patted the spot beside him, saying 'Chair!' That's his word for 'Sit with me'.

'Come on, Ollie,' I replied. 'I don't have time for that.'

'No. Nana chair,' he insisted. And then he held up the mini-ature forefinger of his left hand, his eyes sparkling with a good idea. 'Book!' he announced. He knew I wouldn't be able to resist that. So I sat down on the step, and off he trotted to fetch *More Bugs in Boxes*, which was Anna's favourite book when she was two.

Ollie is a bit of a star at the prison, where the staff have watched him grow since he was less than a week old. You could feel hearts melting beneath prison officer uniforms when Ollie, at around eleven months, toddled through the metal scanner all by himself and climbed the three steps up onto the platform to be scanned with the wand.

Ollie has plenty of fun there, part of a rambunctious clan of kids who visit their mothers every weekend. Probably it won't be long before we'll need to answer his questions about why Mumma can't come home with us. But we think with his sunny nature, he'll be able to handle the answers. And we're glad to see he already has a better sense of direction than Anna. He is the light of all our lives, our gorgeous boy.

Author's Notes

At last, my stacks of journals dating back to 1965 have come in handy. With rare exceptions, the events and conversations detailed in this book were recorded the morning after they occurred. In a couple of scenes, Katie was with Anna when I wasn't. For these, Katie took over the keyboard and wrote the memory herself.

There are no amalgamated characters in this memoir. In almost all cases, people have given permission for their real names to be used. I am deeply grateful, and touched, that so many friends and professionals agreed to be identified as part of our story. For those few whom I could not contact or pre-ferred anonymity, names and some inconsequential details have been changed.

I wrote this book for many reasons, but financial gain was not one of them. All proceeds will be donated to charities that help people struggling with mental illness or addiction, includ-ing women who are or have been incarcerated. These include beyondblue and Prison Network Ministries.

So many people deserve my thanks, for walking beside me and holding me close during the hard years with Anna. I think it's obvious from reading our story who these are, and words cannot say how much I appreciate them. But I do want to formally acknowledge those who helped me with the actual writing of this book. First, there is Dr Julie Marsillo, a community psychologist and my dear friend from the Moreland Baptist Church. I mentioned one Sunday morning that I wanted to write about our saga but didn't know where to begin. A few days later Julie appeared at my door, drove me to a cafe at the top of Mount Macedon, got out her iPad and instructed, 'Just start talking.' She typed while I blathered on about my eating disorder and my unhappy mother and how Anna was such a delightful child to adults but was ostracised by other kids from the time she went to kinder . . . Through dozens more lunches and many kilometres of walking through local parks, Julie helped me sort all this into some sort of order. She gave me amazing practical and emotional support through the entire planning and writing of the first draft.

Then there is John. I couldn't have embarked on this project without his blessing and encouragement. I thank him for only rolling his eyes a little and usually becoming just mildly grumpy on the hundreds of occasions over the past two years when he wanted to do something fun with me and I would say, 'I have to work on the book.'

Katie was also at the heart of this project. She lived through every minute of Anna's story as it unfolded, and passionately discussed with me the writing of it. Like Julie, Katie gave me practical as well as emotional support. When the torn rotator cuff in my shoulder would not allow me to use my right arm any longer, Katie would type while I dictated.

I'd like to thank my counsellor, Chanel, for reading and commenting on sections of the manuscript as it progressed. My newest good friend, Ricki, also read the manuscript and said what anyone should when a friend asks them to look at their book in progress, 'It's great!'

I'm grateful to my publisher at Penguin, Ali Watts, for recognising the potential of this story as soon as she heard about it, and for guiding me through to the best version I could produce. And thumbs up to my meticulous editor, Meaghan Amor. She is a literary warrior in her relentless search for repeated words, unchecked references and confusing construction.

I also owe a thank you to David Sheff. His memoir, *Beautiful Boy*, was a great comfort to me and afforded me many insights, as well as inspiring the title of this book.

Finally, I would like to thank Anna herself, who would have preferred for me not to write about and offer to the public all that she did, and for which she is now profoundly sorry. But she gave me her permission, because she knew it was important for our family. Recently, in one of the beautiful cards she sends me from prison, she said, 'I'm proud of you for trying to help other people with my story.'